T0272749

BUZZING

BUZZING

THE STORY OF BRENTFORD'S
FIRST PREMIER LEAGUE SEASON

NICK BROWN

First published by Pitch Publishing, 2022

Pitch Publishing
9 Donnington Park,
85 Birdham Road,
Chichester,
West Sussex,
PO20 7AJ
www.pitchpublishing.co.uk
info@pitchpublishing.co.uk

A CIP catalogue record is available for this book
from the British Library.

ISBN 978 1 80150 152 1

Typesetting and origination by Pitch Publishing
Printed and bound in Great Britain by TJ Books, Padstow

CONTENTS

PROLOGUE

THE WORLD was a very different place in 1947 to the one in which we now live. The slow recovery process after the Second World War was under way with prime minister Clement Attlee two years into his tenure after Winston Churchill winning the 1945 Genereal Election. The school-leaving age was raised to 15, child benefits were introduced and the National Health Service was still a year away from being founded. King George VI's daughter Princess Elizabeth married Philip Mountbatten, the newly appointed Duke of Edinburgh, in a ceremony at Westminster Abbey. Five years later, Princess Elizabeth would become Queen Elizabeth II and go on to become Britain's longest-serving monarch.

Elsewhere, outside of British shores, the Dead Sea Scrolls were discovered by Bedouin shepherds Muhammed edh-Dhib, Jum'a Muhammed and Khalil Musa in caves near the Khirbet Qumran on the north-western shore of the Dead Sea in Israel; the Cold War began as US President Harry S. Truman signed an Act of Congress to stop the spread of Communism, with the National Security Act creating the CIA (the Cold War ended in 1991); and in New Mexico, the American army issued a press release stating that they had recovered a 'flying disc' from a crash site in Roswell, quickly retracted the statement and insisted it was nothing more than a conventional weather balloon, thus starting the 'Roswell Incident' rumours and conspiracy theories.

And 1947 was also the last time that Brentford Football Club played a match in the top flight of English football.

Rewind 58 years to 1889. A new recreation park was opened in the town of Brentford and the local rowing club got together with the cricket club to decide how best to utilise the new facility. An application to use the ground was submitted to the Chiswick Local Board but their board meeting failed to reach a conclusion. The founders of the rowing club, Archer Green and John Henry Strachan, chaired a meeting of club members to decide whether they would form a new football or rugby club and when put to the vote, it was the round ball that was decided upon. Brentford Football Club was born and it was decided that their colours would be the same as the rowing club's colours – salmon, claret and light blue. Newly elected club president Edwin Underwood promised to allow them the use of a field behind the offices of the Local Board as their home ground. The new club's first official match was played on 23 November 1889 against Kew and ended in a 1-1 draw. The honour of being the first goalscorer in Brentford's history belongs to T.H.M. Bonell.

Brentford led a bit of a nomadic existence early on and made the first of their many moves to Benn's Field in Ealing, west London, and entered the West London Alliance League for the 1892/93 season. They finished the campaign as champions. However, after not being awarded a trophy, they decided not to defend their title, resigned from the league and continued on playing friendlies and entering cup competitions.

In 1896 they were elected into the London League. Their first season saw the club finish as runners-up in the second division and, following promotion, they also secured second spot in the top division at the end of the next season. That year also saw the club achieve a cup double as Brentford won both the London Senior Cup and Middlesex Senior Cup.

The 1898/99 season saw Brentford play in the Southern League and also make their first appearance in the FA Cup. The next few years heralded many changes both on and off the pitch. They changed their colours to dark blue and gold stripes in 1903, settled at Griffin Park in 1904, reached the third round of the FA Cup in the 1905/06 season before being beaten by Liverpool and again changed their colours, this time to gold shirts with blue sleeves, in 1909.

The outbreak of the First World War in 1914 disrupted Brentford's plans, as it did for pretty much the rest of the world. They took part in the London Combination League during the war and, after hostilities ended, resumed playing in the Southern League. In 1920, the Third Division of the Football League was founded and Brentford, along with their Southern League rivals, were the founder members. The club once again changed their colours, this time to white shirts and black shorts. They finished the season in 21st position and only remained in the league due to the other clubs re-electing them. In 1925, the kit changed once more, to the now familiar red and white stripes.

The appointment of Harry Curtis as manager in 1926 marked a turning point for Brentford. Slow but sure progress saw the team climb through the league structure and in 1935 they won promotion to the First Division. Ground improvements were made to Griffin Park that saw the capacity rise to 40,000 and the team responded by ending the season in fifth position, the highest finish in the club's history. The following season saw a sixth-placed finish and an FA Cup quarter-final appearance.

With the outbreak of the Second World War, the Football League programme was decimated and Brentford took their place in the Football League South and the London League, with the team being full of guest players. At the resumption of the league proper, they were relegated from the First Division at the end of the 1946/47 season and from that day on the club floated around the lower reaches of the Football League, occasionally flirting with the idea of promotion back to the big time but dropping away when it mattered.

Things began to change for the better in 2014/15 with Brentford reaching the play-offs for a place in the Premier League before being beaten in the semi-finals by Middlesbrough. Now established as a force in the Championship, Brentford toyed with promotion for the next few seasons, being regulars in the play-offs, and were beaten by Fulham in the play-off final at the end of the 2019/20 season and had to see their west London neighbours promoted instead of them.

Before the start of the 2020/21 season, Brentford moved out of Griffin Park after 116 years and moved into the all-seater Brentford Community Stadium, just half a mile away. Another finish in the play-off positions once again saw them reach the final but this time it was Brentford's turn to triumph. Goals from Ivan Toney and Emiliano Marcondes earned a 2-0 victory over Swansea City to secure a return to the big time after 74 years.

An entire lifetime has passed since the Bees were last in the top echelons of English football. There are supporters who would have to ask their grandfathers what it was like to watch their club play against the likes of Arsenal, Liverpool and Manchester United. Since then, virtually every other team in London who have been part of the Football League has been in the First Division as was or the Premier League as is. The only exceptions are Barnet, Dagenham & Redbridge and Sutton United, who have only amassed 31 years of league football between them, with the 2021/22 season being the first in Sutton's history.

So how will this momentous season pan out? Will they crash the party or will it be a step too far? Would the players who did so well in the Championship be able to cut it in the Premier League? Would manager Thomas Frank be out of his depth among his world-famous counterparts? Would the team struggle against the big boys or would they take everyone by surprise?

So many questions, but only time will tell. The only certainty is that whatever happens, the 2021/22 season marks a milestone in the club's history. After 74 years, the Bees are back in town.

PRE-SEASON

STRENGTHENING a squad after promotion to the Premier League is always a tricky business. What does the manager do? Does he show faith in the players who helped to get the club up, even though they may be untested at that level, or does he bring in lots of players with experience who have been there before? In the past we've seen various clubs try out both strategies only for them to backfire and win nothing but a return ticket to the Championship. In preparation for the 2021/22 season Brentford visited a halfway house, bringing in four players who would realistically be looking for a first team spot along with one or two others with an eye on the future. The new first team squad members were Kristoffer Ajer, Frank Onyeka, Yoane Wissa and Myles Peart-Harris.

Ajer is a Norwegian international who had spent the last five years in Scotland with Celtic. A towering defender, he is used to playing in big games and winning things, having secured three Scottish championships, three Scottish Cups and three Scottish League Cups during his time in Glasgow. Midfielder Onyeka is also no stranger to winning medals, having won two Danish titles with FC Midtjylland, from whom he joined Brentford. The pacy forward Wissa joined from French club Lorient, and Peart-Harris, an attacking midfielder, was a product of Chelsea's academy before moving across west London.

A few players also made their way out through the exit door. Two goalkeepers left on loan – Ellery Balcombe to Burton Albion and Patrik Gunnarsson to Viking Stavanger – while the experienced defender Winston Reid saw his own loan period to Brentford expire and he returned to parent club West Ham. Three players also left due to their contracts coming to an end. Luke Daniels, another goalkeeper, joined Middlesbrough, Henrik Dalsgaard went home to Denmark to ply his trade with FC Midtjylland, and Emiliano Marcondes signed a contract with Bournemouth.

In preparation for the Premier League season, several friendlies were arranged before the big kick-off. First up was a trip to south London to take on AFC Wimbledon. As is usual for these matches, especially this early in the proceedings, the line-ups contained a mixture of first-team squad members and youngsters, and it was two such players who combined for the only goal of the game. Finley Stevens's lob caught AFC Wimbledon goalkeeper Nik Tzanev – a product of the Brentford academy before his move across the capital – off his line but, unfortunately for Stevens, the ball bounced back off the crossbar. Quickest to react, though, was Joel Valencia who dived to head in the only goal of the game.

A few days later, the Bees travelled to Hertfordshire for a match with National League side Boreham Wood. As expected, Brentford had most of the play and came away with a 2-0 win thanks to goals from Ivan Toney and Tariqe Fosu. The opener came when Sergi Canós found some space and played in Toney who curled a nice finish in off the far post, and Brentford's second arrived when Fosu got on the end of a cross from Dominic Thompson.

As the season approached, the intensity of the friendly matches grew. The final three saw the Bees take on top-class opposition in Manchester United, West Ham and Spanish team Valencia.

The trip to Old Trafford saw an end-to-end match finish in a 2-2 draw. The home side took the lead with a stunning strike from young forward Anthony Elanga, who met Aaron Wan-Bissaka's cross to fire home an unstoppable volley. The equaliser came shortly after when Toney headed on for Shandon Baptiste to slam the ball in off the crossbar past United goalkeeper Tom Heaton. In the second period United once again took the lead, this time courtesy of Andreas Pereira. He fired the ball past David Raya after the Brentford keeper had originally thwarted Jesse Lingard's effort. The loose ball was only half cleared by Ethan Pinnock and Pereira pounced. The visitors equalised for the second time when Bryan Mbeumo cut in from the right to curl a shot past Heaton and Brentford could head home satisfied that, even though they hadn't come up against a full-strength Manchester United side, they could leave Old Trafford undefeated.

The next friendly match saw West Ham make the trip across from east London and inflict Brentford's first pre-season defeat. Saïd Benrahma notched the only goal of the game, but it could have been so different had Baptiste converted rather than hit the post. A defeat but, at this stage, the main thing is the development of the team and the fitness of the players leading into the big curtain-raiser.

The final game of the pre-season campaign saw Spanish side Valencia visit the Community Stadium. Thomas Frank fielded virtually a full-strength team and the reward was a 2-1 victory. Brentford thought they had taken the lead when Marcus Forss converted after some good work from Saman Ghoddos but the goal was ruled out by VAR – the first time the Video Assistant Referee had been deployed at the new stadium. It was Valencia, though, who went ahead when Diego López broke into the penalty area and slotted past Raya. In the second half Brentford slowly took control of the game and Ethan Pinnock connected with Canós's corner and his header gave keeper Cristian Rivero no chance. The winner was scored by Frank Onyeka who pounced after Rico Henry's cross was only half cleared.

So then, pre-season over, squad prepared, fans excited. Let the fun begin.

SEASON 2021/22

Friday, 13 August 2021

Here we go then, the wait is over. After 27,109 days, Brentford make their long-awaited return to English football's top division. And not only that, but being the Friday night game, it is the opening match of the season. And not only not only that, but they couldn't have chosen a much bigger one to begin with as Arsenal visit the Community Stadium. OK, it could have been the champions Manchester City, but a big London derby is the perfect way to welcome the Bees to the party. And not only not only not only that, but guess who their last top-flight match on 26 May 1947 was against? That's right – it was Arsenal. That game finished 1-0 to the Gunners with Paddy Sloan scoring the only goal. But that was then and this is now.

The Community Stadium was absolutely jumping with 16,479 fans packed in for this historic occasion and if there were any first-night nerves then Brentford certainly didn't show it. Right from the start they went toe to toe with their illustrious visitors. The first real chance of the season fell to Frank Onyeka but his header was just too high. Not long after, Ivan Toney released Bryan Mbeumo who fired past Arsenal goalkeeper Bernd Leno only to see his shot rebound back off the near post. The pressure finally told midway through the half when a poor Arsenal clearance was knocked back into the danger zone and the ball reached Sergi Canós who cut inside and fired in a low shot past Leno. If the Community Stadium had a roof the fans would have blown it off.

Seventy-four years of waiting coupled with last year's frustrations of not being able to see their team play live due to the COVID restrictions were released in one huge roar. Just before half-time it could, and maybe should, have been two. Kristoffer Ajer played a long ball for Mbeumo who, after outpacing his marker, was left one-on-one with Leno but he pulled his shot wide of the post.

After the break the Gunners pushed for an equaliser with Kieran Tierney and Gabriel Martinelli both going close and David Raya saving well from Emile Smith Rowe, but the hosts were not to be denied on their big day. The points were secured when Mads Bech Sørensen launched a long throw into the Arsenal goalmouth, the ball bounced to the far post and Christian Nørgaard headed in.

Speaking on Sky Sports, Canós was understandably delighted after the match, 'This is amazing. I've been dreaming about scoring the first goal in the stadium and these people deserve it, we deserve it. Great three points, we need a bit of calm and then we go again next week. It is such an incredible moment. Fantastic for me and my family who've come all the way from Spain and all my other family in Spain are watching the game. For the club it's a step forward.'

The post-match press conference saw Thomas Frank understandably delighted with how the game went. 'I have such a big belief in this group of players and this team,' he told reporters. 'I know we are going to face Arsenal, a massive club with better individual players, unbelievable players, top coach, but I just had this feeling that I would be disappointed if we didn't beat them before the game. Maybe I would have had an unbelievable reality check but on the day – because it is only one day, one game – I think we thoroughly deserved to win the game. One of the things where we were unbelievable was in the high pressure, we pressed with massive intensity more or less throughout the game, and then the fans were electric. They created a great atmosphere.'

When asked about the atmosphere created, he said, 'I think it is a combination of so many things. It's the first game in the Premier League for us, the opening game in the Premier League, an evening game, a full house, a top performance. Everyone in the stadium today will never forget this and I'm proud to be part of that. We're number one in the Premier League and that's a fantastic story. We're just a bus stop in Hounslow!'

Whatever happens in the rest of the season, one thing is for sure – it's going to be a party zone in west London.

Brentford: Raya; Ajer (Bech Sørensen 71), Jansson, Pinnock; Canós, Onyeka (Bidstrup 80), Nørgaard, Janelt, Henry; Toney, Mbeumo (Forss 86)

Arsenal: Leno; Chambers (Tavares 81), White, Pablo Marí, Tierney; Lokonga, Xhaka; Pépé, Smith Rowe, Martinelli (Nelson 71); Balogun (Saka 58)

Tuesday, 17 August 2021

Another new signing arrives at the Community Stadium. Goalkeeper Álvaro Fernández joins from Spanish club Huesca. The transfer is initially a one-year loan deal but with an option to make the signing permanent. Fernández has one full international cap having been promoted from the Under-21s for Spain's friendly against Lithuania in June after some of the senior players were forced to withdraw due to COVID isolation rules. He became the first Huesca player to represent the national side. The match finished in a 4-0 Spanish victory.

Friday, 20 August 2021

David Raya is today featured in the newspaper *Metro*. 'I have been working for this ever since I came to England,' he is quoted as saying. 'The chance of playing in the Premier League, collectively, is massive for the club. During the summer it didn't really hit me, but you see things like the Premier League signs around the place and then you begin to realise we are Premier League players now.'

Speaking about his own role in the team, Raya says, 'My role when we're not on the ball is to get everybody switched on. I can't let anybody switch off and we don't like to let the other team create a chance, let alone score a goal. Even a chance can boost their confidence. The manager wanted me to be positive, aggressive and be the type of goalkeeper who plays out from the back rather than be reactive. I have to anticipate and prevent chances as well as make saves. I like to be involved in our build-up. Growing up in Spain, that's the way we played.'

Raya was born in Barcelona and began his playing career with Catalan side Unión Esportiva Cornellà. He came over to England in 2012 to join Blackburn Rovers and, after almost 100 appearances for Rovers, he signed for Brentford in 2019. He was a key player for the Bees in their promotion season, keeping 17 clean sheets.

Saturday, 21 August 2021

After last week's win against Arsenal, there is another connection with the Gunners in today's game at Crystal Palace as the Eagles' new boss is Arsenal legend Patrick Vieira. It is Vieira's first home match after taking over from Roy Hodgson in the summer.

Thomas Frank names an unchanged team from the Arsenal game and, once again, the Bees show that they are not in the Premier League just to make up the numbers. A 0-0 draw makes it four points from six. Both teams came close to breaking the deadlock but saw the ball bounce back off the crossbar. Wilfried Zaha broke away for Palace and played in the onrushing Conor Gallagher who hammered his shot past David Raya only to see the ball bounce down off the bar and out, and Bryan Mbeumo's free kick hit the top of the bar and rebounded over.

The chances continued to come for Brentford, with Ivan Toney firing wide, Sergi Canós just unable to direct Vitaly Janelt's cross goalwards and Palace keeper Vicente Guaita saving from Toney, Frank Onyeka and Ethan Pinnock.

It wasn't all one-way traffic, though, as Raya was called into action to thwart both Gallagher and Christian Benteke.

Speaking to the BBC after the match, Frank says he thought Brentford were the better team, 'I think we slightly edged it to be the better side, I think we pressed fantastic. We only gave one big chance away. We won the ball a lot of times in good areas but didn't quite have the quality to put good counter attacks together. We definitely ended the first half on top but we need a little bit more coolness and composure, but I think it's positive that we still have an extra level to take from this game.'

Crystal Palace: Guaita; Ward, Guéhi, Andersen, Mitchell; Gallagher, Kouyaté, MacArthur; Zaha, Benteke, Schlupp (Ayew 68)

Brentford: Raya; Ajer, Jansson, Pinnock; Canós, Onyeka (Ghoddos 70), Nørgaard, Janelt (Bidstrup 87), Henry; Toney, Mbeumo (Wissa 77)

Tuesday, 24 August 2021

Cup action tonight as League Two side Forest Green Rovers visit in the League Cup, currently being sponsored by Carabao, the energy drink company.

The Carabao story is a bizarre yet strangely brilliant one. Carabao are a popular rock group from Thailand that were formed in the early 1980s and their lead singer, Yuenyong Opakul, now in his 60s, also became the founder of the drinks company that took the same name. Since the company's inception in 2002, they have overtaken Red Bull as Thailand's most popular energy drink, bringing in millions of pounds. In 2015 they moved into the English football market by becoming a sponsor of Reading and then, in 2017, they became the sponsor of the League Cup. They also have deals with Tajikistani team FK Khujand and the famous Brazilian side Flamengo.

There were nine changes made by Thomas Frank to the team that drew with Crystal Palace at the weekend, and it was the visitors who took the early initiative when Jack Aitchison latched on to a defensive error to fire Forest Green into the lead. It could have been even worse had Ebrima Adams been able to convert Nicholas Cadden's cross.

As expected, Brentford came back into it and Forest Green goalkeeper Lewis Thomas saved at the feet of Marcus Forss before Saman Ghoddos headed Dominic Thompson's cross wide. Thomas once again came to the visitors' rescue when he denied Yoane Wissa.

The second half saw Brentford up the tempo with the introduction of both Sergi Canós and Frank Onyeka and the equaliser came when Ghoddos played a ball into Wissa who turned and shot into the corner of the net. Once the equalising goal arrived it seemed almost inevitable that the Bees would go on to win the game. Bryan Mbeumo went close before his header from Thompson's cross found the net to make it 2-1 and Forss sealed the win with a third after some good approach work from Canós.

'It was a tough first half,' said Frank afterwards. 'Forest Green Rovers deserve a lot of praise, Rob Edwards and his staff and the players, they made it difficult for us – I think they were the better side in the first half. In the second half we brought on some of the more experienced guys and after that second half performance I think we deservedly went through to the next round.'

Brentford: Fernández; Roerslev (Canós 45), Bech Sørensen (Ajer 45), Pinnock, Thompson; Ghoddos, Bidstrup (Onyeka 45), Janelt; Wissa, Forss, Dervişoğlu (Mbeumo, 68)

Forest Green Rovers: Thomas; Bernard, Moore-Taylor, Cargill; Edwards (Matt 79), Diallo (March 34), Hendry, Cadden (Allen 74); Adams, Young (Wilson 59), Aitchison

Friday, 27 August 2021

A familiar face will be welcoming the Bees for tomorrow's league match at Aston Villa. Dean Smith was Brentford manager between 2015 and 2018, during which time he made them one of the top teams in the Championship, challenging for the play-off places in each of his three seasons in charge. Smith's efforts earned him a move to

Villa, the team he had supported since boyhood. His father was a steward at Villa Park and he used to earn tickets for matches by cleaning seats in the stands. He guided Villa to promotion to the Premier League in 2019 and now comes face to face with his former club in the top echelons for the first time.

Thomas Frank, Smith's number two before replacing him as head coach, is naturally looking forward to renewing acquaintances. In his press conference, Frank was full of praise for his former colleague:

'I am happy for him, he has done so well. I know how brilliant he is as a manager to build a culture and building a belief in how he wants to play. Dean and Richard O'Kelly [one of Smith's assistants at Brentford] were a massive help for me when I joined the club. It was the first time for me out of Denmark. Since we have split, I have been on the phone with Dean asking for advice. He has always been helpful.'

Not only will Smith be in Brentford's way tomorrow, but striker Ollie Watkins will also be hoping to get one over on his former club. Watkins played 132 time for the Bees, scoring 49 goals before Smith took him to Villa for £28m.

'I wish Ollie all the best,' says Frank, 'I'm so happy he is having success. It was a sad moment when he had to leave. Even though we got a good price, I still think it was a bargain for Villa.'

In this age of social media and millions of television channels and ways of communicating with virtually anyone anywhere in the world, there seem to be no surprises anymore. Go back, say, 25 years and beyond, and things were a lot more 'under wraps' shall we say. You could watch the World Cup and not know every single thing about every single player and, as a consequence, be surprised and delighted by results such as Cameroon beating Argentina, as they did in 1990. Nowadays we would have all the information on players like Thomas N'Kono and François Omam-Biyik, whereas back then they were all new and exotic to us. It was the same with transfers. You would see on the evening news and in the newspapers the following day that Manchester United had signed Andy Cole and be amazed that Newcastle let their top scorer go to their biggest rivals, without the days and weeks of speculation and quotes and insider information that we get now. Today, though, something happened that came right out of the blue.

There had been rumblings for a couple of days that Manchester City were sounding out Cristiano Ronaldo about a move after their failed attempt to land Harry Kane from Tottenham, but there was nothing concrete. But then – bang! A statement from Old Trafford says that Ronaldo would be joining United. You what?! Where did that come from? Ronaldo posted a farewell video to the Juventus fans on his social media accounts and that was that – job done, Manchester here we come. I'm actually really pleased that this happened. Not necessarily because I want to see him back in a United shirt, but just because it seems that these sorts of deals can still be made outside of the public consciousness. This is what the transfer window should be all about, not long, protracted drawn-out deals that just get boring after a while. Welcome back to England, Cristiano, and see you at the Community Stadium in December.

Saturday, 28 August 2021
Frank Onyeka is ruled out of the game at Villa Park due to testing positive for COVID, meaning that Saman Ghoddos

plays from the start after his showing against Forest Green on Tuesday.

It looks like positive COVID tests are something we are going to see throughout the season as Onyeka is by no means the only player to already miss games this season. Among others, Arsenal's Ben White, Alexander Lacazette and Pierre-Emerick Aubameyang, along with Manchester City's Aymeric Laporte, have all returned positive tests and missed Premier League action due to their having to isolate.

An entertaining game sees Brentford collect another point and keep up their unbeaten run. They started on the front foot and within seven minutes had the lead. A corner was cleared only as far as Sergi Canós who fired it back into the danger area. The ball came to Ivan Toney who delightfully shot into the top corner. The same player might have had a second shortly after, but his effort was blocked. Villa's equaliser came when Danny Ings played a neat one-two with Anwar El Ghazi and then found Emi Buendía who slammed the ball past David Raya. It was Buendía's first goal for the club following his summer move from Norwich.

Brentford had a couple of chances to retake the lead when Christian Nørgaard almost turned a long thrown into the Villa net, but Alex Tuanzebe intercepted just in time, and Bryan Mbeumo was denied by a good save from Villa keeper Emiliano Martínez. The closest they came, though, was when Vitaly Janelt touched the ball away from Martínez as he threw it into the air when attempting a volleyed clearance. Janelt knocked the ball into the net, but the goal was disallowed. This is one of those things that will always split opinion. As such, the ball was in play as

Martínez had released it from his hands and Janelt didn't actually foul him. However, the rule insists that in these situations the ball is the goalkeeper's property until he has actually kicked it. In an England v Northern Ireland match in 1971, George Best did the same thing to Gordon Banks and his goal was also chalked off.

The second 45 minutes continued where the first left off with both Ghoddos and Canós having half chances and Thomas Frank brought on both Mathias Jensen and Shandon Baptiste from the substitutes' bench for their Premier League debuts. As for the hosts, they also could have taken all three points, but Raya saved well from Ollie Watkins.

Speaking to BBC Sport, Thomas Frank said he was happy with most of the performance but recognises that in this division the concentration needs to be constantly and completely switched on.

'I think we started the game brilliant,' he said, 'Coming to Villa Park we know is a very difficult place to play. We're brave, we're pressing high, we're getting in front 1-0 and I actually felt we were really on top of the game, but then one slight bit of miscommunication – maybe the first time in three games where we slightly open up a bit – and it gave them the chance and that is the quality of the Premier League.'

Aston Villa: Martínez; Cash, Konsa (Hause 89), Tuanzebe, Targett; Douglas Luiz; Buendía, Chukwuemeka (Nakamba 63), Young (Watkins 79), El Ghazi; Ings

Brentford: Raya; Ajer, Jansson, Pinnock; Canós, Nørgaard, Ghoddos (Wissa 66), Janelt (Baptiste 89), Henry; Toney, Mbeumo (Jensen 80)

Tuesday, 31 August 2021

Today sees the close of the transfer window. Deadline day deals include Crystal Palace buying striker Odsonne Édouard from Celtic, Arsenal signing defender Takehiro Tomiyasu from Italian club Bologna and Manchester United midfielder Daniel James joining Leeds. More than £1bn was spent during the window, the biggest transfers being Manchester City's acquisition of Aston Villa's Jack Grealish for £100m and Chelsea paying only slightly less for striker Romelu Lukaku from Inter Milan.

It's a quiet day in Brentford, with the business sensibly having been done before the season kicked off. I can never understand why clubs wait until the last minute before strengthening, particularly as the season is already three games old. Yes, I know that selling clubs often want replacements signed up before letting their players go, but surely it's best all round to get their deals done early, isn't it? That way you have pre-season to integrate the new players, get your game plan sorted and then hopefully hit the ground running. In this respect, well done to the Bees. The only movement was the exit of Halil Dervişoğlu, who rejoined Turkish side Galatasaray on loan until the end of the season.

Wednesday, 1 September 2021

It is the international break, with World Cup qualifying games being played around the world in the next few days. There is Brentford interest when Christian Nørgaard comes off the bench for Denmark as they beat Scotland 2-0 and in a friendly as Marcus Forss starts for Finland in their 0-0 draw with Wales.

Thursday, 2 September 2021

Once again, it is racism rather than the football action that makes the headlines. England's 4-0 victory in Hungary was marred when the abuse from the stands started as soon as Raheem Sterling scored the first goal. Substitute Jude Bellingham was also targeted as he warmed up along the touchline. I mean, seriously – in this day and age how can it be acceptable? Having said that, it has never been acceptable. Not now, not 100 years ago, not ever. Aside from the racist chants, missiles were thrown on to the pitch at the England players. The sad thing is that this wasn't entirely unexpected as Hungary are already under a UEFA order to play their next three European competition matches behind closed doors after the behaviour of their fans during Euro 2020.

After the match, England boss Gareth Southgate called for FIFA to take tough action.

'There's no more this group of players or staff can do in the fight against racism,' he said. 'Other people have got to take the right action to try and make progress. They shouldn't have to be subjected to any form of racism. It's not fair to criticise all the Hungarian fans – a lot were very generous and behaved extremely well. The individuals that are responsible need to be dealt with. I think there's some evidence that people have been filmed and we've got to hope the authorities deal with that in the right way.'

For the record, Harry Kane, Harry Maguire and Declan Rice added to Sterling's goal for a comfortable victory.

In today's other games, Brentford were represented by Samam Ghoddos, who played for Iran in their 1-0 win over Syria in the race for qualification for the 2022 finals in Qatar.

Saturday, 4 September 2021

A five-minute walk from the Community Stadium is the London Museum Of Water And Steam, and today it opens an exhibition called 'Farewell Griffin Park – The Fans' Story'. Open for the remainder of the season, the exhibition is a collection of memories about Griffin Park, Brentford's former home, using photographs, videos and various pieces of memorabilia.

In today's international matches, Christian Nørgaard and Mathias Jensen are both in the starting XI for Denmark in their 1-0 victory over the Faroe Islands, with Jensen's free kick setting up the winner, scored by Jonas Wind. It is the Danes' fifth win out of five qualifying matches and they look certs to take their place in the 2022 World Cup. Kristoffer Ajer's Norway were also victorious, beating Latvia 2-0, and Marcus Foss came on as a late substitute in Finland's narrow 1-0 win over Kazakhstan.

Sunday, 5 September 2021

Ethan Pinnock today won his second international cap for Jamaica, but they were beaten 3-0 by Panama in the CONCACAF qualifiers.

England recorded their second 4-0 win in four days with goals from Jesse Lingard (two), Harry Kane and Bukayo Saka as they beat Andorra at Wembley.

With regards to the smaller countries and qualifying competitions for major tournaments – no offence to Andorra here, but with the area being only 180 square miles and having a population of about 78,000, you are a small country – there have been, in recent years, calls for them to take part in pre-qualifiers before the actual qualifying tournament begins. It is pointed out in some quarters that countries such as Andorra, Malta, the Faroe Islands and North Macedonia are, basically, whipping boys and that only the best of these should make it to the stage where they take on England, Germany, Italy and the like. The thing is, why shouldn't they be allowed into the qualifiers proper? They are, after all, countries in their own right, the same as anyone else.

It seems that football has, presumably unintentionally, become somewhat elitist at the highest level. What a waste of time it is for England to have to go to Estonia or Spain having to travel to Kosovo, seems to be the attitude. The thing is, the same was being said of countries like Cameroon and Turkey years ago, and they are now established international football nations.

It is the same with the Champions League. What does the name suggest? A league full of champions, perhaps? But look who are granted entry every year. The 32 teams that make up the first group stage include four each from the top leagues in England, Spain, Italy and Germany. How can that be a Champions League? Not only that, but many actual champions from the leagues that are not quite as, shall we say, 'showbiz' as certain others, have to play qualifiers to gain entry to the competition. We therefore have a Champions League competition full of teams who are not champions playing at the expense of many who are.

In the days before the format was changed, the European Cup, as it was then called, was a straight knockout competition between the league champions of each UEFA-affiliated country the previous season. We therefore had more chances of upsets as each team only had a home and away tie to negotiate before advancing to the next round. Surely that is what a cup competition should be all about, should it not? Nowadays, though, if Real Madrid suffer a shock defeat by FC Copenhagen, say, they have a further five games to recover and get the points needed to progress, which they invariably will. I may be cynical here, but it sort of guarantees the top 16 clubs in Europe get into the knockout stages every year, bringing in bigger television audiences and more money. But that can't be the reason for the current format, can it?!

Tuesday, 7 September 2021

The international fixtures continue and another victory is recorded by Denmark, with Christian Nørgaard coming off the subs' bench for the last ten minutes of their 5-0 victory over Israel in Copenhagen. Norway, with Kristoffer Ajer at the back, also hit five in their group match against Gibraltar. In the Asian qualifying section, Saman Ghoddos played the last 30 minutes for Iran as they beat Iraq 3-0.

Thursday, 9 September 2021

Brentford announce that they have signed the Danish international defender Mathias Jørgensen. Even though the transfer window is closed, Jørgensen is able to join as he is a free agent and currently without a club having left Turkish club Fenerbahçe in the summer. He has played in the Premier League before, having been with Huddersfield between 2017 and 2019. When Jørgensen plays, he may well have the name Zanka on his shirt rather than Jørgensen. Why is that, then?

'My former youth coach had seen the movie *Cool Runnings*,' he explained to Radio Leeds during his time at Huddersfield, 'and we had to cram a lot of people in the car. I was sat in front of the passenger seat in what seemed like a bobsleigh and he looked down and said "Zanka" and it just caught on. By the end of high school everyone was calling me Zanka and when I signed my first contract at Copenhagen they asked me what I wanted on my shirt. Zanka is more recognisable than Jørgensen as a lot of people are named Jørgensen in Scandinavia.'

So there you go, mystery solved. For those who may be uninitiated, *Cool Runnings* is a film from 1993 inspired by the true story of the Jamaican bobsleigh team who qualified for the 1988 Winter Olympics. I won't give the rest of plot away, so anybody who is now desperately trying to get a copy can watch it without spoilers. The character Zanka Coffie is played by Doug E. Doug.

Saturday, 11 September 2021

It's back to Premier League action today after the international break and Brentford play host to Brighton.

A good first half sees the Bees create a few chances, but they go begging. Following some good build-up work from Ethan Pinnock and Bryan Mbeumo, Ivan Toney came closest when he hammered his shot just over the bar with Brighton goalkeeper Robert Sánchez beaten, and Mbeumo himself had a couple of sights at goal. Just before the break, Sánchez came to Brighton's rescue when he got down to Vitaly Janelt's fierce drive and the deadlock remained unbroken.

As the second half wore on the sides began to cancel each other out somewhat and clear-cut chances were few and far between. Just as the match was petering out into a goalless draw, Brighton's Argentinian midfielder Alexis Mac Allister made inroads into the Bees' defence and found Leo Trossard who bent his effort round David Raya and into the Brentford net. Not long after the final whistle blew and a late, late goal meant Brentford suffered their first Premier League defeat. But this is what happens in the Premier League – if you don't take your chances you will be punished. It's how you respond that shows your character. Brentford's next game is away at Wolves which won't be easy as they registered their first win of the season today, 2-0 at Watford.

'It was an even game between two sides that wanted to get on top,' said Thomas Frank after the match. 'Up until the 75th minute we were better, or at least had more dangerous situations. Defensively we set high standards – just four shots away. Offensively, in spells we were good but need to be better. One moment decides the game and that is the Premier League.'

Brentford: Raya; Ajer, Jansson, Pinnock; Canós (Roerslev 61), Nørgaard, Baptiste (Onyeka 75), Janelt (Jensen 68), Henry; Toney, Mbeumo

Brighton & Hove Albion: Sánchez; Webster (Moder 37), Duffy, Dunk; Veltman, Lallana, Bissouma, Cucurella (March 82); Trossard; Maupay, Welbeck (Mac Allister 64)

Saturday, 18 September 2021

'I think this was our best performance so far in the Premier League, I'm crazy proud,' said Thomas Frank today on *Match of the Day*. 'The way they perform and express themselves is very impressive.'

Brentford's first away win of the season is secured with a 2-0 success at Wolves, and it could have been so many more. Not only did goals from Ivan Toney and Bryan Mbeumo secure the three points, but two further strikes from Toney were both ruled out.

Brentford took the lead when Sergi Canós's cross found Toney in the box, but the striker was bundled to the floor. He picked himself up to stroke home the penalty. Immediately from the restart, Brentford won the ball back and Vitaly Janelt found some space inside the Wolves penalty area. His shot was saved by José Sá but, as the ball bounced out, Canós played it back into the danger area and Toney back-heeled it into the net. VAR was consulted and Toney was adjudged to have used his arm to control the ball before netting.

Wanderers were close to getting back on level terms when Adama Traoré hammered in a shot that flew past David Raya but, unfortunately for the Wolves man, he saw the ball bounce back off the crossbar. With Raúl Jiménez lurking, Rico Henry made a timely interception to preserve Brentford's lead. After the danger was cleared, Toney rampaged down the left, leaving Max Kilman in his wake. As Sá came out to close the angle, Toney rolled the ball across for Mbeumo to knock it into the empty net to make it 2-0.

After the break, Mbeumo almost made it three when he bent a shot just over the bar with Sá beaten after Janelt had robbed playmaker Rúben Neves, and Wolves themselves might have pulled one back but for an excellent challenge from Kristoffer Ajer on Francisco Trincão just as he was about to pull the trigger.

Toney did have the ball in the net for the third time but, once again, he saw his strike ruled out. Canós slid Mbeumo in behind the Wolves defence and he pulled it back for Toney to slot it home. This time the decision was offside against Mbeumo.

Mathias Jørgensen came off the substitutes' bench to replace Pontus Jansson for his Brentford debut as the Bees saw the game out. The only blot on Brentford's day was the second-half dismissal of Shandon Baptiste after he collected two yellow cards in quick succession.

It was Toney who won all the plaudits after the match. Speaking on Radio 5 Live, the former Rangers and Tottenham defender Alan Hutton said, 'When you've got someone like Ivan Toney up front, who is built for this league – he's big, he's calm and he can pick a pass – you're in with a chance.'

Ex-Arsenal defender Martin Keown agreed. Speaking as a *Match of the Day* pundit, he compared Toney to Chelsea's Romelu Lukaku, 'Toney caused real problems and Wolves were frightened to death of him. He's got all the qualities you need. We talk about Lukaku a lot of the time, but Toney caused panic. If you look at his pace, power and intelligence, he knows what he's good at. He belongs at this Premier League level, there is no doubt about that. He's going from strength to strength.' Considering Lukaku is Belgium's all-time leading goalscorer and cost Chelsea almost £100m in the summer, that is one mighty compliment.

Wolverhampton Wanderers: Sá; Kilman, Coady, Saïss (Hwang 45); Semedo (Silva 82), Moutinho, Neves, Marçal (Podence 72); Trincão, Jiménez, Traoré

Brentford: Raya; Ajer, Jansson (Jørgensen 82), Pinnock; Canós (Onyeka 68), Baptiste, Nørgaard, Janelt, Henry (Roerslev 75); Toney, Mbeumo

Tuesday, 21 September 2021

After Ivan Toney took all the headlines at the weekend, tonight it was Marcus Forss's turn. For the League Cup match against Oldham, Thomas Frank completely changed his team from the one that beat Wolves, and Forss took centre stage as he banged in four goals in an amazing

7-0 win. Yes, Oldham are currently bottom of the entire Football League, but even so, a seven-goal victory isn't easy to come by.

It took Brentford only three minutes to open the scoring. Yoane Wissa was tripped in the penalty box and Forss converted the resulting spot-kick. The second also came from Wissa's approach play when his shot beat the Oldham goalkeeper and bounced back off the post. The rebound landed at Forss's feet and he knocked in number two. Wissa himself notched the third after being put through by Mathias Jensen and the fourth came courtesy of an own goal from Raphael Diarra who, when attempting to intercept a ball meant for Forss, turned it into his own net. Four became five almost instantly when Forss found himself with the freedom of Oldham's penalty area to complete his hat-trick. The second half saw two further goals, Forss firing in his fourth and Brentford's sixth with Wissa's spectacular overhead kick rounding off the scoring.

After the match, Frank was understandably delighted, 'Marcus is doing everything he can in training every day. He's a really good player we have big belief in. He scored four really good goals, showed a top work rate and was very aggressive in pressure with good link up play, so I guess that has to be ten out of ten.'

The draw for the next round takes place after tomorrow's ties.

Brentford: Fernández; Jørgensen, Goode, Thompson; Roerslev (Bidstrup 71), Ghoddos, Jensen, Onyeka (Peart-Harris 71), Fosu (Stevens 71); Wissa, Forss

Oldham Athletic: Leutwiler; Fage, Clarke, Piergiani (Da Silva 45), Jameson; Kiellor-Dunn, Bowden, Diarra, Whelan, Bahamboula (Couto 45); Dearnley (Vaughan 45)

Wednesday, 22 September 2021

Kristoffer Ajer has given an interesting interview to Norwegian television channel TV2, talking about Brentford's scouting system prior to his transfer from Celtic. He said, 'Brentford said they had been to 123 matches with Celtic and provided feedback on which ones were green and approved and which ones were red and unacceptable. They analyse everything. What I liked about this club compared to others was that they said there was a lot of excitement with me. They were interested in me but also there was a lot I had to improve.'

It strikes me as astounding that a club would watch a player over 100 times. That's two seasons and more! That's certainly thorough, I'll give them that. I just wonder how often they have watched a player they are really interested in, say, 80 times and then suddenly he has transferred to another club somewhere who has 'only' watched them 50 times. In the old days, a manager would get a scouting report, go and watch the player themselves or send a club representative a couple of times and act upon that. Times they are a-changing.

The draw for the next round of the League Cup gives Brentford an away match at Stoke City. Stoke have made a decent start to the season in the Championship so it will be a tricky tie.

Elsewhere, it has been announced that FIFA have fined the Hungarian Football Federation £158,000 and their next two matches will be played behind closed doors. This is a result of the racist chanting aimed at England players during their World Cup qualifying match at the start of the month. The FIFA statement read, 'The FIFA Disciplinary Committee has imposed a ban and substantial fine on the Hungarian Football Federation in relation to the racist behaviour of numerous supporters during the FIFA World Cup Qatar 2022 qualifying match between Hungary and England on 2 September 2021. After analysing and taking into consideration all the circumstances of the case, specifically the seriousness of the incidents (racist words and actions, throwing of objects, lighting of fireworks, blocked stairways), the Committee decided the MLSZ would play its next two home matches in FIFA competitions without spectators, the second match being suspended for a probationary period of two years. In addition, the Committee imposed a fine of 200,000 Swiss Francs. FIFA's position remains firm and resolute in rejecting any form of racism and violence as well as any other form of discrimination and abuse. FIFA takes a clear zero-tolerance stance against such abhorrent behaviour in football.'

Saturday, 25 September 2021

This is exactly what it was all for. All the hard work, the lessons learned, the blood, sweat and tears and everything else that was involved in getting Brentford up into the top division. Days like today show it was all worthwhile. A packed Community Stadium for the visit of Liverpool, and a barnstorming end-to-end six-goal thriller. Today was everything we dared hope for, and perhaps a little bit more besides.

The game started as it meant to go on. Liverpool looked to put Brentford under pressure from the off, but the home side were dangerous on the break. Andy Robertson fired a dangerous ball that fizzed across the Brentford goalmouth missing everyone and Kristoffer Ajer reached Jordan Henderson's dangerous ball just before Curtis Jones could turn it in. Jones then threaded a ball through to Mo Salah who rolled it past David Raya. He was already turning away to celebrate what would have been his 100th league goal for Liverpool only to see Ajer race back to hook it clear. Moments later the tables were turned when Bryan Mbeumo knocked the ball past visiting goalkeeper Alisson Becker, but this time it was Joel Matip who made the last-ditch clearance.

The opening goal came from a Brentford set piece straight off the training ground. Vitaly Janelt played a free kick to Christian Nørgaard who slid the ball in to Sergi Canós. The Spaniard's cross was flicked on by Ivan Toney to Ethan Pinnock who arrived at the back post to knock the ball in. The joy, though, was short lived as a few minutes later Liverpool's Diogo Jota powered a header into the Brentford net for the equaliser. Once again it was Henderson who was pulling the strings and he placed his cross directly on to Jota's head.

The action continued relentlessly. Toney narrowly failed to connect with Mbeumo's lay-off, just beaten to the ball by Alisson, and Raya produced a great save from Jota's follow-up after Jones had seen his shot deflected on to a post by Pontus Jansson.

The second half carried on where the first half left off, with end-to-end stuff producing chances for both sides. It was the visitors who got their noses in front when Salah's run beyond the Brentford defence was spotted by Fabinho who lofted a pass into the area for the Egyptian to touch the ball past Raya. This time there was no recovering defender and his century of Premier League goals was completed.

Liverpool looked to capitalise on their advantage and pressed for a third. Raya saved from Jota, Trent Alexander-

Arnold had a shot blocked and Robertson saw his effort fly past the post. The Bees, however, refused to lay down and let the former champions take control. Canós's cross was met at the far post by Mbeumo who saw his effort blocked. The rebound fell to Pontus Jansson whose effort came back off the crossbar straight to Vitaly Janelt who nodded the ball over the line to restore parity.

Still the action continued unabated. Sadio Mané laid up a chance for Jones who shot over the bar but, just moments later, he made amends. He cut inside from the left wing and fired home a long-range effort that flew past Raya via a slight deflection off Jansson.

With time running out, Brentford attacked down the right and Shandon Baptiste's cross was just too high for Toney, but substitute Yoane Wissa reacted quickest to the loose ball to dink it over Alisson as he came out to make it 3-3.

In the final couple of minutes both sides might have taken all three points. Jørgensen headed a half-cleared corner back into the danger zone and Toney fired it past Alisson but was thwarted by an offside decision, his third disallowed goal in two league games. There was just enough time for Raya to get down to Roberto Firmino's low shot before the referee's whistle finally brought an absolutely breathless encounter to an end with honours even, points shared and a standing ovation for both teams all round the stadium.

'Fantastic performance, in many ways extremely proud of the players,' said Thomas Frank after the game. 'They were brave, they played with determination throughout the game. We went up 1-0, they equalised quickly after, in the second half when they're going up 2-1 we are still staying in the game, still going, still believing and we're hanging in there and, in the end, we're playing 3-3 with Liverpool, one of the best teams in Europe, and I think it was a completely fair result. In the end we could have potentially won the game.'

His Liverpool counterpart, Jürgen Klopp, was very complimentary towards Brentford. 'Brentford deserved a point,' he said. 'They deserved a point as well because they put up a proper fight. I respect that a lot.'

Alan Shearer agreed with Klopp. Speaking on *Match of the Day*, he said, 'They were intelligent, they were brave, they played very well and, yes, they caused Liverpool all sorts of problems. And they had a game plan, and that game plan worked to perfection at times. Yes, they were direct, but why shouldn't they be when they have players who can attack the ball? They get balls into the box because Toney can do that.'

Let's just take a deep breath and think about this for a moment. Brentford 3 Liverpool 3 at the Community Stadium in the Premier League. The visitors were Premier League champions two seasons ago. They won the title by 18 points, an absolutely huge margin. They could have forfeited their last five games and still been champions. They have won 19 league championships, just one behind Manchester United's record of 20. They have won six European Cups and Champions Leagues, behind only Real Madrid, who have won 13 and AC Milan with seven, and level with Bayern Munich. The famous names in Liverpool's history read like a who's who of the English game – the likes of Kevin Keegan, Tommy Smith, Kenny Dalglish, Ian Rush, Robbie Fowler, Michael Owen, Steven Gerrard and many more. And today Brentford stood toe to toe with them, giving them a real fright. And it was no fluke. No, Brentford didn't win the game but, when today's euphoria dies down and this match is looked at in the cold light of day, it will absolutely highlight just how far the Bees have come and what a momentous season this is for the club.

Brentford: Raya; Ajer, Jansson, Pinnock (Jørgensen 43); Canós, Onyeka (Baptiste 68), Nørgaard (Wissa 78), Janelt, Henry; Toney, Mbeumo

Liverpool: Alisson; Alexander-Arnold, Matip, Van Dijk, Robertson; Henderson, Fabinho, Jones (Firmino 67); Salah, Jota, Mané

Monday, 27 September 2021

Speaking on talkSPORT this morning, Ivan Toney tells breakfast show host Laura Woods that he was disappointed Brentford didn't win on Saturday. 'It was crazy,' he said, 'to think we were going toe to toe with Liverpool. With the chances we had and the way the game panned out, we were kind of disappointed. It sounds crazy to say that we should have taken all three points from one of the best teams in the world. But it was a great experience and the boys enjoyed it.'

Co-host Jamie O'Hara, a former Tottenham midfielder, reacting to his old team's 3-1 defeat at the hands of their north London rivals Arsenal, asked Toney to sign for Spurs. He probably didn't get the reaction he was after as Toney just laughed!

Friday, 1 October 2021

Thomas Frank's press conference today focused on Sunday's match with West Ham, extolling the job that his counterpart David Moyes is doing in east London:

'David Moyes, with his staff around him, has shown what a great coach he is. I am really pleased for him. He is soon to pass the milestone of 1,000 games. He did a fantastic job at Everton, an unbelievable job at Preston but then suddenly, because it didn't work out at Manchester United, it seems like he wasn't recognised as a proper coach. What he has done at West Ham is fantastic – he's taken them to their second best position in the Premier League, they have sold players in every position and he's continued this season. What he's done is remarkable and he deserves a lot of praise.'

Frank also spoke about Saïd Benrahma, a former Brentford player who is now starring for the Hammers, 'I am so pleased that he is doing well. I always thought his abilities on the ball were Premier League class and he's showed that. His one v ones, his assists and his goalscoring is at a very high level. I hope he does very well, except on Sunday.'

Sunday, 3 October 2021

The *Mail on Sunday* today carries an interview with Thomas Frank. In it he explains the 'bus stop in Hounslow' reference that he used after the victory over Arsenal on the opening day. It began as an insult from Queens Park Rangers supporters – 'You're just a bus stop in Hounslow' they sang sarcastically – but it has been since used as a motivation.

'The bus stop in Hounslow is, in many ways, a very good analogy of what kind of club we are compared to all the big ones we're competing with,' says Frank. 'When Leeds went up – massive club; when Wolves went up – massive club; when Sheffield United went up – massive club. We are just little Brentford. Of course, we know within the club, with the knowledge, with the hard work, quality players, fantastic staff, we have quality. We know that. But we need to understand we are a small club. If I was head coach of Leeds, I would never say it we're just a bus stop, that would never work. But this can work in our favour as every single time we get a point it's a fantastic performance.'

The journey across town to West Ham is already Brentford's third London derby of the season. No other city in the world has so many such matches in its footballing calendar. In the Premier League alone, Arsenal, Brentford, Chelsea, Crystal Palace, Tottenham and West Ham play in the capital, meaning each has ten league derby matches per year. Fulham seem to be bouncing between the top two divisions in recent years as well, so maybe next season there will be even more.

And let's not forget the lower-league sides, either. Add Charlton Athletic, Leyton Orient, Millwall, Queens Park Rangers, Sutton United and AFC Wimbledon and that makes a total of 13 Premier League and Football League teams playing in London. There is an argument for placing Sutton United in Surrey which, a few years ago, would have been the case but, as London has expanded outwards, Sutton has been swallowed up and is now just on the London side of the London/Surrey border. Two other London teams have also been floating between the Football League and non-league football in recent seasons in Barnet and Dagenham & Redbridge, and Bromley are among the favourites to be promoted from the National League this year so, potentially, there could be 16 London teams playing in the Football League at any one time.

No other city in Europe has so many professional clubs, certainly not so many at the top end of their football hierarchy. Moscow boasts 14 professional clubs but of those only CSKA Moscow, Dynamo Moscow, Lokomotiv Moscow and Spartak Moscow play in their Premier League, and Istanbul has 13, including the big three of Turkish football – Galatasaray, Beşiktaş and Fenerbahçe – but Istanbul is in both Europe and Asia as the Bosphorus Strait, the border between the two continents, splits the city in half.

The sheer amount of London clubs is the reason why not every team is considered deadly rivals with one another and that the city, at least for footballing reasons, is split into the four compass points – north, south, east and west. For instance, the Arsenal-Tottenham rivalry is the one that matters to both clubs whereas, when either team plays against, say, Crystal Palace, yes, it is a London derby, but that intense feeling of rivalry is not there.

Brentford started the game on the front foot and the strike force of Bryan Mbeumo and Ivan Toney caused the West Ham defence problems. Mbeumo had a chance from Rico Henry's cross, but his header flashed wide of the post and, shortly after, his long range effort flicked the crossbar with Hammers keeper Łukasz Fabiański beaten. Toney, for his part, forced Fabiański into action with a volleyed effort.

For all Brentford's early dominance, West Ham themselves had a couple of chances to take the lead as they grew into the game. Kurt Zouma's header fell just the wrong side of the post and Pontus Jansson was well-placed to block Michail Antonio's effort. Just as it seemed the momentum was swinging the way of the home team, Brentford struck. Sergi Canós ran beyond the Hammers' defence and Toney's pass was perfectly weighted for Canós to strike low to Fabiański's right. Somehow he managed to get a hand to it but the rebound fell kindly for Mbeumo. Still Fabiański managed to get down to Mbeumo's effort to scoop it away but the Goal Decision System showed that the ball had clearly crossed the line before Fabiański's intervention.

The second half saw West Ham begin to dominate the possession and press for the equaliser. David Raya was called into action to deal with a Saïd Benrahma free kick and he also reacted smartly to thwart Jarrod Bowen. Michail Antonio might have done better than volley an effort wide and Tomáš Souček's header failed to test Raya. Inevitably, though, the pressure finally told. Aaron Cresswell's corner found Declan Rice at the near post and his flick found its way to Bowen who slammed his shot past a helpless Raya.

The game could easily have swung away from Brentford, but their fighting spirit kept West Ham at bay as the home team pressed for the winner. Rice almost set up Bowen for what may well have been that crucial goal, but Pontus Jansson did enough to put him off and his header went wide of the target. When the winner did come, though, it was via Yoane Wissa. Just as he did against Liverpool, he climbed off the bench to grab his goal, this time earning all three points. Mathias Jensen's free kick picked out Jansson whose header was kept out by Fabiański. The rebound, though, fell to Wissa who drilled the ball back past him into the net. There was just time enough for West Ham to kick off again and the final whistle blew. A last-gasp victory for Brentford, but today they showed they're certainly up for the fight.

This Premier League malarkey is easy, isn't it? What's all the fuss about? Three more points, another away victory, give us the championship trophy now!

'We went to a difficult place, West Ham away,' said Thomas Frank afterwards. 'A very, very good team. The way we approached it, brave, aggressive, taking control of the game to go 1-0 up. West Ham took over in the second half and we had to show togetherness. But we did that. We weathered the storm after they scored but that mentality to go again for the win was fantastic.'

It was put to Frank that Brentford are becoming everyone's second favourite team. 'I guess that's OK,' he agreed. 'It's nice and I understand why. I think we're a good story. We are approachable and positive, so I understand it. But I'm also very aware everything changes very quickly in football so we must keep on working. I'm always honest, so I believe in the team and the players massively and I believed that we could do something in the Premier League. Also, from the beginning, I knew we would be strong defensively and pressing forward and aggressive. I also knew that we would try to be brave, that's my biggest message to the players. But, of course, 12 points – that's a lot. We are proud but I think it's also a truly deserved 12 points.'

West Ham United: Fabiański; Coufal, Zouma, Ogbonna, Cresswell; Souček, Rice; Bowen, Benrahma, Fornals; Antonio

Brentford: Raya; Jørgensen, Jansson, Pinnock; Canós, Baptiste (Jensen 29), Nørgaard, Onyeka (Bidstrup 81), Henry; Toney, Mbeumo (Wissa 81)

Today also saw the Premier League's first managerial casualty of the season. Watford have parted company with Xisco Muñoz after ten months in charge, despite his leading them to promotion last season. It seems to be par for the course at Watford, the club having had four managers in just two years. It is expected that Claudio Ranieri, who led Leicester City to their remarkable Premier League victory in 2016, will be appointed his successor.

Saturday, 9 October 2021

It is international break time again and in the match in Moldova, Christian Nørgaard scores his first international goal in Denmark's 4-0 win. Skov Olsen's corner found Nørgaard at the back post and he turned the ball in to open his account with the national team.

England secured a comfortable 5-0 victory in Andorra with Gareth Southgate pretty much playing a second-string side. Goals from Ben Chilwell, Bukayo Saka, Tammy Abraham, James Ward-Prowse and substitute Jack Grealish secured the points and put England within two victories of qualifying for the tournament as group winners.

Monday, 11 October 2021

Cadena SER, the Spanish radio network, broadcasts an interview with David Raya. He is asked about rumours that have begun to circulate about a move away from Brentford to either Arsenal or Everton.

'I'm happy at the club,' Raya confirmed. 'I want to have a good season this year. We'll see what happens in the summer. My ambitions are great, I'd like to play at the top. You always want to play for big clubs.'

On his international ambitions, Raya says, 'For me it'd be a dream to represent Spain. I've dreamed of it since I was little. If this is the case, I'm delighted. I have to keep working and competing to please Luis Enrique [the Spanish national team manager].'

Fin Stevens, on duty for Wales Under-21s, says that he hopes the progress Brentford are making can help him force his way into his country's full squad.

'We're doing really well in the league,' he says, 'and I was lucky enough to be on the bench once, at Aston Villa.

It was a great experience. Getting minutes in the B team and being in and around the first team at training is a really good experience.'

On Brentford's start to the Premier League campaign, he says, 'We've just got to keep doing what we're doing. The way we're playing is obviously working. Playing off Ivan is the main thing, but I think we can give anyone a run for their money in the league.'

Tuesday, 12 October 2021

Brentford will be represented at the World Cup next summer as Denmark ensured their qualification with a 1-0 victory against Austria in Copenhagen. It was the Danes' eighth victory in eight matches and they now cannot be caught as they are seven points ahead of second placed Scotland with only two games remaining. Christian Nørgaard and Mathias Jensen both came on as late substitutes.

England drew 1-1 with Hungary at Wembley, John Stones equalising Roland Sallai's penalty. They are three points clear of Poland at the top of the table with games against Albania and San Marino to come in November, so qualifying should – *should* – be a formality.

Fin Stevens doesn't enjoy such a successful night with the Welsh Under-21s as they are beaten 5-0 by the Netherlands in Nijmegen and he unfortunately puts one in his own net.

Friday, 15 October 2021

Brentford face Chelsea at the weekend and Thomas Frank has been looking forward to the big game, but also highlighting the task that Brentford face.

'The day we won promotion through the play-off final they won the Champions League,' he points out. 'With the offensive threat that they possess we need to defend very well. We also need to be brave and press high when we can. We have to want the ball in as many moments as possible. Most importantly, we need to be brave. We are playing against a world class team and, on paper, they are much better than us but in the end it is 11 v 11. The braver we can be, showing the right mentality, the better chance we have of winning the game.

'I believed that we could get something out of the game against Liverpool, and I also believe we can get something out of the game against Chelsea. The odds are more towards a win for Chelsea than a win for Brentford but I 100 per cent believe we can get something out of the game, hopefully three points. We are not going out there to put in a nice performance, do well and everyone likes Brentford. We are going out there to try to win.'

Saturday, 16 October 2021

Let's get this into context, then. For years now, Chelsea have been able to take their pick from some of the world's best talent, both playing and managerial, and were able to spend almost £100m on a star striker in the shape of Romelu Lukaku during the latest transfer window. They have won six championships, eight FA Cups, six European trophies and they are the current European champions. Brentford, by contrast, are in the top division for the first time in most people's living memory, have never won the league, their best performance in the FA Cup is reaching the quarter-finals and their record signing, Kristoffer Ajer, cost them £13.5m. So, a walkover of a victory, then?

Chelsea began strongly, Timo Werner almost finding a way through only for Mathias Jensen's challenge to halt his run to goal. As the half wore on, though, Brentford came more and more into the game and started to threaten the visitors' defence. Ivan Toney saw a header deflected wide and, from the resulting corner, the Bees came even closer to breaking the deadlock. The delivery itself was cleared, but only as far as Sergi Canós. He returned the ball into the danger area where Ethan Pinnock nodded it across goal to Christian Nørgaard who in turn touched it into the path of Bryan Mbeumo. His shot beat Chelsea goalkeeper Édouard Mendy but bounced away to safety off a post. Not long after, Werner broke free and crossed for Lukaku to steer the ball past David Raya to give Chelsea the lead. Or did he? VAR returned an offside verdict and the game remained all square.

As the half-time interval approached, both teams had opportunities to open the scoring in quick succession. Mateo Kovačić saw his free kick deflected wide and, at the other end, Nørgaard won possession and freed Mbeumo, but Mendy got down to save. It proved to be a vital stop as, just as the first 45 minutes were almost up, N'Golo Kanté played the ball wide to César Azpilicueta whose cross was only half cleared and Ben Chilwell fired the ball past Raya. This time there was no VAR intervention and the Blues went in one up.

The second half saw Brentford take the game to their illustrious rivals and Mendy come to Chelsea's rescue time and time again. As the half progressed, Chelsea's defending became more and more desperate and Mendy's keeping more and more heroic as they found their goal under siege. Only a flying save stopped Toney's effort from arrowing into the top corner, Mbeumo hit the post for the second time in the game after being released by Marcus Forss and

Saman Ghoddos saw Mendy block his effort down at the near post. The chances continued to come with Nørgaard coming close three times. Firstly, his flick was cleared off the line by Trevor Chalobah, then he had another attempt blocked and finally an overhead attempt was acrobatically tipped over the bar by Mendy. It was a cracking finish to the match but somehow Chelsea's defence remained unbroken. They will not play many other matches this season where they will be so reliant on their goalkeeper to preserve their three points.

Quite understandably, Thomas Frank was very proud of his players afterwards. Speaking on *Match of the Day*, he said that he was very proud of the performance and that Chelsea were very lucky to win the game.

'We kept the champions of Europe to five shots in the whole game,' he said, 'and that's very impressive. I know they dominated a little bit more in the first half but, in the end, we were all over them and that's very, very impressive. If we play this game again we win it. It is what it is. We really want to build on this.'

Brentford: Raya; Jørgensen, Jansson, Pinnock; Canós (Ghoddos 72), Onyeka (Forss 66), Nørgaard, Jensen, Henry; Toney, Mbeumo

Chelsea: Mendy; Chalobah, Christensen, Sarr; Azpilicueta (James 89), Kanté, Loftus-Cheek, Kovačić (Mount 65), Chilwell; Lukaku (Havertz 77), Werner

Friday, 22 October 2021
Ahead of Brentford's match against Leicester on Sunday, Sergi Canós is interviewed in *The Sun* about his reunion with Brendon Rodgers. At the age of 16, Canós spent some time at Liverpool, then being managed by the now Leicester boss.

'Brendon had a very good impact at Liverpool,' he remembers. 'He wanted a lot of academy players training with him regularly. He was really good with us. He gave us hope that if you worked hard, you would get your chances. I'm not surprised about what he has done at Leicester. The way he likes to play is how football now is. He was a revolutionary in that respect.'

Canós played in every game of Liverpool's 2014/15 UEFA Youth League campaign and, after spending most of the 2015/16 season away on loan, made an appearance for the Reds' first team on the last day of the season, coming on as a substitute in a 1-1 draw with West Brom. The following season was spent on loan at Brentford before transferring to Norwich where he made three appearances in 2016/17.

He moved back to west London the following season. It was during his time at Norwich that he was a team-mate and room-mate of James Maddison, whom he will also be facing at the weekend.

'We would both be in the group of 20 travelling to games, but the coach then chose his squad of 18 and Madders and me were always the two left out. They were hard times, but we had a really good relationship and we supported each other,' Canós said.

He also spoke about Brentford's great start to the season and their determination to put up a good fight:

'We have been working so hard to get to this league and we are here now. We can't disappoint people. It is our responsibility to show we can compete. We can compete against Chelsea, we drew against Liverpool, we beat West Ham who finished in the top six. But without that spirit we are no one.'

Sunday, 24 October 2021

Leicester's visit to the Community Stadium provided another end-to-end game that could have gone either way. Brentford dominated for long periods of the first half and almost took an early lead. Mathias Jørgensen's long throw fell to Christian Nørgaard whose volley looked a certainty for the bottom corner, but Leicester keeper Kasper Schmeichel got down smartly to deny him. Shortly afterwards, though, a helpless Schmeichel was unable to stop Ivan Toney's tap-in after Mathias Jensen set Rico Henry away down the left. Henry's cross found Toney unmarked at the far post to touch the ball home. Unfortunately, though, the flag was up and Toney was ruled offside.

Bryan Mbeumo also had a good opportunity to open the scoring after he left Çaglar Söyüncü for dead, but Schmeichel narrowed the angle and Mbeumo's effort ended up wide of the far post.

When the opening goal came it was the visitors who scored it. James Maddison swung a free kick into the Brentford penalty area but the ball was headed out of the danger zone by Henry. The immediate danger zone, that is, as the ball fell to Youri Tielemans who thundered a first-time shot into the top corner of David Raya's net from fully 25 yards. There was absolutely nothing he could have done about it and Leicester had the lead.

The rest of the first half saw Brentford push for the equaliser and come close on a couple of occasions. Schmeichel produced a flying save to tip a header from Toney over the bar and from the resultant corner Henry shot wide from the edge of the box.

The second half saw a more even spread of possession. Raya thwarted Maddison after he had produced a strong run from midfield and was again on hand to stop Boubakary Soumaré extending Leicester's lead. Schmeichel, on the other hand, was powerless to prevent the Brentford equaliser. Mathias Jensen swung in a corner which was flicked into the net at the near post by Mathias Jørgensen for his first Brentford goal.

The winning goal may well have come from either side. Kristoffer Ajer saw a shot deflected wide and Toney lashed an effort just past the post. When the winner did come, it was from a swift counter attack from the visitors. Schmeichel kicked a quick clearance to Kelechi Iheanacho who knocked it inside for Tielemans. The Belgian picked out the run of Patson Daka and, as Raya came out to meet him, he laid the ball across for Maddison to knock the ball into the empty net.

'It was a very good performance, I'm very proud of the players. Chelsea are number one in the Premier League and Leicester became the fifth last season, they are a very good side, very well coached,' was Thomas Frank's post-match verdict.

On the reaction to the disappointment of the defeat, he said, 'That's why it is difficult in sport because now you can feel that I'm irritated, my body is burning and the same is with the players. It's about getting that out of the system, be rational, evaluate, reflect on the game. Good performance – can we do that again? If we put that determination in again we'll be absolutely fine.'

Brentford: Raya; Jørgensen, Jansson, Pinnock (Ajer 45); Canós, Onyeka (Ghoddos 77), Nørgaard, Jensen, Henry; Toney, Mbeumo (Forss 57)

Leicester City: Schmeichel; Amartey, Evans, Söyüncü (Vestergaard 68); Pereira, Tielemans, Soumaré, Castagne; Maddison (Pérez 78); Vardy (Daka 45), Iheanacho

Monday, 25 October 2021

There are a few words from Mathias Jørgensen in today's *Evening Standard* about the need for Brentford to capitalise on their chances during matches.

'I think the Premier League is all about being clinical,' he says, 'having that guy who wins the game for you. Whether that being a keeper that makes a great save or a defender that makes a great block, a striker that gets that goal. I think we have so much quality up front and we'll keep scoring goals, I'm not worried about that. But obviously, on a day like this, it does hurt that we don't get anything or any more out of all the chances and ball we had today.'

In the Premier League that might be easier said than done. Last season in the Championship, out of the 46 league matches, Brentford scored two or more goals in 23 of them and in the other 23 where they didn't, they were still able to take points from 18 of them, including five 1-0 wins. Of course, in the big league they are regularly coming up against many of the world's top players but, so far, have acquitted themselves brilliantly and have won many admirers.

In his press conference today, Thomas Frank looked ahead to Wednesday's cup game at Stoke, anticipating another tough match, 'It's going to be an unbelievable physical battle, not only tough duels but the running, pressing, defending and attaching, so we need to be absolutely on it. We need to put a strong team out there. We want to have a chance to progress to the next round so you will see exactly how the team looks on Wednesday. I will definitely not make as many changes as I've done in the first two rounds.'

There will certainly be at least two changes forced by injury. Frank added, 'Bryan Mbeumo and Ethan Pinnock will miss Wednesday, hopefully they can be available for Saturday although that is too early to say yet. Mbeumo suffered a minor hamstring issue so it is not a big one because I would just rule him out for the next couple of weeks.'

Wednesday, 27 October 2021

The trip to the Potteries proved as tough a game as Thomas Frank predicted it would be, even though the Bees started the game quickly. Only two minutes had been played when Saman Ghoddos found some space on the right and he picked out Ivan Toney who, at full stretch, could only direct the ball agonisingly wide at the far post with Sergi Canós also lurking.

Brentford continued to put the home side under pressure and Marcus Forss came close after being set up by Mathias Jensen. It was not long, however, until the breakthrough came. Ghoddos and Mads Bidstrup linked up in the midfield to find Mads Roerslev in space on the right wing. His cross found Toney whose shot was blocked, and the ball rebounded to Canós but Stoke goalkeeper Josef Bursik did well to turn the ball wide. Jensen's corner caused panic in the Stoke penalty area but neither Toney nor Forss could find room to get a shot away. Toney, though, was able to set up Canós to lash his shot in past Bursik.

Having taken the lead, Brentford did not rest on their laurels. Jensen came close with a long-range effort and also saw a free kick saved by Bursik, and Toney was crowded out when it looked that he would make it 2-0. Inevitably, the second goal did eventually come. Ghoddos won the ball in the midfield and freed Forss to make inroads into the Stoke defence. He found Toney who this time made no mistake when firing home.

After the break, though, Stoke stepped up the momentum. Following a corner, Romaine Sawyers pulled one back when he rifled a shot past Álvaro Fernández, who has been deputising for David Raya in the Carabao Cup games.

With the clock beginning to run down, Brentford could have wrapped the game up when Ghoddos made his way into the penalty area and found Frank Onyeka. His shot was blocked and Rico Henry hit the rebound over the crossbar. Had the score gone to 3-1 the game would have been safe but the final ten minutes were nervous ones. A frantic finish to the game saw Mario Vrančić collect Sawyer's through ball but fire over, and Abdallah Sima headed only just wide. Time finally ran out for the home team and a tough night saw Brentford through to the quarter-finals in what was their first away win at Stoke at the 15th attempt.

From here on in things are going to get more difficult. The three ties so far have all come against lower-league opposition but, out of the eight teams left in the competition, only Sunderland are not from the Premier League.

Thomas Frank was pleased how his team had conducted themselves. 'I think it was actually a very impressive first half,' he told reporters afterwards. 'I am pleased with the attitude, the discipline, the intensity. We played with a very good intensity in our pressure, we created chances and we scored two really good goals, so first half, bang on. They score, it's probably a little more scrappy, a little more second ball game. We handled that well because we gave nothing away and we still created three or four big chances. I think it was a massive win.'

Stoke City: Bursik; Østigård (Brown 82), Souttar, Wilmot; Duhaney, Sawyers, Thompson (Ince 82), Doughty (Vrančić 56); Campbell (Sima 63), Fletcher (Surridge 63), Tymon

Brentford: Fernández; Ajer, Goode, Jørgensen; Roerslev, Ghoddos, Bidstrup (Nørgaard 62), Jensen (Onyeka 72), Canós (Henry 72); Toney, Forss (Fosu 72)

Thursday, 28 October 2021

After yesterday's win over Stoke, goalkeeper Álvaro Fernández says that he is ready to step into David Raya's boots as the club have announced that Raya sustained knee ligament damage in the game against Leicester last weekend and could be out for up to five months.

'First of all, I wish David a good recovery,' Fernández told the *Evening Standard*. 'We are team-mates but friends as well. Now it's a good opportunity for me, I'm going to try my best and in football you have to be ready always. I've worked every day as hard as possible and I'm ready so let's go.'

It's a big blow for Brentford as Raya has been one of the stand-out performers so far this season but, on the other hand, it is also a big chance for Fernández to make his mark.

Friday, 29 October 2021

Today's *Evening Standard* features an interview with Ivan Toney regarding his international ambitions. Toney qualifies for both England and Jamaica due to his heritage on his mother's side.

'People are saying "should he go to England or Jamaica",' says Toney, 'but I think it is crazy for my name to be out there like that, let alone considering who I'm going to choose. When the time's right, and whatever the future holds, it'll just fall into place. I'll have to have a long chat with my family first, see what goes on and how things pan out. I'm sure the right international side will come forward and I'll choose them.'

Saturday, 30 October 2021

Before today's league action gets under way, the draw for the quarter-finals of the League Cup is made. Brentford's reward for their victory over Stoke is a home tie against Chelsea. It's sure to be another cracking evening at the Community Stadium – a west London derby and the smell of Wembley hanging in the air. The ties are due to be played the week of 20 December.

Brentford were given their first real lesson in the Premier League as Burnley claimed a comfortable 3-1 victory at Turf Moor. The game was over by half-time as goals from Chris Wood, Matt Lowton and Maxwel Cornet put Burnley in a commanding position.

Burnley opened the scoring after just four minutes. Lowton's long pass evaded Ethan Pinnock's attempted clearance and landed nicely into the path of Wood, who hammered his shot past Álvaro Fernández, giving the keeper no chance.

Brentford's brightest spell in the game came at 1-0 down. Frank Onyeka was denied by the offside flag when he got on the end of an Ivan Toney knock-down, and Toney himself was just short of connecting with a cross from Rico Henry. Toney was then denied by a flying save from Nick Pope in the Burnley goal following some good work from Sergi Canós.

Burnley survived Brentford's flurry and their second came just at the right time for them. Charlie Taylor picked out Lowton, who had made space for himself in the Brentford penalty area, and he headed powerfully in. The two-goal lead only lasted for four minutes though, but unfortunately for Brentford it was turned into a three-goal advantage. Dwight O'Neil's through ball found Cornet and he smashed home past Fernández from the edge of the penalty box.

Things could have been even worse had Burnley not had another goal chalked off by VAR after Cornet touched the ball home from close range when latching on to Wood's header. The Video Assistant Referee showed that Wood had been in an offside position when setting up Cornet.

After the break, Brentford did have chances of their own with Ivan Toney being thwarted by Pope, who was called upon again to push away a Christian Nørgaard effort at full stretch. When the Bees did break through, it was a cracking strike. Vitaly Janelt's ball into the penalty area was head back by Nørgaard for Saman Ghoddos to volley an acrobatic scissor kick into the net, giving Pope no chance.

Thomas Frank was in no doubt that the home team deserved the points today. 'One hundred per cent, fair and square win to Burnley,' he said afterwards. 'Big congratulations to Sean Dyche, his staff and Burnley because it was a well deserved win. When you look into the performance, especially in the first half, it wasn't good enough for our perspective. We are normally very solid defensively and yet we are conceding three goals. The first two goals and the offside situations is a situation we knew Burnley would do. We trained it, we talked about it and then it's a combination of we executed it badly and Burnley executed it perfectly and then it was difficult to come back.'

That's three league defeats in a row and the next match will be a very important one. Norwich City visit the Community Stadium next week as the only team in the top flight without a victory to their name. They were promoted to the Premier League last season as champions, with Watford six points behind them and, of course, Brentford accompanied them through the play-offs. After ten games the Canaries have just two points, having drawn with Brighton and Burnley. Brentford sit in 12th position with 12 points, the highest of the three promoted teams. As expected, the top three spots are occupied by Chelsea, Manchester City and Liverpool, with West Ham, Manchester United and Arsenal making up the top six.

Burnley: Pope; Lowton, Tarkowski, Mee, Taylor; Guðmundsson, Brownhill, Westwood, McNeil; Wood, Cornet (Vydra 68)

Brentford: Fernández; Zanka, Jansson, Pinnock; Canós (Roerslev 77), Onyeka (Ghoddos 58), Nørgaard, Jensen (Janelt 68), Henry; Toney, Forss

Thursday, 4 November 2021
Thomas Frank reveals that the hamstring injury suffered by Kristoffer Ajer that forced him to miss the game with Burnley will keep him out until the new year. It's a blow for Brentford, especially coming so soon after David Raya's injury.

Saturday, 6 November 2021
Norwich visit the Community Stadium for what is traditionally a tight match between the two teams. Brentford and Norwich have met six times in the Championship in the last five years – all in the Championship – and in those

games there hasn't been a victory for either side by more than a single goal. So what about today?

Norwich got off to a flyer. Only six minutes were on the clock when Milot Rashica advanced down the left. His cross wasn't dealt with properly and the loose ball fell to Mathias Normann who, after getting it under control, unleashed a shot that arrowed into the bottom corner of the Brentford net.

Just moments earlier it was very nearly Brentford not Norwich who took the early advantage as, just before the Canaries went ahead, Ivan Toney connected with Mathias Jensen's cross but saw the ball bounce away to safety off a post.

As Norwich looked to build on their advantage, Álvaro Fernández was forced into action to deny Rashica. Brentford, though, weren't without opportunities of their own. Charlie Goode, on as a substitute after Mathias Jørgensen had limped off, launched a long throw into the Norwich penalty area that Christian Nørgaard helped towards the corner of the net, but Norwich goalkeeper Tim Krul managed a last gasp block to preserve his team's lead. Ethan Pinnock also came close with a header from a corner and Jensen saw an effort blocked.

The Bees were left to rue their missed chances as Norwich grabbed a second after a quick counter attack. Normann's pass released Teemu Pukki who was adjudged to have been unfairly stopped by Goode and a penalty was awarded. Pukki picked himself up to take the spot-kick and confidently tucked it away for 2-0. Pukki had the chance to make it three early in the second half, but his shot flew wide of Fernández's far post.

Bryan Mbeumo thought that he had halved the deficit when he raced on to Toney's flick and shot powerfully past

Krul but the goal was ruled out for offside. Krul then came to Norwich's rescue when he made an excellent save from Nørgaard following Jensen's corner and he also rushed out to save at Toney's feet.

Brentford did pull one back, though, when Saman Ghoddos's cross found a stretching Rico Henry arriving at the far post to knock the ball in and give the Bees a way back into the game.

They pushed for the equaliser but the Norwich defence held firm. Pinnock's header was saved by Krul and he was also called upon to further deny both Nørgaard and Toney and the three points headed to East Anglia.

Sometimes, though, football is a funny old game. A struggling team produces their best performance of the season, registers their first win and then promptly sacks their manager. After the 2-1 win at the Community Stadium, Norwich City parted ways with Daniel Farke as the spate of Premier League dismissals continues. He follows Xisco Muñoz, Steve Bruce, Nuno Espírito Santo and Dean Smith, formally of Watford, Newcastle, Tottenham and Aston Villa respectively, to the dole queue. He clearly had no idea it was coming as his last act as Norwich manager was to tell the press, 'We definitely have a chance of survival. It's a long marathon. The longer we work together, the better we will be as a team. I can't guarantee we'll stay in the league but don't write us off.'

Brentford: Fernández; Jørgensen (Goode 12), Jansson, Pinnock, Canós, Jensen, Nørgaard, Janelt (Ghoddos 45), Henry (Forss 69); Toney, Mbeumo

Norwich City: Krul; Aarons, Gibson, Omobamidele, Williams; Normann, McLean; Dowell (Giannoulis 74), Lees-Melou, Rashica (Idah 90); Pukki (Sargent 78)

Monday, 8 November 2021

Another international break as England play their last two qualifying matches for next year's World Cup. The break has probably come at a decent time for Brentford as it gives them a chance to regroup after the four straight losses, have a talk with each other and get some good training in. The next league game is at Newcastle on 20 November and is another big one as they are nestled in among the clubs at the wrong end of the table.

It will also be their new manager Eddie Howe's first in charge.

Mathias Jensen has tested positive for COVID after arriving in Denmark for his country's forthcoming international matches. He must now undergo a period of isolation before returning to England. This will put his participation against the Magpies in doubt.

Thursday, 11 November 2021

Brentford's B team will shortly be heading out to Cyprus to take part in the Korantina Homes Cup, where they will compete against local teams Pafos FC and Aris Limassol, as well as other visitors Riga of Latvia, Rodina Moscow from Russia, and a squad from the Asociación de Futbolistas Españoles.

The teams will be split into two groups of three and a final game will be against the team from the other group that finished in the same position, to produce a one-to-six ranking table. For example, if Brentford finish runners-up in their group, they will play the team that finish second in the other group to see who ends the tournament in third place. Brentford's first game is on Sunday, 14 November.

Friday, 12 November 2021

England's penultimate qualifying match for next year's World Cup against Albania ended in a comfortable 5-0 victory with Harry Kane taking the goalscoring honours as he registered a hat-trick to move to joint fourth on the all-time list with Jimmy Greaves. Only Gary Lineker with 48, Bobby Charlton on 49 and Wayne Rooney, the leading scorer with 53, are ahead of him. It will surely be only a matter of time before Kane is topping that list and probably sooner rather than later. With one last qualifying match to go, the World Cup being staged next November and December, along with any friendlies that will be arranged beforehand, could he be topping the international scoring chart next season?

Harry Maguire opened the scoring after nine minutes with a header from a free kick, Kane added the second from Jordan Henderson's cross before Henderson himself knocked in the third and two more Kane strikes wrapped up an easy victory.

Saturday, 13 November 2021

A piece of history was made today as Halil Dervişoğlu became Brentford's all-time record international goalscorer. Dervişoğlu, who is currently on loan at Galatasaray SK, scored twice for Turkey in their 8-0 win over Gibraltar to take his international tally to four.

He had previously held the record jointly with Dai Hopkins who netted twice in his 12 appearances for Wales in the 1930s.

Marcus Forss was also on target for his country as Finland beat Bosnia-Herzegovina 3-1.

Sunday, 14 November 2021

In their first match in the Korantina Homes Cup in Cyprus, Brentford B were comfortably beaten 5-1 by local team Pafos FC. The Cypriots fielded an experienced side including the former Southampton and Crystal Palace midfielder Jason Puncheon. The Bees were four down at the break, the game all but over. The second period was a lot more even and Nathan Young-Coombes pulled one back from the penalty spot before the home side netted another to complete their victory. Brentford's second fixture is on Wednesday against the Russian side Rodina Moscow.

Monday, 15 November 2021

England gained the point they needed against San Marino – was it ever really in any doubt that they would? – and qualified for the World Cup. Once again it was Harry Kane who stole the headlines. His four goals moved him level with Gary Lineker as England romped to a 10-0 victory. Here's a thought – with his early season form at Tottenham being substantially less Kane-like than in previous seasons on the back of his collapsed move to Manchester City that looked like it would happen in the summer, perhaps Brentford should put in a bid during the January transfer window. You never know, Tottenham *might* accept.

England's other goals came from Harry Maguire, Tammy Abraham, Bukayo Saka, an own goal, and both Tyrone Mings and Emile Smith Rowe registered their first for their country. England top the group and it's off to Qatar for the World Cup.

The choice of Qatar as hosts of the 2022 World Cup has, since it was announced, been a constant source of criticism. For the first time since the first tournament took place in 1930, the World Cup will be played in the winter. To be fair, it is sensible to have it at that time of year due to the climate in that part of the world. Normally the tournament would be played in June and July but, if that was the case in Qatar, the teams would be playing in average temperatures of 36°C, 97°F. With that in mind, it is sensible to move it to winter when temperatures are at an average of 24°C, 75°F. However, this does cause disruption in virtually every league programme of the countries that will be taking part. The opening match is scheduled for 21 November, with the final due on 18 December. A couple of days ago, the Premier League announced that the 2022/23 season will begin on a little earlier than usual on 6 August, will stop on 13 November, just eight days before the World Cup kicks off, will restart again on 26 December, eight days after the World Cup Final, and will run until 28 May.

England manager Gareth Southgate, along with his counterparts around the world, must be wondering how on earth their preparations are going to go. There will be next to no time for the squad to gather, train together, play a couple of practice matches to hone the tactics and to just get in the mood for a World Cup. Every other tournament previously has seen the various managers have time to go to a training camp, get some public relations in with the locals to get them on their side and tune their minds into the task ahead of them. We all know that FIFA want to promote the game in parts of the world where football isn't necessarily as big a market and popular as in other places, but you really have to ask yourself if this was a wise move.

Wednesday, 17 November 2021

Brentford B suffered their second defeat in two matches in the Korantina Homes Cup in Cyprus as they were beaten 3-1 by Russian team Rodina Moscow. The Muscovites went ahead when Denis Tikhonov turned in a cross from the right, but Brentford were not behind for too long. Ryan Trevitt finished off a good passing move and, shortly afterwards, provided a chance for Dom Jeffries but his volley flew just the wring side of the post.

Despite the match being pretty even, it was Moscow who had the killer touch and two second-half goals from Stanislav Kraphuin wrapped up the points. Brentford will play Limassol tomorrow in their final game to decide fifth and sixth place.

Thursday, 18 November 2021

A 3-2 victory over local team Aris Limassol ensured that Brentford B wouldn't be bringing the wooden spoon back to west London. Despite having less than 24 hours' rest, the Bees put in a spirited performance to end their Korantina Homes Cup campaign. Two goals from Lachlan Brook and another from Tristan Crama gave Brentford the win. Of course, everyone wants to win every game, but the results are not necessarily the be-all and end-all of tournaments like these. The players will gain good experience that will only help their development into, hopefully, Brentford stars of the future.

Saturday, 20 November 2021

Another big game for Brentford after the international break as they travel up to St James' Park to play Newcastle. For the last few seasons, the Newcastle supporters have been actively showing their discontent at the way the club has been run with Mike Ashley as owner. It was seen by many that the limit of his ambitions for Newcastle was to stay up rather than push on and challenge the big boys.

On the face of it, Newcastle really should be one of the big clubs – they have a big and loyal fanbase, they are the biggest club in the north-east and they have a good stadium. The last time they were league champions was in 1927, however, and their last FA Cup win was in 1955. They briefly flirted with the big time during the mid-1990s when Kevin Keegan was the manager, finishing runners-up in two consecutive seasons, both times to Manchester United. That might all be about to change, though, as they now have a Saudi-backed consortium running things, having just bought the club for £300m. Eddie Howe has been installed as manager, taking over from Steve Bruce, and Ashley's days on the Newcastle board are over. Today is Howe's first day in the dugout. Or it would have been had he not tested positive for COVID.

As expected, Newcastle started the game buoyantly and were in front after ten minutes. Joelinton's shot was deflected wide but, from Matt Ritchie's corner, Jamal Lascelles leapt to head the ball past Álvaro Fernández.

Given the situation, it had potential to become a really awkward afternoon for Brentford, but an almost instantaneous equaliser dampened the home side's enthusiasm. Ivan Toney won an aerial duel with the loose ball dropping for Sergi Canós. Toney received it back from Canós and fired past Newcastle keeper Darlow to level the scores. Toney almost had a second when he knocked in the rebound after Bryan Mbeumo's shot came back off a post but VAR ruled that he was offside.

The game continued at a frantic pace with Mbeumo and Rico Henry combining to present Toney with another opportunity, only to see defender Ciaran Clark getting back to block his effort and keep parity. At the other end, Fernández saved from Allan Saint-Maximin. Inevitably, considering the amount of chances being created, it wasn't long before the third goal did come and when it did it was Brentford's. Just after the half hour, Canós crossed to the far post for Rico Henry to nod past Darlow.

The action continued relentlessly and Newcastle notched the game's fourth goal, all before half-time. Saint-Maximin made inroads down the left, cut inside and fired towards goal. His effort was blocked but the ball fell to Joelinton who turned the ball in past Fernández. There might have been more goal action had Ethan Pinnock not got in the way of Joe Willock and Toney blocked an effort from Callum Wilson on the goal line.

The chances continued to come in the second half. Fabian Schär's header was stopped by Fernández and Saint-Maximin saw a shot fly just wide after good work from Willock. It wasn't all Newcastle, though, as Brentford also had their opportunities. Mbeumo looked to be through before an out-rushing Darlow beat him to a Canós through ball. The danger had not been completely cleared, though, as Henry found himself in a lot of space on the left, the ball was worked to Frank Onyeka, on as a substitute for Saman Ghoddos, whose shot was unintentionally turned into his own net by Lascelles.

Such was the nature of the game that the action continued end to end. Fernández was in the way to deny Saint-Maximin after his effort deflected off Pontus Jansson and Canós had a chance to wrap up the points, but his free kick flew just over the crossbar. There was one further opportunity for Saint-Maximin, but this time he made it count. Ryan Fraser's cross picked out the Frenchman who unleashed a shot that gave Fernández no chance to level at 3-3.

The last 15 minutes saw both teams push for the victory. Darlow denied both Onyeka and Mbeumo with Fernández thwarting Joelinton and Wilson. Eventually time ran out and a breathless encounter ended up all square.

Speaking after the match, Ivan Toney insisted that he didn't have a point to prove to Newcastle after his former club sold him to Peterborough in 2018 with him having just five minutes of Premier league action under his belt. 'There's no hard feelings against the club,' said Toney. 'They hold a place in my heart and I wish them all the best throughout the season. Maybe I wasn't ready, maybe I wasn't good enough, who knows. At the time the club had a decision to make and the decision was to let me go.'

Toney's only league appearance for Newcastle came as an 85th-minute substitute in a 2-2 draw with Chelsea. He had made the move north after beginning his career with hometown club Northampton Town and joining Peterborough came after having been out on various loan spells at Barnsley, Shrewsbury, Scunthorpe and Wigan. Forty goals in 76 league games at Peterborough won him his transfer to Brentford in 2020.

Newcastle United: Darlow; Schär (Longstaff 71), Lascelles, Clark; Murphy, Shelvey, Willock (Fraser 71), Ritchie; Joelinton, Wilson, Saint-Maximin

Brentford: Fernández; Roerslev (Goode 80), Jansson, Pinnock; Canós, Janelt (Baptiste 89), Nørgaard, Ghoddos (Onyeka 59), Henry; Toney, Mbeumo

Monday, 22 November 2021

With the mid-season transfer window opening in January, reports are beginning to emerge of potential targets for various clubs. Today Brentford are being linked with Dante Vanzeir who plays as a forward for Royale Union Saint-Gilloise in the Belgium league. There is always a lot of paper talk around this time of year, so let's just wait to see if anything happens.

There is big news from Old Trafford today as Ole Gunnar Solskjær has been sacked as manager of Manchester United. After five losses in their last seven Premier League matches and continued unrest among the supporters, the board have relieved him of his duties. The calls for his head got louder after their 5-0 home defeat by Liverpool followed by their conceding four against both Leicester and Watford and a home derby defeat to Manchester City. The talk is that the former Tottenham and current Paris Saint-Germain boss Mauricio Pochettino and Ajax manager Erik ten Hag are the frontrunners to take over permanently, although it is also suggested that, as it is unlikely anyone would like to lose their manager to another club mid-season, an interim coach may be installed until the end of the campaign. Solskjær's number two, Michael Carrick, has taken temporary charge of the team.

Thursday, 25 November 2021

Brentford have received favourable headlines today by saying that they will not be changing their home kit for next season. It has recently become practice for teams to change their shirts every year, thus raking in bundles in sales. Gone are the days when clubs would only change kits every so often, perhaps when they had a new shirt sponsor.

Brentford, though, are keeping this season's for next season. On the club website, brentfordfc.com, chief executive Jon Varney said, 'Whilst it is not normal for Premier League clubs to roll a kit over for two seasons, fans have told us that they would be in favour of the savings that a two-season shirt would provide. When we discussed the idea, everyone at the club was fully behind it. We also think this is a step in the right direction to help the environment a little. It can only be good to reduce kit cycles.'

Sunday, 28 November 2021

Everton come to town today as Brentford look to build on last week's draw at Newcastle and get back to winning ways. After a good start to the season, the Toffees have been struggling of late, being winless in their last six matches.

The game was a pretty even one, the early stages mostly being played in midfield with both teams sussing each other out. Chances were few and far between until Bryan Mbeumo won a corner. Sergi Canós's cross was punched away from underneath his crossbar by Everton goalkeeper Jordan Pickford, with the loose ball falling to Frank Onyeka.

A high challenge came in from Andros Townsend – so high that he actually kicked Onyeka in the head! – the ball dropped to Pontus Jansson but his shot was saved by Pickford. Everton broke away and Salomón Rondón was denied by a last-ditch challenge from Mbeumo, who had tracked him almost the length of the pitch. It was at this point that VAR alerted referee Darren England to the fact that he had missed a possible foul on Onyeka, he rechecked the footage and awarded the penalty for Townsend's high challenge. Ivan Toney placed the ball on the spot and coolly slotted it home without taking his eye off Pickford to see which way he was diving.

Everton almost immediately replied but were denied by a double save from Álvaro Fernández. Firstly, Rondón found a bit of space in the Brentford penalty area, swivelled and fired in a shot that Fernández got down to, and then, from the rebound, Townsend played it back into the danger zone only for Rondón to once again be denied by the Brentford keeper.

All of a sudden the game came to life. Onyeka played a one-two with Toney and crossed for Mbeumo but Pickford denied him a tap-in at full stretch. Abdoulaye Doucouré's desperate last-ditch challenge stopped Vitaly Janelt getting a shot off and then Pickford kept out Ethan Pinnock's header. As for the Toffees, Lucas Digne's free kick cleared the crossbar and Charlie Goode made a great interception to stop Doucouré getting on the end of a Townsend cross.

After the break, Canós sent in a blistering volley that was just too high and, from then on, Everton pushed for the equaliser. Rondón had a couple of efforts but saw the first fly over the crossbar when he latched on to a loose ball and the second saw Janelt in his way just as he was pulling the trigger. Alex Iwobi tested Fernández with a low shot and the Bees' keeper also kept out an effort from Demarai Gray that took what could have been a wrong-footing deflection. The last action of the game saw Brentford break away and Yoane Wissa sting Pickford's hands after he was found by Shandon Baptiste.

Thomas Frank was understandably pleased with the result. He told reporters afterwards, 'I am so pleased we got the three points today. It is a massive win against a huge club. We got a very important clean sheet also, in the last few games we have conceded too many chances and goals.'

Brentford: Fernández; Goode, Jansson, Pinnock; Canós (Wissa 87), Onyeka, Nørgaard (Baptiste 70), Janelt, Henry (Roerslev 77); Toney, Mbeumo

Everton: Pickford; Coleman, Keane, Godfrey, Digne; Allan, Doucouré; Townsend (Gray 70), Iwobi, Gordon; Rondón

Monday, 29 November 2021

Former Norwich, Celtic and Blackburn striker Chris Sutton is full of praise for Ivan Toney after yesterday's penalty winner. Writing in the *Daily Mail*, Sutton says, 'Eric Cantona used to stare at the goalkeeper when taking penalties. He'd wait for his opponent's knee to give away the direction he was going, then duly stick the ball in the other side. It's an amazing skill to have and one Ivan Toney has very much mastered.'

Toney has scored from 18 of the 19 penalties he has taken in his professional career, a fact not lost on Sutton, 'I used to pick a side when taking penalties and do a slow run-up, but I watch what Toney does in awe. It's perfection the way he executes it, an art form. Having a 12-yard expert is of great benefit to Brentford.'

As a player, Sutton formed a lethal partnership with Alan Shearer when Blackburn won the Premier League in 1994/95. He scored 15 goals alongside Shearer who banged in 34. It was Blackburn's third championship, their first two coming in the 1912/13 and 1913/14 seasons.

Manchester United have appointed Ralf Rangnick as their interim manager until the end of the season. Rangnick has joined from Lokomotiv Moscow where he was working as sports and development manager. As a manager, he had previously been with a series of German clubs, most notably Schalke and RB Leipzig. Part of his commission is to help find a new permanent manager for United for next season.

Wednesday, 1 December 2022

Another transfer link appears in the papers today. It is reported that Brentford, along with Watford and Crystal Palace, are keen on recruiting Joe Aribo. The Nigerian international midfielder is currently playing in Scotland for Rangers. We'll see when the transfer window opens next month if there is any truth in the rumours.

Thursday, 2 December 2022

There have been matches spread out across midweek and tonight Brentford visit Tottenham. With Antonio Conte recently installed in the Tottenham hotseat and his players looking to impress their new boss, it was always going to be a tricky night for Brentford and the last thing they needed was to concede a strange own goal only 12 minutes in. Heung-min Son crossed from a short corner and Pontus Jansson rose to head clear. Unfortunately, his header flew back off the head of Sergi Canós and straight past Álvaro Fernández into the net.

Up until then, the opening exchanges had been a pretty much even affair with lots of possession in midfield but little goalmouth incident. After Tottenham went ahead the pattern of the match didn't change, with both teams almost cancelling each other out. Chances were few and far between and when they did come, both goalkeepers were more than equal to them. Fernández saved well from Lucas Moura after Harry Kane had found him in space in the Brentford penalty area, and he later rushed out to thwart

Emerson Royal by saving at the Brazilian's feet. His most unorthodox piece of goalkeeping, though, came when, after punching a corner kick clear, the ball landed at the feet of Pierre-Emile Højbjerg, who hammered it back towards goal. It beat the keeper's dive but Fernández kept it out with his face. As for Brentford, their clearest sight of goal came from a long throw from Charlie Goode, but Ben Davies's challenge prevented Bryan Mbeumo from heading home.

The second half saw Kane have a chance to wrap the points up but, when put clear by Oliver Skipp, he shot straight at Fernández. The scare jump-started Brentford into life and another long throw caused panic in the Tottenham penalty area but Jansson fired over the bar. Ivan Toney then had an opportunity after combining with Vitaly Janelt but Hugo Lloris was equal to it.

As is so often the way in football, when one team looks like they are beginning to get on top they are hit by a sucker punch. The ball found Kane in some space in the midfield area and he released Sergio Reguilón who raced forward and crossed for Son to score from close range.

As the game entered its final stages, Lloris was forced to tip over from Mathias Jensen and was also called upon to save with his feet from Toney. The last chance fell to Mbeumo, but his curled effort was just too high and the match ended 2-0.

Speaking at his post-match press conference, Thomas Frank was once again impressed by the application of his players even though they came away with nothing. 'I am pleased with the attitude and work ethic,' he said. 'We were very brave. We came here and played our game. If we want to get anything from the game we can't concede the second goal, end of. We shouldn't have conceded the corner for the first goal too, simple. We have to learn from the second goal. I always think you win or you learn and today we definitely learn. We were on top before the second goal and then switched off, didn't track a runner and goal.'

December is going to be a tough month. Having started away at Tottenham, the Bees also face both Manchester United and City in the league and Chelsea in the League Cup. There are also games against Watford, Southampton and Brighton in the traditionally packed end-of-year schedule.

Tottenham Hotspur: Lloris; Sánchez, Dier, Davies; Royal (Tanganga 83), Skipp, Højbjerg, Reguilón; Moura (Winks 76), Kane, Son (Bergwijn 87)

Brentford: Fernández; Goode, Jansson, Pinnock; Canós (Wissa 70), Onyeka (Baptiste 56), Nørgaard, Janelt (Jensen 70), Henry; Toney, Mbeumo

Saturday, 4 December 2022

There's some mutual admiration between Thomas Frank and Marcelo Bielsa in the build-up to tomorrow's Leeds v Brentford match. Bielsa has many high-profile admirers including Pep Guardiola, who admitted, 'My admiration for Bielsa is huge because he makes the players much, much better,' while Mauricio Pochettino once said, 'He is like my football father. We are a generation of coaches that were his disciples.' Even Johann Cruyff, after the 2010 World Cup, said that Bielsa's Chile team played the best football.

So what does Frank like about him? 'His level of detail in and out of possession and the level of detail on his style of play, and just how unique it is. We have never seen anything like that in the history of world football.'

Bielsa, for his part, is equally complimentary about the way Frank sets out his team, 'Anyone who has seen Brentford play this season can see they attack with six players and they always want to keep the ball. That's not common in any league and even more so when that team is not one of the most prestigious clubs in the league.'

Sunday, 5 December 2022

Not exactly the start to the day that Brentford wanted as Ivan Toney is ruled out of the match at Elland Road having tested positive with COVID. Shandon Baptiste takes his place in the line-up.

The match started at breakneck speed, with both teams going for it from the off. Bryan Mbeumo saw his shot blocked and, when Sergi Canós pounced on the loose ball and tried to play in Vitaly Janelt for a tap-in, Junior Firpo just got a toe in and Leeds keeper Illan Meslier was able to gather. Canós then had a shot that was deflected straight into Meslier's arms after he had played a nice one-two with Christian Nørgaard. For Leeds, their closest moment came when Tyler Roberts won the ball deep in Brentford territory, but he sliced his shot and it was easy for Álvaro Fernández.

It was Leeds who took the lead just before the half hour, Roberts making amends for his earlier miss. Raphinha found some space on the right to cross but Pontus Jansson was in the way. The clearance went back to Raphinha again, this time his cross was a good one and Roberts arrived to knock the ball past Fernández at full stretch. There was a bit of conjecture as to whether the goal should have stood as Raphinha appeared to foul Charlie Goode just before Leeds broke away. The referee played the advantage, but

Brentford immediately lost possession and moments later the ball was in the net.

Brentford were almost on level terms straightaway. Rico Henry's cross was cut out by Firpo but he misdirected his header towards his own goal but, fortunately for him, straight into the arms of his own goalkeeper.

It could have been two just after the break, but Fernández came to Brentford's rescue with a flying save from Luke Ayling and Mads Roerslev was on hand to block Ayling's follow-up.

When the next goal came, it was a Brentford equaliser. Henry won the ball in midfield and played it out to Canós. His cross was blocked but it fell to Baptiste on the edge of the area. His shot flew past Meslier and Brentford were level. The visitors now had the upper hand and the chances continued to come. Christian Nørgaard jinked into the penalty area and fed Baptiste. Just as he was working himself a shooting opportunity, Firpo's challenge stopped him in his tracks. The loose ball fell to Janelt who set up Canós but his effort smashed right into Ayling's face.

The pressure eventually told when Nørgaard won possession and set Canós on his way. The ball was transferred to Baptiste and on to Mbeumo who returned it to Canós whose shot flew past Meslier.

The latter stages saw Leeds pile forward for the leveller. Fernández saved from Stuart Dallas, and Goode got in the way of a shot from Mateusz Klich that looked like it might cause Fernández a bit of bother. Just as the points were packing their bags and preparing to head down the M1, with the last action of the game, Leeds won a 95th-minute corner. Raphinha swung it in, Ayling flicked it on and Patrick Bamford – playing in his first game since

September because of an ankle injury – managed to get his knee to the ball. It bounced up on to the underside of the crossbar and, agonisingly for Brentford, back down over the line to steal a point.

A point won or two points dropped? It will feel like a loss but after the excitement has died down, a point at Leeds is never a bad result. With 15 matches gone, the league table is so tight. Burnley, Newcastle and Norwich fill the relegation places with all three on ten points. Watford are just above them on 13, then come Southampton, Leeds and Crystal Palace with 16 and Brentford have 17 in 13th position. Just above them, Everton have 18, Leicester and Aston Villa both have 19, Brighton are on 20 and then we are in the top eight.

The Premier League table seems to be split into three mini-leagues. Manchester City, Liverpool and Chelsea are most definitely the top three; Manchester United, Arsenal, Tottenham and West Ham seem to be fighting it out for the remaining European places; with the rest playing between them for places eight to 20. We're not even halfway through the season yet, but it is shaping up to be an exciting one.

Thomas Frank was once again full of praise for his players, as he told gathered reporters:

'I can't praise the players enough. They gave everything, what an effort. In the first half, we started very well in the first ten, 15 minutes then Leeds were on top, but we didn't expect anything different because they play with this high intensity. Second half, we stepped up, pressed high, got in front after winning the ball high, and we are actually completely in control. They have two chances in the game – the goal and the goal. That's so cruel when it comes from a set piece at the end, but it is what it is. There's so much positive to take from this game. We can't run away from it that we have the lowest budget, and when you have injuries or for other reasons three key players out, coming up here and doing how we do is fantastic.'

Leeds United: Meslier; Ayling, Llorente, Cooper (Harrison 15), Firpo (Bamford 68); Forshaw, Phillips (Klich 55); Dallas, Raphinha, James; Roberts

Brentford: Fernández; Goode, Jansson, Pinnock; Roerslev, Baptiste (Onyeka 69), Nørgaard, Janelt (Jensen 90), Henry; Canós (Wissa 72), Mbeumo

Monday, 6 December 2021
The draw for the third round of the FA Cup was made this evening, with Brentford handed a trip to Port Vale. The ties are to be played over the (long) weekend beginning 7 January.

Friday, 10 December
An important game today as Watford visit the Community Stadium. The matches against clubs like Liverpool and Manchester City are the showbiz games – any points picked up from these type of fixtures are a bonus. However, it is the games against teams like Watford who, you would assume, would be in the mix with Brentford for final league positions, that you would be looking to take points from, especially at home. It is also Bees against Hornets.

Brentford started brightly and Watford goalkeeper Daniel Bachmann was in the thick of the early action. He denied Shandon Baptiste at full stretch after the Brentford man had sent in a volley from the edge of the penalty area, tipping the effort over the crossbar, and he reacted well to get down to a Rico Henry cross with both Bryan Mbeumo and Yoane Wissa lurking for a simple tap-in. Another flying save deprived Mbeumo of a spectacular opener after he sent in a curling effort from 20 yards.

For all Brentford's early pressure, though, it was the visitors that made the breakthrough.. Josh King broke away down the left and sent in a low shot which had Álvaro Fernández beaten but came back off the post and was cleared for a corner. Tom Cleverley delivered the ball into the heart of the area and Emmanuel Dennis headed in to score against the run of play.

The rest of the half saw Brentford continue to apply the pressure and Watford resist. Christian Nørgaard hooked a long throw from Charlie Goode just wide of the post and Goode himself met a corner from Vitaly Janelt but saw his header land on the roof of the net. Watford defender Kiko Femenía also made an important interception when it looked like Nørgaard's through ball had given Wissa a sight of goal.

The second half continued in much the same vein. Brentford had the vast majority of the play but were unable to break through a determined Watford defence. Rico Henry had a shot blocked after he got on the end of a cross from Mads Roerslev, Nørgaard almost found a way through after Goode had found himself in space and Bachmann again came to the Hornets' rescue with another flying save to push Janelt's drive clear.

With the amount of pressure that Brentford were exerting, the law of averages says that the equalising goal must come at some point. To the relief of the home supporters who were fearing an evening of frustration, it duly arrived with only three minutes left on the clock. Janelt's cross landed at the feet of Frank Onyeka but his shot was deflected wide of the post. Janelt swung it in, saw the ball cleared but it worked its way back out to him. His second cross was helped on its way by Marcus Forss and Pontus Jansson charged in to head the ball home. A point was the least that Brentford deserved on the balance of play.

However, as was the case in the last match against Leeds, the winning goal arrived in the 95th minute. This time, though, it was Brentford who were the beneficiaries. Nørgaard freed Saman Ghoddos inside the Watford penalty area, William Troost-Ekong's attempted last-ditch tackle felled the Brentford man and a spot-kick was awarded. With Ivan Toney still missing, Mbeumo took responsibility and slotted the penalty home. There was barely enough time for Watford to restart before the match ended and a vital three points were earned. Two goals in the last eight minutes of the match gave the Bees what could be a very important three points in the final reckoning.

'It's crazy,' said Thomas Frank afterwards, 'but this is what football is all about. These are the moments we are working so hard to achieve. The game against Leeds was cruel, conceding in the last minute and now scoring in the last minute. It's an unbelievable performance and getting three points with the injuries and the COVID cases, we equalise in the 87th minute and still go for the win, that's crazy.'

Brentford: Fernández; Goode, Jansson, Janelt; Roerslev, Baptiste, Nørgaard, Jensen (Ghoddos 69), Henry (Onyeka 76); Mbeumo, Wissa (Forss 69)

Watford: Bachmann; Femenía, Troost-Ekong, Cathcart, Ngakia; Kucka, Sissoko; Hernández (Sema 76), Cleverley (Pedro 57), King; Dennis (Tufan 90)

Monday, 13 December 2021

Today's transfer talk involves two possible ins and one possible out. The *Daily Mail* is reporting that Brentford have opened talks with Brazilian side Grêmio over the possible transfer of defender Vanderson. He was a reported target during the summer but Grêmio's valuation of £13m priced him out of a move.

Another potential signing, according to *The Sun*, is Francisco Moura of Portuguese club Braga. Another defender, previously he almost moved to Barcelona but the transfer was called off due to his suffering a cruciate ligament injury. It is claimed that Brentford are considering whether or not to make their move in January, assuming they would be able to capture him for a cut-price fee.

Meanwhile, *The Guardian* reports that Pontus Jansson has his admirers. Apparently, Leicester, Newcastle and Everton are all interested in luring him away from London.

Tuesday, 14 December 2021

Tonight's home game against Manchester United, one of the matches that everyone associated with Brentford was surely looking out for when the fixture list was released before the start of the season, has been postponed. With the new Omicron strain of COVID sweeping the world, there have been outbreaks at many football clubs. Ivan Toney has been missing for Brentford's last couple of matches, Brighton v Tottenham was called off at the weekend, Burnley v Watford tomorrow is a doubt and United have had an outbreak at their training complex. Public health issues are far more important than a game of football so hopefully all affected will make full recoveries soon.

Thursday, 16 December 2021

Thomas Frank says that he believes the weekend's fixtures, along with the League Cup matches in midweek, should be postponed due to the rising cases of COVID. He was interrupted during his morning press conference to be told of four new positive tests at Brentford, bringing the tally to 13 among players and staff.

'The COVID cases are going through the roof,' he told the gathered reporters. 'Everyone is dealing with it and everyone has a problem at this moment in time. To postpone this round and the Carabao Cup would give everyone a week at least to clean and do everything at the training ground so everything is fine and we break the chain at every club. We fully respect that we want to play. We want to carry on but this way we can have Boxing Day game no problem.'

The government has just introduced its COVID Plan B, meaning that anyone wishing to attend a match must register online first, declaring their COVID status. Also, all fans over 18 must either show that they have an NHS COVID pass or prove that they have had a negative result from a lateral flow test no more than 48 hours before kick-off.

Much of last season was played behind closed doors when sport resumed after lockdown and a few places around Europe are again choosing to do the same now. Markus Söder, head of the Bavarian state government, has already announced that sports events will be held in empty stadiums until further notice, meaning that Bayern Munich's games are currently being played behind closed doors, including a big Champions League clash with Barcelona. It remains to be seen what further measures, if any, the British government or the Premier League will bring in.

Sunday, 19 December 2021

The Premier League programme was almost wiped out this weekend, with only four matches surviving. Brentford's game at Southampton was one of those that fell foul to the ongoing COVID conditions. If it carries on this way, we may well be heading for a bit of a fixture pile-up at the end of the season. Brentford's next scheduled match is the League Cup quarter-final against Chelsea on Wednesday, but Blues manager Thomas Tuchel seems not to be too keen for the tie to go ahead after seven players had tested positive in the lead-up to their game this afternoon.

'If we have the next test and the next positive, I would like to speak to the people from the Premier League about what they expect,' he said. 'Shall we stop and not arrive for the next game if we are made to play? When they make us play against Brentford shall we not arrive? Shall we not train any more? What shall we do?'

The COVID situation has added weight to the annual cry for fewer games to be played. Every single season there are Premier League managers who call for a lighter schedule of games, be it a break over Christmas and the new year period, a reduction of clubs in the division, or whatever. Liverpool manager Jürgen Klopp today had his say after their match with Tottenham:

'If we don't play anymore and we have a break I am completely fine with that as well. I know the problem is now going to be when do we play the games, it's not so easy to find spaces wherever you can fit it in here and there. They said before [COVID] that the schedule was a little busy and now all of a sudden it comes back and gives us another punch. In truth we cannot carry on like this and that's what we have to consider as well.'

The call for less football, or at least a mid-season break, does make me wonder, sometimes. OK, I know the COVID situation has made things slightly different at the moment, but it is a constant theme. It was only for the 1995/96 season that the Premier League was reduced from 22 teams down to 20. Up until then there had always been 22 in the top division, meaning there were four more games than there are now, plus, of course, the squad sizes were that much smaller before then.

Going back to the 1970s, 1980s and back through time, you pretty much knew what each club's first 11 was. Just as an example, Aston Villa last won the league championship in the 1980/81 season and, throughout the entirety of that season, they used only 14 different players. OK, that was an exception, but it does make you think a bit, doesn't it? Add to that the FA Cup and League Cup matches they were involved in – this is when the first 11 would also play in those games as well, there was no mass bringing in of the reserve players – and Villa had seven players who played in every single game that season, each wracking up a total of 46 appearances. Something else to remember from those days is the state that the pitches used to get into. There was no modern technological way of growing grass and making it look like a carpet throughout the whole year. The grass was grown, in the winter it would freeze, in the rain it would get sodden and by February grounds resembled a bowl of porridge rather than a football pitch.

Villa's use of only 14 players was unusual, but just to take a few other random seasons, in 1994/95 Blackburn Rovers won the league using 21 different players; in 1988/89 Arsenal were champions by using 17; and in 1977/78 Nottingham Forest used 16 when taking the trophy. In

2020/21 Manchester City won the league by using 24 players in their 38 games.

There also only used to be one substitute named and permitted per team per game, and that was only introduced for the 1965/66 season. At that time, subs were only allowed to replace an injured player. The first sub used in an English league match was Keith Peacock of Charlton Athletic who came on for injured goalkeeper Mike Rose in their game at Bolton Wanderers. Of course, he wasn't actually a goalkeeper, so Charlton had to have a midfielder between the sticks for the remainder of the game, which they not surprisingly lost 4-2. On the same day, Bobby Knox of Barrow became the first substitute to score when he netted against Wrexham. From 1968/69 subs were allowed for tactical reasons as well as injuries, but still only the one was allowed. It wasn't until 1987/88 that two subs were selected and could be used, and that was increased to three for the 1994/95 season, although one of the three had to be a goalkeeper.

The number of subs to choose from rose to five for 1996/97 – although only three were still permitted to be used – and then to seven, the current amount, from 2008/09. There have been calls from certain quarters to allow five changes per team in each league match, although the Football Association have so far resisted.

It has also been announced that Brentford's co-director of football, Rasmus Ankerson, will be stepping down from his role at the end of the year. Rasmus has been in the job since 2015 since when he has been working alongside Phil Giles, who will continue as sole director of football from the beginning of 2022.

Tuesday, 21 December 2021

The Premier League have issued a statement with regard to the ongoing COVID situation. Some managers have suggested that it might be wise to postpone the forthcoming league matches and restart again in the new year, but that looks unlikely to happen. The statements reads:

'The safety of everyone is a priority and the Premier League is taking all precautionary steps in response to the impact of the Omicron variant. The League has reverted to its Emergency Measures and has increased testing of players and club staff to daily Lateral Flow and twice weekly PCR tests, having previously carried out Lateral Flow testing twice a week.

'The League can confirm that between Monday, 13 December and Sunday, 19 December, a record 12,345 COVID-19 tests were administered on players and club staff. Of these, there were 90 new positive cases.

'The Premier League's COVID-19 Emergency Measures include protocols such as wearing face coverings while indoors, observing social distancing, limiting treatment time, as well as the increased testing. The League is continuing to work with the clubs to keep people safe by helping mitigate the risks of COVID-19 within their squads. We are also liaising closely with the Government, local authorities and supporter groups, while being responsive to any future changes to national or local guidance.

'The Premier League is providing this aggregated information for the purposes of competition integrity and transparency. No specific details as to clubs or individuals will be provided by the League and results will be made public on a weekly basis.'

Going on their press release, it looks, then, that no postponement will happen unless things get totally out of control and the government brings in lockdown measures.

Turning to club matters, the reported transfer of Grêmio defender Vanderson to Brentford now apparently looks like it is on the point of collapse. Brazilian TV network Globo Esporte reports that his preferred destination is Monaco, with an unnamed Italian club also in the frame. Apparently, Monaco have outbid Brentford and the player would prefer the French Riviera to west London!

During Thomas Frank's press conference today, he expanded on why last week he called for the suspension of the scheduled League Cup matches tonight and tomorrow:

'We are in a fine place. I guess there will come a few questions about the COVID situation so I can probably start there. Thursday last week I asked for what we thought was a good thing to postpone the round and we were not that far off, six games were postponed. One was last minute which is unfair for the fans. Clearly our opponents tomorrow were quite unhappy with their game going on so that could so easily have been seven. But we should only focus on ourselves which helped us massively. We closed our training ground later that day on Thursday so that meant that we had Tuesday, Wednesday, Thursday, Friday, Saturday and Sunday not at the training ground which helped us to break that circuit of transmission of the virus. So, from having six or seven positive cases on that Thursday to the next testing round on Saturday with Lateral Flow and PCR tests, we only had one on the Saturday, zero Monday and zero today, so we are definitely in a fine place going into the game on Wednesday.'

Wednesday, 22 December 2021

With the opening of the mid-season transfer window just over a week away, the newspapers are today linking Brentford with a bid to sign Nottingham Forest forward Brennan Johnson. According to the *Daily Mail*, the Bees are up against both Everton and Newcastle in the race for his signature. As with the multitude of possible transfer links that always occur at this stage of the season, we will just have to wait and see if there is anything in it.

Of more immediate concern is the League Cup quarter-final with Chelsea at the Community Stadium. After all the postponement talk, all four quarter-finals are being played. Last night Arsenal beat Sunderland 5-1 and, aside from Brentford v Chelsea, tonight's other matches are Liverpool v Leicester and Tottenham v West Ham.

The match started cagily with the visitors having a lot of possession without much penetration. Álvaro Fernández wasn't really tested, the only moment of concern coming when Ross Barkley met Marcos Alonso's cross, but his header was comfortable for Fernández. Brentford's first real chance fell to Yoane Wissa but, like Barkley before him, he couldn't quite direct his header as he would have liked and Chelsea stopper Kepa Arrizabalaga wasn't really troubled. One moment that did have Kepa's heart in his mouth, though, was when Bryan Mbeumo charged down his attempted clearance but, unfortunately for Brentford, the ball bounced wide. The best chance of the half fell to Rico Henry. Mathias Jensen played him in behind Chelsea's defence, but he shot straight at Kepa with the goal gaping.

The match continued the same way after the break with the chances that were created also being squandered. With ten minutes to go, the breakthrough came. N'Golo Kante played in Reece James down Chelsea's right flank, and he played a low ball into the Brentford box. Pontus Jansson arrived first but his outstretched leg could only deflect the ball into the top corner of his own net. It was a very unfortunate moment for the captain and Fernández was helpless to prevent it.

The goal that put the tie beyond doubt arrived five minutes later. Mason Mount tried to play Christian Pulisic in, but his attempted pass was deflected away from danger. Fernández rushed out to claim the ball but Pulisic hadn't given up the chase and his speed saw him get there just slightly ahead of Fernández and their coming together resulted in a penalty being awarded. Jorginho took responsibility and sent Fernández the wrong way to wrap up a 2-0 Chelsea victory.

Afterwards, Thomas Frank was disappointed that his team were beaten. 'We gave nothing away and had the biggest chances of the game in the first half and should have been in front,' he surmised, 'but in the second half we struggled to create anything and were poor from set pieces which is usually one of our strong points. We need to do better with both goals. Pontus has had a fantastic season and will blame himself, and also the penalty – two minor mistakes cost us. I am really disappointed. We missed a great opportunity against a top side.'

The draw for the semi-final was made after the game. Chelsea came out of the hat against Tottenham and, in the other semi, Arsenal will face Liverpool. The ties will be played over two legs in early January.

Brentford: Fernández; Pinnock, Jansson, Bech Sørensen; Canós, Jensen (Forss 81), Janelt (Nørgaard 65), Baptiste (Onyeka 73), Henry (Ghoddos 73); Wissa (Toney 65), Mbeumo

Chelsea: Kepa; Azpilicueta, Chalobah, Sarr; Simons (James 65), Barkley (Kanté 76), Saúl, Kovačić (Jorginho 45), Alonso; Vale (Mount 65), Soonsup-Bell (Pulisic 45)

Thursday, 23 December 2021

Today's transfer speculation surrounds Deji Sotona who is currently on the books of French Ligue 1 side Nice. It is reported that Brentford are one of the clubs interested in bringing him back to the Premier League – he was a product of Manchester United's academy before crossing the Channel – along with Everton, Chelsea and Tottenham. Unable to make the breakthrough to Nice's first team, Sotona reportedly wants to move to pastures new.

Looking back to yesterday's defeat to Chelsea, Thomas Frank today tells the media, 'I think the game was very important for us to get up to speed. After six days where we couldn't train – yes, they were running, but that's not the same – you saw the impact of that when training resumed. There were quite a few of the players that didn't feel that fresh and were struggling in certain spells. They got through it because it was only six days, but now the system just got that boost and they will be ready to go on Boxing Day.'

Friday, 24 December 2021

Speaking of the forthcoming match with Brighton today, in his press conference, Thomas Frank had this to say:

'I think they have done very well. I think Graham [Potter, the Brighton manager] and his staff are doing a top job down there. They develop their style and play constantly year after year. They have been, a little bit like us, a bit unlucky – they should have had more points, a lot of draws in recent games. The recent games they've struggled a little bit to get over the line to get the win, but this is because football is a random game. A lot of games they've played recently, they should have won as well, but a lot of them they dominated, created chances and play a nice style of football.'

Turning to the COVID issue (how can we possibly escape it?), the suggestion of being allowed five substitutions in Premier League matches is raised.

Frank says, 'I think it would be a positive thing. With COVID, I still think we should have five subs. I just think it will add something new to the game. You can make more tactical changes as well, it is not only fitness, so I think that would be good. We've gone from one sub to three, but the squad just increased and then we have 20 on the bench so I don't understand why it's not five. I think it is very simple. If we want to play and carry on, there'll be lots of cases for the next two to three months. If we do what we do now, I think that's the best way to try to carry on. There will be situations where there are cases every day in different clubs. We test the day before or the day after, so I think we'll be fine, and I think the big thing is that when we actually play the matches, there is a minimal risk of transmitting the virus.'

Sunday, 26 December 2021

The match on the south coast is the first return fixture of the season. In September, Brighton travelled up to west London and inflicted Brentford's first defeat as a Premier League team.

The game started with Brentford having the better of the early chances. Dominic Thompson, making his Premier League debut, played in Bryan Mbeumo who lifted his shot over the out-rushing Brighton goalkeeper Robert Sánchez.

The ball headed goalwards but Dan Burn got back to clear in the six-yard box. Mbeumo also had a headed chance from Mads Bech Sørensen's cross and Shandon Baptiste saw his shot deflected over the bar following a bit of a scramble from a corner.

From then on, the home team started to take control of the game and Enock Mwepu came close, firing into the side netting.

It was two goals in the space of eight minutes that won the points for Brighton, and both had a touch of class about them. The first came when Mwepu played a long ball through the centre of the defence and Leo Trossard got there just before Álvaro Fernández and flicked it over him into the net. The second was a cracking effort from Neal Maupay. Following some good work down the left from Jakub Moder, Maupay hit a first-time shot from the edge of the box into the top corner, giving Fernández no chance. Coming three minutes before the half-time break, it was a bad time for Brentford to concede, although the referee's whistle did interrupt Brighton's flow and prevented any further goal damage.

After the break, Brentford saw more of the ball and fashioned one or two chances. Both Thompson and Sergi Canós fired efforts wide of the target and Sánchez somehow managed to stop a shot from Baptiste with his leg, even though a deflection took the ball away from the keeper's flying dive. Ethan Pinnock also came close when his goalbound header was cleared away by a retreating Marc Cucurella with just inches to spare.

Maupay said afterwards that he didn't celebrate his goal out of respect for Brentford. The Bees had brought him to English football when they paid French side St Etienne

£1.6m to bring him across the Channel in the summer of 2017. He scored 41 goals in two seasons for the club before transferring to Brighton in time for 2019/20.

Maupay explained, 'I did not want to celebrate because they are the club that gave me my chance. Four years ago, nobody wanted to sign me in France and they called me and asked me to come. I didn't know anything about them and I didn't know anything about England. They were the ones that gave me my chance. I respect them so much – everything they have done for me and everything they have done for a lot of players. They deserve to be where they are now and it is a great club.'

Things don't get any easier as next up for Brentford is Manchester City. In their last three league games, City have beaten Leeds 7-0, Newcastle 4-0 and Leicester 6-3.

Brighton & Hove Albion: Sánchez; Lamptey, Webster, Burn, Cucurella; Lallana (Groß 84); Mwepu, Moder, Mac Allister (Alzate 84); Maupay, Trossard (Welbeck 45)

Brentford: Fernández; Pinnock, Jansson, Bech Sørensen; Canós, Baptiste, Nørgaard, Jensen (Onyeka 45), Thompson (Ghoddos 61); Toney, Mbeumo (Wissa 40)

Tuesday, 28 December 2021
Today's transfer link comes courtesy of Ukrainian outlet *Tribuna*. It says that Brentford are interested in recruiting the Shakhtar Donetsk winger Mykhaylo Mudryk. It is reported that the Bees have already had one bid turned down but are expected to return with another.

Wednesday, 29 December 2021
Manchester City are in town for the last home game of 2021. They are currently top of the table, on a run of nine

league wins in a row and are blowing away anyone they come up against. Not only that, but Brentford are without several players who have so far this season been among the first-choice picks. Rico Henry, Charlie Goode, Kristoffer Ajer, Christian Nørgaard, Vitaly Janelt and Bryan Mbeumo miss out due to injury.

As expected, City had the vast majority of the possession, but their usual fluency was missing as the home players got among them and didn't give them time to settle. After a quarter of an hour's play, though, City found the breakthrough. Kevin De Bruyne picked out Phil Foden inside the penalty box with a lovely through pass and Foden turned the ball in at the near post.

It could have been so different as just moments earlier Brentford had a double chance to open the scoring. Frank Onyeka played in Yoane Wissa whose effort took a deflection that almost wrong-footed City keeper Ederson, but he recovered to claw it round the post. From the resulting corner kick, Ethan Pinnock's header found Wissa who again tested Ederson. The Brazilian could only flick the ball upwards, just out of the reach of Ivan Toney, and, as the net was about to bulge, João Cancelo hooked it off the line and out of danger. Before that, Onyeka had a shot palmed away.

After the interval, the game followed much the same pattern. City pushed forward but Brentford's stiff resistance limited them to few chances. Foden had the ball in the net for what would have been his second but VAR adjudged him to have been in an offside position, and Álvaro Fernández saved from De Bruyne. Brentford's closest effort came from Onyeka but his shot was blocked before testing Ederson.

It was a stout effort from Brentford, considering they were up against a team that has cut almost everybody apart in the last few seasons. Strange it may be to say, but the 1-0 defeat might well be good for their goal difference at the end of the season – City have so far scored an average of two and a half goals per game, including four against Newcastle, five against Norwich and seven against Leeds; teams who, you would assume, will be Brentford's immediate rivals for league places come the end of the season.

Thomas Frank was delighted with the way his team stood up to the test. 'Incredible, unbelievable, fantastic performance,' was his summing up afterwards. 'We are playing against the best team in Europe at this moment in time, especially offensively. We all know City, from the last years under Pep, have been fantastic offensively but they have their moments when they are in form and not in form. We met City at their highest, an in-form team and the first half, for me, is a masterclass in defensive organisation and mentality in the low block. We give away one chance in 45 minutes and that's a goal which is marginally onside.'

Regarding his choice of players due to the injuries, he said, 'We are playing with Dominic Thompson, his second start in the Premier League, Mads Roerslev who has never played a full season in any league, Shandon Baptiste the same, Mads Bech Sørensen for his second start. Lacking six starters. It's not the same for City. They play Grealish, Sterling, Foden or Mahrez – I don't know the difference, actually. So, incredibly proud and I think we fully deserved at least a point.'

The result means that Manchester City finish 2021 on 50 points, eight clear of Chelsea at the top of the Premier League. Liverpool are third on 41 and Arsenal are fourth with 35. Brentford are in 14th position on 20 points, but mid-table is very congested and positions are swapping almost daily. To underline this, Wolves are in eighth, six places in front of Brentford, but are just five points further ahead. The bottom four are beginning to get a little bit cut off from the rest although, of course, it could all change in a couple of weeks or so. Norwich are currently bottom on ten points, with Newcastle and Burnley just ahead on 11. Watford are two further clear on 13.

Brentford: Fernández; Pinnock, Jansson, Bech Sørensen; Roerslev, Baptiste, Jensen, Onyeka (Bidstrup 75), Thompson (Ghoddos 81); Toney, Wissa (Canós 69)

Manchester City: Ederson; Cancelo, Dias, Laporte, Ake; De Bruyne, Fernandinho, Silva; Jesus, Grealish, Foden

Thursday, 30 December 2021

Frank Onyeka has received a call-up to the Nigeria squad for the forthcoming Africa Cup of Nations (AFCON). He will join up with the Nigerian squad after Brentford's match against Aston Villa on Sunday. The tournament begins on 9 January in Cameroon.

The AFCON happens every two years, the 2019 winners being Algeria who beat Senegal 1-0 in the final in Egypt. Each time it is held it is one of those things that the managers bemoan due to their players missing up to a month of the Premier League programme. I suspect this time it will cause even more discord as not only will it add to the number of players missing due to injury, but there will also be the COVID absentees, too. There have already been a fair amount of matches postponed because of the combined injuries and COVID factor, so this may well contribute to more fixtures being called off.

Almost every team will be affected by call-ups. For example, Liverpool will be missing Mo Salah, Naby

Keïta and Sadio Mané; Arsenal will have Thomas Partey, Pierre-Emerick Aubameyang, Nicolas Pépé and Mohamed Elneny away; and Leicester will be without Daniel Amartey, Nampalys Mendy, Wilfred Ndidi and Kelechi Iheanacho. Other possible call-ups from Brentford are Tariqe Fosu who has made four appearances for Ghana, Yoane Wissa who has played twice for the Democratic Republic of Congo and Julian Jeanvier who represents Guinea, although he has only just recently resumed training after a long-term injury suffered when out on loan at Turkish club Kasımpaşa. It isn't unknown for certain managers to give their players who are bound for the AFCON more playing time beforehand possibly 'hoping' (whoops – did I say that?) that they might pick up minor niggles that would be enough for them to pull out of their country's squad, but not so bad that they only miss a game or two, rather than the four or five they would miss if they were away at the tournament. That's an unofficial view, of course.

Friday, 31 December 2021

Speaking to the press after the game with City, Ivan Toney explained that the system that Thomas Frank has put in place for Brentford's style of play and the attitude of the players means that every member of the squad can come in and just slot into the team.

'From the starters to the subs we have quality all over the field,' he says. 'We're missing some main players, but the other boys came in and did great. It's not just the quality, though, it's wanting to work hard and knowing your job when you get in the team, and they did both. Everyone is always ready for the opportunity to play and the players who came in did well, but when we get everyone back we have a great squad and can compete at the highest level.'

On yesterday's match, Toney adds, 'We could have scraped something out of it, but we lacked quality in the final third. But to start the year in the Championship and end it in the Premier League, losing narrowly to one of the best teams in the world, is an achievement, and we can hope for better things next year.'

Saturday, 1 January 2022

Hark, what's that creaking sound I hear? Oh, that'll be the transfer window opening, and it might be an interesting one as far as one or two clubs are concerned. Tottenham's new manager Antonio Conte has been vocal about the need to strengthen his squad and Newcastle, now under new megabucks owners, are at the wrong end of the league with relegation currently looking a real threat. It is Brentford, though, who make the first move of the window. Thomas Frank has moved to bring in Midtjylland goalkeeper Jonas Lössl, initially on loan until the end of the season, but with the option to make the signing permanent at the end of the loan spell.

'Jonas is a very good goalkeeper who will bring with him lots of experience,' said Frank about his new signing. 'He has played in England and the Premier League and we also know him from his work with FCM [Midtjylland]. He fits the criteria of what we want in a goalkeeper with his feet and in his penalty area. The most important thing is that he will add to the experience within our goalkeeper group in our first Premier League season. We have David Raya injured and Álvaro Fernández has missed some training recently. This gives us an extra experienced goalkeeper in training and also someone who has played Premier League games and will be used to the matchday environment if he starts a game for us.'

Concerning that Premier League experience, Lössl played 69 games for Huddersfield in the 2017/18 and 2018/19 seasons. He has also been on the books of Everton, although he didn't actually make an appearance for them, and has played in France for Guingamp and in Germany for Mainz 05. He also has an international cap for Denmark having been between the sticks for the second half of a friendly against Scotland in 2016 after he replaced the injured Kasper Schmeichel at half-time.

Not exactly another new signing but Christian Nørgaard has signed an extension to his current contract which now runs to the end of the 2024/25 season. Nørgaard joined the Bees in 2019 from Italians Fiorentina having only made six appearances for the Florence-based club. He started his career at Lyngby in his native Denmark but, after having made just one single appearance, he moved to Germany with Hamburg. After two seasons he returned to Denmark, this time to Brøndby, where he won the Danish Cup before moving to Italy. Nørgaard has been one of the mainstays of the Brentford team since arriving in west London.

'This is a fantastic New Year's Day gift for all Brentford fans,' beamed Frank. 'We are on a great journey here and we are very pleased that Christian is going to stay on that journey with us. Christian has been a key part in the rise of Brentford in the past three years. I think Christian has had a fantastic first half season in the Premier League. He has shown that he can compete in this league against some of the best in the world in his position. He is also consistently working to develop himself. Christian shows great leadership in training every day and he helps build our culture. That is very important to us. He has an unbelievably important role in this team and it is great that he will be part of our future.'

Sunday, 2 January 2022

Before today's match against Aston Villa at the Community Stadium, Sky Sports, who are showing the game live, broadcast an extended interview with Thomas Frank. In it he talks about the last year and what Brentford have achieved in 2021.

'Of course, after the play-off final there was a bit of time to try to absorb anything and understand that this is unbelievable what we have been part of,' he says, 'but then things go so quick. You go into the routine and the hamster wheel again and prepare.'

How does it feel being up against managers such as Pep Guardiola, Jürgen Klopp and Thomas Tuchel?

'Especially the first game against Arsenal because it was the first game of the Premier League season. I tried just to "woah, this is cool, this is the Premier League", and both Chelsea, Liverpool and Manchester City now, it's something you think of for just 30 seconds but, when the game starts, I don't even know who is in the other dugout. It's just a man I want to beat and a team I want to beat out there on the pitch, so you just completely forget.'

The man that Frank wants to beat today is Steven Gerrard, and the match with Villa began with the visitors showing why they have had an upturn in form since Gerrard's arrival as manager. Gerrard replaced Dean Smith after the former Brentford boss was relieved of his position earlier in the season. It is Gerrard's first managerial job in English football following a successful spell at Rangers in Scotland where he led the Gers to their first league championship triumph in ten years.

Villa took control of the game from the off with Danny Ings causing the Brentford defence all sorts of problems with his running off the ball and finding little pockets of space. His first chance saw Mads Bech Sørensen block his goal bound effort, but he made no mistake second time round. Emiliano Buendía made moves towards the Brentford penalty area and played in Ings who fired into the far corner, giving Álvaro Fernández no chance.

Brentford continued to be hemmed in and some frantic last-ditch defending kept the score at just 1-0. Bech Sørensen snuffed out an effort from Bertrand Traoré and John McGinn sent a long-range effort just too high. As the half wore on, though, Brentford gained more of a foothold and when the equaliser came it was a beauty. Mads Roerslev made inroads down the right wing and played the ball inside to Yoane Wissa. The yard of space he was in was enough for him to curl a delightful effort from the edge of the box past Villa keeper Emiliano Martínez. The goal signalled a complete turn-around in play and it was Brentford who finished the half the stronger. They could even have gone in ahead but Pontus Jansson's header from a Mathias Jensen corner fell just the wrong side of the post.

Frank Onyeka might have given Brentford the lead in the second half but for a fingertip save from Martínez and, at the other end, Fernández denied Ings.

With time running out, Saman Ghoddos found Shandon Baptiste on the edge of the Villa penalty area. Baptiste slipped in Roerslev whose shot was well saved by

Martínez. The rebound, however, again fell to the wing-back who knocked it straight back into the net for his first goal in the red and white stripes.

The remainder of the match saw Villa desperately push for the equaliser and Brentford manfully defending as if for their lives. Last-ditch tackles were made, bodies were put on the line and Fernández once more saved well from Ings. A huge roar greeted the final whistle and a very gutsy performance was rewarded with the three points.

This one could turn out to be an important victory. It has given Brentford a bit of breathing space as they are now ten points clear of the bottom four. OK, one or two teams below them have games in hand, but it is still a good position to be in at this stage of the season.

'I think it shows a lot about the mentality of the group,' Frank told reporters afterwards, 'and on the day for whatever reason when we couldn't play quick enough or play forward enough then you need a magic from one of your players and Wissa had that magic moment in him.'

On Roerslev, he said, 'I think Mads deserves a lot of praise, I think it's a very good story but also a very good Brentford story. We take a young player, nobody really knows him, we work hard with him for two years and now he has played I think maybe four or five Premier League starts. He had a good assist, a very good goal and he deserves a lot of praise.'

Brentford: Fernández; Pinnock, Jansson, Bech Sørensen; Roerslev, Onyeka (Janelt 80), Nørgaard, Jensen (Baptiste 61), Canós (Ghoddos 54); Toney, Wissa

Aston Villa: Martínez; Cash, Konsa, Hause, Targett; Douglas Luiz, McGinn; Traoré (Trézéguet 79), Buendía, Ramsey (Sanson 69); Ings

Tuesday, 4 January 2022

Brentford's former director of football, Rasmus Ankersen, has wasted no time in getting back into the game. Having left his post at the Community Stadium only days ago, he is now involved in a consortium who today announced that they have completed a takeover of Southampton. Ankersen's company, Sport Republic, working with the Serbian media magnate Dragan Šolak as their lead investor, have acquired an 80 per cent share in the south-coast side from their former owner Gao Jinsheng for £200m.

Henrik Kraft, co-founder and chairman of Sport Republic, said in his press release, 'We will be an active and engaged owner, but we will not be starting any revolutions. We were attracted to Southampton because it is already a well-run club that follows a clearly defined strategy. Our ambition is to build a portfolio of high-influence stakes in football clubs and other sporting assets across the world. Southampton is a great first step.'

Wednesday, 4 January 2022

The German channel Sport 1 is reporting that Brentford are showing interest in the young Schalke midfielder Mehmet-Can Aydin. His contract expires at the end of the season and it is said that he has received what are termed 'attractive offers' from clubs around Europe, who are named as Anderlecht, Lille, Marseille, Parma and Real Betis as well as Brentford.

Moving across Europe from Germany to Portugal, and the Portuguese newspaper *Record* claims that the Bees are also keeping an eye on another up-and-coming youngster in the guise of SC Braga striker Vitor Oliveira, known as Vitinha. Reports are that not only Brentford are showing interest, but that Tottenham and West Ham are also monitoring his progress.

Thursday, 6 January 2022

The FA Cup starts for the big boys this weekend, with clubs from both the Premier League and the Championship joining the competition for the third round. The FA Cup is the oldest cup competition in the world, with the first final being played in 1872. The first winners were The Wanderers who beat Royal Engineers 1-0 in the final played at the Kennington Oval. Arsenal have won more FA Cups than anyone else, having amassed 14, and they have also played in most finals, being runners-up in a further seven. Brentford have never been in a final, nor indeed a semi-final, with the quarter-final being the furthest they have progressed. Four times they have reached the last eight, in the 1937/38, 1945/46, 1948/49 and 1988/89 seasons.

Thomas Frank today tells his press conference that he will be treating their third-round opponents, Port Vale, with respect, even though they are currently playing in the bottom tier of the English professional structure.

'We truly respect Port Vale,' he told reporters. 'A good team that are doing well in League Two. I'll put a strong team out there, a strong squad to travel because I believe in keeping the momentum. I think about the next game, that is now the FA Cup game against Port Vale, and we have to do everything we can to win and give it maximum focus. After that, it is on to the next game against Southampton.'

Regarding his cup opponents, he says, 'I've heard that playing away to Port Vale is tricky. It's a tricky ground and will be lively. I hope we have a very fantastic cup atmosphere. We're up for it, we know how they like to play and try to attack. We'll be ready. I'm 100 per cent sure that Darrell Clarke will put his strongest side out because they had been hit by COVID then had a lot of games postponed because other teams have COVID. He needs a game with his starting 11 which we are looking forward to facing.'

Friday, 7 January 2022

Thomas Frank's press conference today continues with the FA Cup focus today, with the manager saying that he will treat the competition with the respect it deserves.

'We know it is the oldest tournament in the world and I would say the one with the biggest prestige to try to win,' he says. 'I know the story about cup tournaments and especially the FA Cup. Of course, I followed the FA Cup a lot, especially when I was younger in Denmark, so I'm excited. For whatever reason, since I've been here it's only the Carabao Cup we've been quite successful in, so I'd like to change that with the FA Cup. This year I'd like to see us have a nice run.'

Changing the subject to the victory over Aston Villa, Frank says he wasn't surprised at Yoane Wissa's stunning strike, 'That's why we brought him in and paid quite a lot of money, to produce some of these magic moments. A little bit out of nothing he produced a goal we needed the most that also changed the momentum of the game. I think he's getting better and better, but I still think he's not as sharp as he was just before he got injured against West Ham. What I see in training, he's doing well but he lacks the last ten or 15 per cent of that when he was banging goals in in training. But it's nice to know he can still get better.'

Saturday, 8 January 2022

The FA Cup is famous for its giant killings. It isn't exactly unknown for a team from the higher echelons of the league structure to be beaten by those who are lower-ranked. There have been a few famous examples of this down the years. For instance, in 1989, non-league Sutton United beat Coventry City, who were at that time in the old First Division and had won the competition two years previously; Arsenal, the reigning league champions, lost in 1992 to Wrexham, who had finished bottom of the entire Football League the previous season; and Stevenage, in their first season as a Football League club, beat Premier League Newcastle 3-1 in 2011.

For all the giant-killing exploits, it still does tend to be, at least in recent years, that the cup winners come from among the powerhouses of English football. In the last 30 years, going back to the 1992 final, Arsenal have won the competition on nine occasions, Chelsea have won seven, Manchester United five, Liverpool three and Manchester City two. The only clubs outside of those five to have won the FA Cup in that time are Everton in 1995, Portsmouth in 2008, Wigan in 2013 and Leicester, who are the current holders.

You can see how the game has changed and how the same clubs are tending to win all the trophies, be they championships or cups, if you look back another 30 years to 1962. In that period, 15 different teams carried off the trophy – Tottenham and Manchester United (five each), Liverpool (four), West Ham (three) and Arsenal and Everton (two), with Chelsea, Coventry, Ipswich, Leeds, Manchester City, Southampton, Sunderland, West Brom and Wimbledon winning once each.

What about this year's competition, then? Would the FA Cup of 2021/22 produce any surprise results, or will the bigger teams assert their authority on their not-so-recognised peers? As it happens, this weekend's third-round ties do not disappoint, with two non-league teams beating league opposition. National League side Boreham Wood were 2-0 winners against AFC Wimbledon of League One and the lowest-ranked team still left in the competition, Kidderminster Harriers of the National League North, overcame Championship Reading 2-1. Two Premier League teams also went out at the hands of lower-league opponents. Burnley were beaten 2-1 by Huddersfield Town of the Championship, but what about Newcastle United 0 Cambridge United 1? Newcastle didn't weaken their team, they gave a debut to new signing Kieran Trippier who has just joined them from Atlético Madrid – you would assume the first of many signings under the new owners – and they had home advantage. Cambridge, on the other hand, are in the lower half of League One.

What about Brentford, then? They were up against lower-league opposition in Port Vale. Was their match added to the list of shock results?

Brentford, with Kristoffer Ajer back in the team and new signing Jonas Lössl making his debut in goal, took control of the early exchanges but clear-cut openings were few and far between. The first real sight of goal came when a long thrown from Mads Bech Sørensen was flicked on by Fin Stevens for Marcus Forss. His effort was helped on by Yoane Wissa but Vale keeper Aidan Stone got down well to save.

The breakthrough came when Mads Bidstrup advanced into the Port Vale half and found Forss in space in the penalty area. He took one touch before clinically dispatching the ball into the roof of the net. Wissa almost added a second on the stroke of half-time. Vitaly Janelt swung in a corner which Stone came to punch clear. The ball dropped to Wissa who instantly lobbed it back over him only to see his effort bounce back off the crossbar. Ajer pounced on the loose ball and hit his shot on the turn only to see a scrambling Stone block his effort.

The second half saw Vale step it up and really exert some pressure on Brentford. Ajer intervened just as Tom Pett was steadying himself to convert David Worrall's cross and Mads Roerslev blocked an effort from the same player shortly after.

With the home side building up the pressure, Thomas Frank sent on Bryan Mbeumo, a decision that almost immediately paid dividends. Bidstrup found Janelt who in turn slipped the ball through to Mbeumo. As the keeper came out to meet him, Mbeumo knocked it passed him to make it 2-0. Instead of taking the wind out of the home team's sails, though, the second goal just spurred them on to intensify their efforts and, almost straight from the restart, Dennis Politic crossed from the left and Kian Harratt headed in. They kept coming at Brentford and pushed and pushed for the equaliser, Lössl denying Worrall and Lewis Cass shooting just wide.

Just when it was looking like the last 15 minutes would be very awkward for Brentford, Bidstrup and Shandon Baptiste combined to set up Mbeumo to hammer the ball home and restore the two-goal cushion. Ivan Toney came off the bench and hadn't been on the pitch long before he was hauled to the ground inside the box. The regular penalty taker, he gave Mbeumo the chance to get his hat-trick which he duly did by converting the spot-kick and the game was done and dusted. It was the first time a Brentford substitute had climbed off the bench to score a hat-trick. On paper the 4-1 victory looked a comfortable one, but in reality Port Vale certainly gave them a game.

Port Vale: Stone; Cass, Martin, Smith; Worrall, Pett (Walker 81), Conlon, Gibbons (Benning 59); Garrity; Wilson (Harratt, 54), Amoo (Politic 59)

Brentford: Lössl; Ajer (Roerslev 62), Bech Sørensen, Pinnock; Stevens, Ghoddos (Peart-Harris 81), Bidstrup, Janelt (Baptiste 71), Thompson (Toney 81); Forss, Wissa (Mbeumo 62)

Brentford's next scheduled match is against Southampton in the Premier League on Tuesday but Saints manager Ralph Hasenhüttl is unsure whether or not they will have to ask to have the match postponed. Speaking after their cup win over Swansea in extra time, he said, 'At the moment it's all about lottery. You wake up in the morning and go to the training ground. You sit at breakfast and you are waiting for new cases. The problem is with the fixtures coming up it doesn't get any easier. We have had a long game, overtime. It's super tough and we have to definitely recover well because a strong team is waiting for us. We must hope that we don't get any more COVID cases because on a few positions we are running out of players.'

Sunday, 9 January 2022

And still the shocks come. Today it is the turn of Nottingham Forest who are 1-0 victors over Arsenal. Forest are doing well in the Championship but, even so, it is a lower-league team beating a Premier League rival. Arsenal have only gone out of the FA Cup in the third round once in the last 25 years. That was in 2018, ironically also against Nottingham Forest.

There are no further unexpected results in today's ties, but Tottenham are given a fright by Morecambe. The League One side took the lead at the Tottenham Hotspur Stadium and were still ahead until the last 15 minutes before finally giving way and Tottenham ended up winning 3-1. Liverpool also found themselves behind at home to Shrewsbury Town but, like Tottenham, came back and eventually won 4-1.

The draw for the fourth round gives Brentford a tough tie away at Everton. The tie of the round, at least for the romantics, sees West Ham drawn away at Kidderminster Harriers. What a brilliant reward for the Harriers' victory over Reading yesterday.

Monday, 10 January 2022

A video is circulating on the internet today, courtesy of Brentford's Twitter account, of David Raya's arriving for his first day back at training since his injury lay-off. It shows Raya joining the other players while dressed in a Tyrannosaurus Rex costume. He says 'good morning' and we can hear somebody off camera reply 'good morning T-rex'. The thing that strikes me most about this video is the lack of surprise or amazement on anyone else's face. If I was at work and a dinosaur arrived to join in, I think I would at least think to myself, 'Hang on, what's going on here?' Perhaps, though, the other players are used to it. Perhaps this is the sort of clothing that Señor Raya tends to wear. I mean, why wouldn't you shun jeans and a t-shirt when there is a dinosaur costume just laying around doing nothing? Maybe it is just normal for him to dress as some long-extinct creature before hitting the town. 'Hey lads, I'm off to the West End for a meal and then on to a musical in Shaftesbury Avenue. I've got a spare ticket and Dodo costume if anyone fancies it.'

Looking forward to tomorrow's match with Southampton during his press conference, Thomas Frank has special praise for the Saints' playmaker:

'James Ward-Prowse is maybe the best set-piece taker in the league, maybe he's even the best free-kick taker in the world. There's one left-footer at PSG [Lionel Messi] who is right up there and is pretty good as well. So maybe Ward-Prowse is the best right footed free-kick taker in the world. So many times he just puts the ball into the top corner. It's not the same as a penalty but it's pretty close to it for Ward-Prowse, so we've got to be aware of that, trying not to give a foul away around the box.'

Frank also has praise for his Southampton counterpart, Ralph Hasenhüttl, 'I think Southampton are a good, experienced Premier League side. Ralph Hasenhüttl and his coaching staff have done a top job down there. His team is very well-organised, very well-drilled. We know they are coming most likely in a 4-4-2 formation, but they can change very easily to, for example, a 4-3-3. But the energy and structure in the middle, their high press is very impressive. They are one of the best or maybe, even at some stages, the best high energy pressing team in the league. It's very impressive so we need to deal with that.'

Frank insists that he isn't setting any targets for his team for the rest of the season. He just wants them to continue on in the same vein, 'I think it's been a good first half to the season. We have tried to become an asset to the Premier League, we have tried to attack it, being positive and brave.

Maybe we could even have had a few more points, which is quite impressive. And with the injury list, taking that into mind as well, that's been good. Looking forward, only one game at a time, we are trying to maximise everything and we will try to get three points tomorrow. We only have two targets: one, to focus entirely on the next game, and two, to end as high as possible. So instead of only going for a certain points target, we just push to go as high as possible and to maximise every single day.'

On the subject of suffering injuries, he also had a bit of good news regarding Josh Dasilva. After moving across London from Arsenal in 2018, Dasilva had made nearly 100 appearances in the Bees' midfield before sustaining a hip injury in March 2021 having played 30 times in what would become the promotion-winning campaign.

'I said to Josh the other day that he will be our best signing this year when he returns,' Frank recounted. 'When he comes back it will be like having a new player with top quality and I really hope he will come back in a fantastic place. We are on track with him. We are progressing fine. He was with the team yesterday so hopefully in five or six weeks, if everything goes to plan, he will potentially be available. We have to be careful with him and make sure he is strong. He needs almost a pre-season.'

Tuesday, 11 January 2022
Despite Ralph Hasenhüttl's reservations at the weekend, the Southampton v Brentford match does indeed go ahead tonight. And regardless of Thomas Frank's warnings at his press conference yesterday about the expertise of James Ward-Prowse at dead balls, he provided the ammunition for the Saints to open the scoring. It was a corner rather than

a free kick that Word-Prowse swung in dangerously, Jan Bednarek heading up from the back and getting the vital flick to deflect the ball into the Brentford net.

The warnings were there as, before Bednarek's intervention, Nathan Redmond almost found a way through the Bees' defence only for Kristoffer Ajer's challenge to bring his run to a halt just as he was getting ready to pull the trigger, and Ward-Prowse saw his effort deflected wide of the target.

Brentford weathered the storm and managed to get back on level terms thanks to an expertly volleyed strike from Vitaly Janelt. Shandon Baptiste found some space on the left and switched play to Mads Roerslev on the other side of the pitch. Roerslev fed Bryan Mbeumo who sent in a dangerous cross that was met sweetly by Janelt. His volley into the bottom corner gave Fraser Forster no chance in the Southampton goal. A little while later, Janelt set his sights on a second but this time his long-range effort was saved by Forster.

Southampton retook the lead in strange circumstances, again from a corner. This time the ball found its way to Ibrahima Diallo who fired in a shot from the edge of the penalty box. The ball beat Álvaro Fernández but came back off the post. Unfortunately for the Spanish keeper, it came straight back at him and rebounded back into the net off the back of his still-outstretched hand. It will go down as an own goal but was a very unfortunate one at that. Moments later, though, Fernández made amends by somehow pushing a header from Romain Perraud to safety when it looked like Southampton might be extending their lead.

The second half saw Brentford pushing for their second equaliser of the evening, and it was this that lead to the game's fourth goal. It was, though, a third for the home team as they caught Brentford on the break. As an attack broke down, Oriol Romeu spotted the run by Armando Broka and played him in with a defence-splitting pass. Broka bided his time, waited for Fernández to come out and meet him and slid the ball past him into the far corner for 3-1.

There was more to come as, once again, Brentford were caught pushing forward and a long ball this time found Ché Adams who lifted it over Fernández as he came out to try to narrow the angle, and Southampton had a three-goal cushion. There were a couple of half chances for Brentford in the closing stages, but Forster thwarted both Mbeumo and then Ivan Toney.

'Fair play to Southampton,' said Frank after the match, 'they did their job, but it is my job to look at our performance and that was definitely not good enough today. I think we know that we need to be playing every second of every Premier League match 100 per cent and we definitely didn't do that today. In terms of focus and winning the duels, in a very basic first half we were not winning any second ball all over the pitch more or less.'

Turning to Fin Stevens, who made his Premier League debut tonight when he came on as a substitute for Sergi Canós, Frank said, 'I think he did a decent job. I think he earned that in the game against Port Vale where he played a very good game, especially the first half, so I think he is a promising young player.'

Southampton: Forster; Bednarek, Lyanco, Salisu; Tella (S. Armstrong 69), Ward-Prowse, Romeu, Diallo, Perraud; Redmond (Adams 64), Broja (A. Armstrong 78)

Brentford: Fernández; Ajer, Jansson, Pinnock (Jensen 68); Roerslev, Baptiste (Wissa 56), Nørgaard, Janelt, Canós (Stevens 76); Toney, Mbeumo

Wednesday, 12 January 2022

It is reported that Brentford are one of the clubs keeping an eye on the young Sheffield Wednesday forward Bailey Cadamarteri. His form for Wednesday's Under-18 team has apparently attracted interest from a few clubs, including the Bees and fellow Londoners West Ham. Bailey is the son of Danny Cadamarteri, who played as a striker for Everton, Bradford City and Huddersfield, among others.

While on the subject of footballing offspring, in the weekend's FA Cup ties, Stoke City gave a debut to D'Margio Wright-Phillips, the son of Shaun Wright-Phillips, who played for Manchester City, Chelsea and Queens Park Rangers. Shaun's brother Bradley also played at the top level for, most notably, Southampton before becoming a star in Major League Soccer in America. He is currently New York Red Bulls' all-time leading goal scorer. Both Shaun and Bradley are the sons of former Arsenal hero Ian Wright, the club's second all-time top scorer behind only Thierry Henry. So, a third generation of Wrights (Wright-Phillipses) is upon us. Interestingly, also playing for Stoke that day was Tyrese Campbell, the son of another former Arsenal player and Wright's former team-mate, Kevin Campbell. Not only that but Tom Ince, the son of the ex-Manchester United and England midfielder Paul Ince, was in their line-up too.

There have been a few father/son top-level dynasties. The most famous current example is Peter and Kasper Schmeichel. Peter played in goal for Manchester United during their glory days under Sir Alex Ferguson, winning five Premier League championships, three FA Cups and the Champions League, while Kasper is currently the Leicester City number one who famously helped his team to the Premier League title in 2015/16 the FA Cup in 2020/21.

Between them they have so far earned 207 international caps for Denmark and counting.

Another few notable examples include Alex Bruce, currently plying his trade at Macclesfield Town after having previously starred for Hull City and Ipswich Town among others, the son of Steve Bruce, another former Manchester United favourite; Norwich City goalkeeper Angus Gunn is following in the footsteps of his father Bryan, who made almost 400 appearances between the sticks for the Canaries; Huddersfield striker Jordan Rhodes is the son of the ex-Oldham goalkeeper Andy Rhodes.

Then, of course, we have the Lampard/Redknapp connection. While Harry Redknapp and Frank Lampard were starring for West Ham in the 1960s, they married twin sisters. Redknapp's son Jamie played for Liverpool and England, while Lampard's son Frank junior is Chelsea's all-time record goalscorer. So this means that Harry Redknapp and Frank Lampard senior are in-laws, Jamie Redknapp and Frank Lampard junior are cousins, with each of the seniors being uncle to each of the juniors. Phew!

And if you think *that* was complicated, don't even begin to try to work out the Allen family. Oh, go on then. Les Allen played for Chelsea, Tottenham and Queens Park Rangers in the 1950s and '60s, with his brother Dennis starring for Reading. Les had sons called Clive, another Tottenham hero from the 1980s, and Bradley, who is best known for his days at QPR. Dennis's son Martin also represented QPR, as well as West Ham. Then there's Paul, the nephew of both Les and Dennis, who was a midfielder with both West Ham and Tottenham. Descending a further generation, we find Clive Allen's son Oliver who represented Barnet. So here we have fathers and sons, uncles and nephews, grandfathers, grandsons and a frazzled brain!

Friday, 14 January 2022

This weekend's Premier League action sees Brentford travel to Anfield to play Liverpool in what will be Jürgen Klopp's 350th match in charge of the Reds. In their respective press conferences, both managers seem to be looking forward to it. Thomas Frank spoke of the atmosphere he was expecting to experience.

'It's the first time we are going to Anfield,' he said, 'we all know it's one of the most iconic stadiums in the world. We are all looking forward to that and we want to go there and express ourselves and attack, because we want it to be a fun and good experience at two o'clock but also at four o'clock. It's not that fun if we go there and get beaten 4-0, it's only a fantastic experience if you go there, perform and get a result, and that's what we're aiming for. It's also about the atmosphere. It's one of the stadiums where what I've heard – I've been there a few times – that the atmosphere when the fans are really on it, which they normally are, is unbelievable. Plus, the way Liverpool play under Klopp makes it so hectic, so intense, that it's going to be a very big experience, I'm 100 per cent sure of that.'

Klopp, for his part, was complimentary about how Brentford have acquitted themselves so far.

'They play a brilliant first season in the Premier League,' he said. 'Thomas Frank is doing a brilliant job there. The squad is well set up, interesting players there, the way they want to play. So many things really work together there that we have to be really aware of.'

The only time in Brentford's history when they have beaten Liverpool at Anfield was in the old First Division in November 1937. The score that day was Liverpool 3 Brentford 4. Some more of that would be a bit tasty.

There was a piece of good news for Brentford today when it was revealed that Pontus Jansson has put pen to paper with a year's extension to his current contract, which had been due to expire at the end of the season. There had been a bit of paper talk a few weeks ago that Everton, Leicester and Newcastle were interested in trying to lure him away, but now it seems that he will be staying at the Community Stadium until at least the end of next season.

'I am very pleased that Pontus has signed a new contract,' said Frank. 'He has been a big part of the success we have had over the last three years. He has been important to our defensive improvement in the last three seasons. Pontus has done well for us in the Premier League, and we are all pleased that he will be with us next season. His leadership and communication in defensive situations and his positioning are very important for us.'

One player who didn't sign for the Bees when the opportunity was there is also in the news today. Hugo Siquet, a full-back who was the product of the youth system at Belgian club Standard Liège, has given an interview to *Het Belang Van Limburg*, a Dutch language regional newspaper in Belgium, and explained why he chose to move to German club Freiburg instead of west London in the close season.

'There were a lot of advantages to Brentford,' he told the paper, 'but I didn't feel ready to jump straight into the Premier League at the time. That's a different world. Freiburg were interested for some time. It's a very stable club. The coach [Christian Streich] has been here for more than ten years. Financially and sportingly it was interesting. Life is quiet here and there is less pressure.'

Sunday, 16 January 2022

Brentford are at Anfield for the first time in 84-and-a-bit years but, unlike the first match earlier in the season at the Community Stadium, Liverpool were in no mood to take anything other than the three points. Diogo Jota was a constant thorn in Brentford's side and twice in the first half he threatened to break the deadlock. Firstly, his shot from a Jordan Henderson corner was scrambled clear and then, again after having been set up by Henderson, Jota was denied by a block from Kristoffer Ajer.

The pressure continued to mount and Rico Henry, back in the team for the first time since picking up an injury in the League Cup match with Chelsea, had to intervene to stop Trent Alexander-Arnold getting his shot in. Álvaro Fernández also had to be in top form to stop Virgil van Dijk. A corner from Alexander-Arnold was flicked on past Fernández at the near post to Van Dijk who looked certain to open the scoring but, somehow, Fernández recovered to stop his effort on the line. As the first half progressed, though, Brentford began to get a foothold and started to test the Liverpool defence. Ivan Toney saw a long-range effort fly just the wrong side of the post and Vitaly Janelt's shot was just too high.

Just before the half-time break, Roberto Firmino played in Jota once again, but Henry got back to intervene. The resulting corner found its way past a whole host of bodies to Firmino at the far post and he nodded the ball over the line to give Liverpool the lead.

The opening exchanges in the second half saw Fernández stop efforts from Fabinho and Curtis Jones, while Brentford came close when Bryan Mbeumo latched on to a pass from Christian Nørgaard. He made a bit of space for himself, but his shot flew just wide of the post with Liverpool keeper Alisson beaten.

As the game progressed, Liverpool's chances kept coming. Alexander-Arnold caused trouble in the area before setting up Jota, who looked sure to double the lead, but his shot came back off the post. Shortly afterwards, Firmino found himself in the clear but Fernández produced another fine stop when it looked to be a certain goal.

The Reds continued to turn the screw and eventually the pressure told. Andy Robertson produced a fine cross from the left and Alex Oxlade-Chamberlain was on hand at the back post to head in the second, and the game was finished as a contest when Takumi Minamino knocked the ball in from the edge of the six-yard box after a mix-up in the Brentford defence presented him with an unmissable chance.

After the game, Thomas Frank admitted his team need to tighten up defensively.

'It's not the first time a team has lost 3-0 at Anfield but it is irritating me a lot because especially the third goal was completely avoidable and should never happen,' he said. 'We conceded in a set piece. That should never happen. If you want to get a good result against a world-class team, one of the best in the Premier League, you can never concede on a set piece. Unfortunately, we did that. I said to Jürgen I would love to have seen what would have happened had it been 0-0 at half-time. We had a chance through Mbeumo and then they scored for 2-0 and it was a done deal. We are very aware of it and if you want to be a good team in the Premier League you have to do all the phases well. If you are a newly promoted team you need to be very good at defending set pieces and you can't concede soft goals. I felt that in the first ten to 12 games we were brilliant at them and then, for whatever reason, we have conceded from set pieces in recent weeks and we need to do better.'

Regarding Henry's comeback to the team and his having to be taken off again shortly into the second half, Frank reassured reporters that it shouldn't be a big deal:

'It was more precautionary to take him off. It was planned that he would pay 60 minutes, but he got a contact in the first half, and we decided it was not worth the risk. It was fantastic to have him back. He is a big player for us, and we don't have anyone else like him. It will be good to have him back and playing more games.'

Despite the seeming comfort of the win, Liverpool manager Jürgen Klopp admitted to not being completely at ease.

'They are extremely uncomfortable to play against, to be honest,' he told BBC Sport. 'All these high balls, long balls, the constant fight for second balls and there were so many moments when the ball was five or six times in the air where you just go for the header, go for the header, and we obviously have to play football.'

Liverpool: Alisson; Alexander-Arnold, Matip, van Dijk, Robertson; Henderson, Fabinho, Jones; Oxlade-Chamberlain (Minamino 74), Firmino (Milner 78), Jota (Gordon 82)

Brentford: Fernández; Ajer, Jansson, Pinnock; Roerslev, Baptiste (Wissa 67), Nørgaard, Janelt, Henry (Canós 49); Toney, Mbeumo (Jensen 75)

Over in the blue half of Merseyside, Everton today sacked manager Rafael Benítez. He was only appointed in June as successor to Carlo Ancelotti. Even though they started the season well – they won four and drew one of their first six games – they have since fallen into an alarming slide that sees them in 16th place in the Premier League table, only six points above the relegation places. It was seen by many as a strange appointment in the first place due to Benítez's association with Everton's rivals Liverpool, with whom he won the Champions League in 2005 and the UEFA Super Cup and FA Cup the following season. Until a permanent successor is named, former Everton centre-forward Duncan Ferguson, who has been on the coaching staff since the days of David Moyes's managerial reign, will be in charge of first team matters.

Monday, 17 January 2022

It is being reported in some sections of the media that Brentford have offered a six-month contract to Christian Eriksen. The Danish playmaker has openly said he is hoping to resume his professional career sooner rather than later and is even looking at a return to international football.

'My goal is to play in the World Cup in Qatar,' he told Danish Broadcaster DR1. 'That has been my mindset all along. It's a goal, a dream. Whether I'll be picked is another thing, but it is my dream to come back. I'm sure I can come back because I don't feel any different. Physically, I'm back in top shape. That has been my goal and it is still some time away, so until then I'm just going to play football and prove I am back at the same level. My dream is to rejoin the national team and play at Parken again and prove that it was a one-time and that it won't happen again. I want to prove that I can move on and play for the national team again. It is up to the manager to assess my level, but my heart is not an obstacle.'

Eriksen refers, of course, to his collapse on the pitch during last summer's European Championship. While playing for Denmark against Finland at the Parken Stadium in Copenhagen, Eriksen suffered a cardiac arrest a few minutes before half-time. The match was immediately stopped and his life was saved after CPR and defibrillation were performed on him on the pitch. Eriksen is a free agent as his contract with Inter Milan was terminated by mutual consent due to the Italian authorities not allowing sportsmen to play in Italy with implanted heart-starting defibrillators. He has recently been training with Danish team Odense and Chiasso in Switzerland. Now that *would* be an interesting signing. Let's see if there are any legs in this one.

And from Scandinavia to Scotland. The *Scottish Herald* reports that Kristoffer Ajer is thoroughly enjoying his time at Brentford. Ajer made 170 appearances in the Scottish League with Celtic before making the trip south.

Ajer is quoted as saying, 'Especially when you meet [teams like Liverpool], they keep the ball so well, they attack with so many players and they tire you out. It is, of course, difficult but we have to be better throughout the 90 minutes, but I love every single minute at Brentford. It doesn't matter what team you play, we have to show ourselves and the quality we've got. I look forward to every single game.'

Another piece of good news is that Josh Dasilva came through 45 minutes of a friendly against Havant &

Waterlooville unscathed. The match was played behind closed doors and provided a good run-out for Dasilva and one or two others who have been short on first-team playing time recently.

Dasilva, who hasn't played since March due to a hip injury, was taken off at half-time as a precaution to ease him back to action gently. Also involved in the game were Saman Ghoddos, Mathias Jensen, Mads Bech Sørensen, Yoane Wissa, Marcus Forss, Mads Bistrup, Dominic Thompson and Jonas Lössl. Brentford beat Havant 2-1.

Tuesday, 18 January 2022

A couple more pieces of transfer speculation appear via various media outlets today. Firstly, there is heavy coverage of a possible move for Bologna's Scottish defender Aaron Hickey. He moved to Italy from Hearts in time for the 2020/21 season, but it is now being said that both Brentford and West Ham are interested in bringing him to London.

The other player being mentioned is Keane Lewis-Potter who is currently with Hull City. The completion of any possible deal may be made more complicated by the fact that Hull are currently in the process of a takeover by the Turkish businessman and media mogul Acun Ilıcalı.

There is, though, only one rumour that takes the spotlight in Thomas Frank's press conference today. When asked about Eriksen, he neither confirmed nor denied interest:

'I can tell you that Christian is a really good player, everyone knows that. A top Danish player. I've worked with him in the past. He needs to find a club. This is a player that only plays for the top clubs. Something unfortunate happened with Christian and things changed a bit. He deserves to play at the highest level, and I hope that he is going to play at the highest level. Under normal circumstances there would be no rumours with a club like us, so I guess we should be flattered. If Brentford had been linked with Christian ten or even five years ago, the fans would say you were crazy.'

Wednesday, 19 January 2022

Today is the visit of Manchester United. What a throwaway comment. Let's just repeat that again. Today is the visit of Manchester United. It's funny how quickly you get used to this, isn't it? 'Oh, Manchester United today, is it? Well, we've already played Arsenal, Liverpool, Chelsea, Tottenham and Man City so, yeah, bring it on.'

Just take a moment and think about what this actually means. Brentford v Manchester United in the Premier League. Yesterday in his press conference, Thomas Frank said of being linked with a move for Christian Eriksen, 'If Brentford had been linked with Christian ten or even five years ago, the fans would say you were crazy.' So how about five years ago saying this fixture would be a thing? Five years ago, the 2016/17 season, saw Brentford finish tenth in the Championship, while Manchester United won the League Cup and the Europa League. The season before they lifted the FA Cup and they had only just come out of a period where they finished no lower than third place in the Premier League for 21 years in succession, during which time they twice won the Champions League. Today they visit the Community Stadium with Cristiano Ronaldo in their ranks, thought by many to be one of the greatest players who has ever lived, and spoken in the same breath as such legendary luminaries as Pelé, Diego Maradona and Lionel Messi.

From the first whistle, Brentford took the game to their illustrious opponents. Their first opportunity fell to Mathias Jensen. A long throw from Mads Bech Sørensen into the United goalmouth was only cleared as far as Jensen but he shot just the wrong side of the post. It was the same player who had a clear-cut chance midway through the half from a passage of play that caused panic in United's defence. Bryan Mbeumo was challenged by Victor Lindelöf and the ball broke to Christian Nørgaard who played in Jensen with only David De Gea to beat. Jensen shot low but the United keeper saved with his leg. The loose ball eventually found its way to Vitaly Janelt but his effort was deflected wide. From the corner, Bech Sørensen saw his shot bounce agonisingly past the post via a United leg. The next corner was knocked clear but only straight to Janelt. He returned the ball into the danger zone to Nørgaard but his shot flew over the bar.

The Bees kept up the pressure, desperately looking for the opening goal. From a breakaway from a corner, Janelt knocked the ball forward to Ivan Toney who steered it into Jensen's path. With only De Gea to beat, Jensen shot straight at the Spaniard and Toney was unable to convert the follow-up. The resulting corner found the head of Ethan Pinnock but once again De Gea was equal to it.

The second half began with United fortunate to still be on level terms, and they knew it. They upped the tempo and Ronaldo headed against the crossbar from Bruno Fernandes's corner. Shortly afterwards, Fred was afforded space in the midfield and picked out Anthony Elanga. He accelerated through, the ball bounced up and he nodded it past Jonas Lössl to give the visitors the lead. Lössl saved a long-range effort from Scott McTominay but was powerless to act when Ronaldo turned the ball into Fernandes's path.

He raced clear, squared for Mason Greenwood and he knocked it past Lössl.

Two goals in eight minutes put United in the driving seat in a match where they could easily have been at least two down themselves. Still Brentford kept pushing and Shandon Baptiste laid the ball across to Toney, but his shot was blocked on the line by Raphaël Varane. Bech Sørensen played it back in to Mads Roerslev at the far post but he sliced his shot and another chance went begging.

United wrapped up the points when McTominay burst through, knocked the ball to Fernandes who, in turn, played in Marcus Rashford who slammed it home. Brentford did, however, manage a consolation goal with five minutes remaining. Another long throw did the damage as it dropped to Pinnock. His shot was blocked, the ball eventually landing at Toney's feet who fired in.

Speaking to BT Sport after the game, Thomas Frank made it abundantly clear that he was delighted with the performance, if not the result.

'I'm unbelievably proud of my team,' he said. 'I think we are the smallest club in the Premier League and Manchester United are probably the biggest. I think the way we played in the first half I think we destroyed them. We should have been up at least 2-0, they didn't have a sniff, nothing. We created five, six chances, and three were huge chances. They changed their system against little Brentford. I'm so, so proud of my team.'

The result leaves Brentford in 14th position on 23 points after 22 games. It is a decent enough return considering they are a newly promoted club and were, realistically, let's be honest, being mentioned in the conversation before the season kicked off about who would be among the relegation candidates. But how is that conversation going now? Actually, it's really quite difficult to tell. Normally most, if not all of the teams, would have played the same number of matches as they would all be playing at the weekends and in any midweek fixtures, and it would be easy to see how the rest of the season may well pan out. This year, however, due to all the COVID postponements that have been happening, it is a lot more difficult to predict.

For example, Burnley are currently bottom of the league with only 11 points, but their matches have been particularly badly affected and, as a result, they have only played 17. Norwich, in 18th position, have played four matches more than Burnley but only have two more points. So, on the face of it, Burnley are in a much better position, but they still have to get points from their postponed games when they are eventually played. Plus, as the season goes on and more matches are potentially called off, it means that certain teams could be playing every three or four days for the last few weeks. Therefore, tiredness and fatigue may well be a factor in determining the final outcome. Is it better to have the points in the bag now or have the games in hand? This season, more than any other, nothing is certain. The only thing that *does* seem to be certain is that, come April and May, it's going to be a frantic and exciting finale.

Brentford: Lössl; Pinnock, Jansson, Bech Sørensen; Roerslev, Jensen (Wissa 67), Nørgaard, Janelt (Baptiste 64), Canós (Henry 64); Toney, Mbeumo

Manchester United: De Gea; Telles, Lindelöf, Varane, Dalot; Fred, McTominay (Matić 84); Greenwood (Rashford 71), Fernandes, Elanga; Ronaldo (Maguire 71)

Meanwhile, 3,800 miles away from the Community Stadium in Garoua, Cameroon, Frank Onyeka came off the substitutes' bench to make his first appearance for Nigeria in the Africa Cup of Nations. He was a 76th-minute replacement for Kelechi Nwakali, who plays in Spain for Huesca, where he is a former team-mate of Brentford goalkeeper Álvaro Fernández. Nigeria beat Guinea-Bissau 2-0, meaning they won all three of their matches in the opening group phase. They now go on to the second round where they will meet Tunisia.

Thursday, 20 January 2022

The media today is full of Cristiano Ronaldo's reaction at his being substituted during yesterday's match. Having been replaced by Harry Maguire after 71 minutes with the score at 2-0, Ronaldo was clearly unhappy as he walked off the pitch and the television cameras caught him in discussion with Ralf Rangnick, his expression not exactly one of joy. Some sections of the media are saying that it shows how much he cares, while some are saying that it was a show of petulance. Those viewers who are able to lip read and, actually, those not able to lip read, could quite clearly see him asking, 'Why me?'

Rangnick gave his answer to the press when questioned about it:

'I have to make my decisions in the interest of the team and club. We had the same situation at Aston Villa when we were 2-0 up in the second half and I didn't want to make the same mistake [the match ended 2-2]. It was the right decision. Cristiano is a goalscorer but it was more important to be compact at this moment. When we scored a third, I said this exactly to him, "I know you are ambitious to score but maybe in two years' time when you are a head coach like me and in the same position, you will understand.'"

So there. That's you told, Cristiano!

The *Daily Mail* today reports that Hull City's new owner, Acun Ilıcalı, seems to have ruled out Brentford transfer target Keane Lewis-Potter leaving the club, at least in this transfer window. The newspaper quotes him as saying, 'There is a logic point in football that sometimes you have to sell a player, but this logic moment at the moment is not soon for us. He is so young, he is not in a rush, so we are not in a rush, so why sell him in the short term?'

The *Mail* says that as well as the Bees, Southampton, West Ham and Tottenham are all interested in prizing Lewis-Potter away from the MKM Stadium.

With regards to any potential incomings, the news at Thomas Frank's press conference today was that there is no news.

'There is no further development in any of the rumours about transfers to Brentford,' he said. 'I will look forward to speak about any transfer that is possible to happen when they happen. I said it before the season and also in this transfer window, I think we have a strong enough squad to compete in the Premier League. I think we have shown that last night. I think the first 60 minutes were absolutely amazing, they showed what these players are capable of. I do think a player or two would bring extra energy and awareness to the squad, but I don't think it is essential. We are always prepared, we are always in the market, and if we find the right player for the right position, with the right character, then we will do it.'

Looking forward to the weekend's match against Wolves, Frank acknowledged the job that Bruno Lage has done since being installed in the Molineux hotseat in the summer:

'It will be a huge challenge. I think their foundation Nuno [Espírito Santo] built when he was there, and Bruno Lage has very smartly built on that. They defend unbelievably well with a good structure and big desire, so it is a big challenge. We, first and foremost me, and our players, need to bring the same energy as we did against Manchester United, and the fans need to bring the same performance off the pitch, because we are going to face a team who I think has performed as good as Man United this year.'

Elsewhere, the League Cup Final will be between Chelsea, Brentford's conquerors in the quarter-finals, and Liverpool. They overcame Tottenham and Arsenal in their respective semi-finals, Chelsea 3-0 on aggregate against Tottenham and Liverpool 2-0 on aggregate against Arsenal. The final is due to be played on Sunday, 27 February.

Friday, 21 January 2022

The Premier League have released their latest statement on the current COVID-19 situation, and it is good news. The statement reads:

'The Premier League has confirmed that between Monday, 10 January and Sunday, 16 January, 13,625 COVID-19 tests were administered on players and club staff. Of these, there were 33 new positive cases. This is the third week in a row the number of positive results has decreased, and the lowest number of positives in a week since 5 December.

'The safety of everyone remains a priority and the Premier League is taking all precautionary steps in response to the impact of the Omicron variant. The League has reverted to its Emergency Measures and has increased testing of players and club staff.

'The Premier League's COVID-19 Emergency Measures include protocols such as wearing face coverings while indoors, observing social distancing, limiting treatment time, as well as the increased testing. The League is continuing to work with clubs to keep people safe by helping mitigate the risks of COVID-19 within their squads. The League is also liaising closely with the Government, local authorities and supporter groups, while being responsive to any future changes to national or local guidance.

'The Premier League is providing this aggregated information for the purposes of competition integrity and transparency. No specific details as to clubs or individuals will be provided by the League and results will be made public on a weekly basis.'

Saturday, 22 January 2022

If it's incident you want, then the Community Stadium is definitely the place to be today. Wolves are in town boasting the meanest defence in the Premier League apart from that of Manchester City, so it was always going to be a difficult afternoon. As it turned out, 'difficult' became 'crazy'.

Brentford started the game well and had an early chance when Vitaly Janelt made a burst from midfield and played the ball into the penalty area for Sergi Canós but the attentions of Wolves defender Rayan Aït-Nouri were enough to put him off and the chance was gone.

Just when it looked like a normal football match, Rico Henry and Mathias Jensen both went up for a long ball, collided into one another, clashed heads and went down concussed. The medical attention quite rightly took a fair amount of time, and both players were replaced, by Mads Roerslev and Shandon Baptiste repectively, who came on as concussion substitutes. No sooner did the match restart than it was stopped again. This time a drone was being flown over the stadium, so the referee brought a halt to the action and the players left the pitch.

After the enforced break, the nearest either side came to a breakthrough was when Fábio Silva was afforded too much space on the edge of the Brentford penalty area. He took the ball down on his chest but saw his shot fly just wide of the far post. When the first half eventually ended, 72 minutes had passed since the kick-off.

The second half began with Wolves on the front foot and it took them only three minutes to open the scoring. Rúben Neves found João Moutinho 20 yards out, Moutinho played a neat one-two with Nélson Semedo and curled the ball with the outside of his foot into the bottom corner of the net, using Kristoffer Ajer as a shield to block his intention from Jonas Lössl.

Brentford brought on Yoane Wissa and he had a sight of goal but saw his effort fly over the bar. In keeping with what had gone on before, though, it was a strange incident that got the Bees back on level terms. Ajer brought the ball out of defence, advanced deep into Wolves territory and played the ball to Bryan Mbeumo just as a challenge came in from Toti. He went sprawling and the referee stopped play, even though Mbeumo was in a dangerous position in the penalty area. Toti was shown the red card, the Video Assistant Referee called for a review and the red was changed to a yellow. Mbeumo floated in the free kick, Ivan Toney found some space at the back post and he volleyed low into the far corner.

The winning goal came when Semedo was released on the right and crossed into the Brentford area. It was knocked clear but only as far as Moutinho who slid a ball to Neves to strike his shot past Lössl. The goalkeeper got a hand to it but was unable to stop it nestling in the corner.

When the final whistle went, it signalled the end of the match but not the end of the unusual occurrences. Thomas Frank marched on to the pitch, got involved in a confrontation with Moutinho and was sent off. The incident may have been sparked when Moutinho went down for some treatment in the closing stages, during which time Frank stood on the touchline and tapped his watch in the direction of the referee.

When questioned about his dismissal afterwards, Frank told the media, 'I was frustrated we didn't get a point, but I was relatively calm and there was a situation which triggered it. I got a yellow card after a confrontation with a Wolves player, then I turned round to Peter [Bankes, the referee] and said, "You can give me a second one as well." He said it was because I was turning around too aggressive. I want the players to control their emotions and not get silly cards, so it is disappointing I could not control my emotions.'

With regard to the concussed players, he said, 'It was horrible. When they were running I was thinking, "Oh God, this is going to be bad." But they are good. Mathias is clear of concussion and Rico will be assessed.'

Brentford: Lössl; Ajer, Jansson, Pinnock; Canós (Ghoddos 83), Jensen (Baptiste 27; Forss 79), Nørgaard, Janelt, Henry (Roerslev, 26; Wissa 58); Toney, Mbeumo

Wolverhampton Wanderers: Sá; Kilman, Coady, Toti; Semedo, Dendoncker, Neves, Moutinho, Aït-Nouri; Podence (Trincão 90), Silva (Traoré 75)

Sunday, 23 January 2022

The Independent today quotes Ivan Toney on yesterday's defeat to Wolves and whether or not the incident with the drone adversely affected Brentford's concentration.

'It was tough, but we can't use that as an excuse,' he said. 'Both teams had the stoppage. Obviously, you have got to stay focused and keep on the move. I felt that when we came back out from the pause for the drone, we started sloppy. It's stops and starts but we can't do anything about that. You've got to go out and continue with the game and they coped with it well and got the three points. I felt there's something we can take out of the game. We have to look forward now and try to change it in the next game.'

About getting on the score sheet again, he said, 'On a personal note it was another one for the tally, but it is much sweeter when there are three points behind it. It's time to reset. Obviously, we are on a bad run, we know that, but it's not like we've been playing badly, we're just conceding silly goals. If we cut that out we've got a great chance. It's time to restart and go again.'

Over at the Africa Cup of Nations, Frank Onyeka's Nigeria are on the receiving side of a surprise result in their second-round match and are out of the competition. The Nigerians had been the only side to win all three of their group matches and were strong favourites to overcome Tunisia in the round of 16. Their opponents only qualified as one of the five best third-placed teams but scored a 1-0 victory thanks to Youssef Msakni's long-range effort with only two minutes left. Onyeka was an unused substitute. Everton's Alex Iwobi probably wishes he was also an unused substitute as he came on after 59 minutes and just seven minutes later was shown the red card.

There is a saying in football, 'never go back'. Not often does a player or manager return to a club where they have been successful and replicate that success during their next stint. I wonder what John Sheridan thinks of that saying. He has today returned to Oldham Athletic for his sixth managerial appointment there. Oldham are currently bottom of League Two, holding up the entire league, and seven points from safety.

His first post was in 2001 when he was very briefly (as in one week) assistant to Billy Urmson when he was still actually playing for the club. Two years later he was given a co-caretaker position with David Eyres after Iain Dowie left to be Crystal Palace manager before Brian Talbot was brought in. He returned to Oldham as manager in his own right in 2006 for three years before leaving by 'mutual consent' after there were reports of his fighting with some of his players at a race track. His fourth appointment was in 2016 when he led them to safety in League Two. Sheridan left to join Notts County at the end of that season and rejoined Oldham in January 2017. This time he lasted eight months. Now, for his sixth spell, he replaces Selim Benachour who was made interim boss after Keith Curle left his post in November. I wonder how this one will end.

Monday, 24 January 2022

News emerges today that Thomas Frank and his assistant Brian Riemer have both signed new contracts that will run until the end of the 2024/25 season. They have been working together since 2018 when Riemer became the first new addition to the coaching team after Frank took over as manager from Dean Smith. He had previously been at FC Copenhagen.

'On behalf of everyone at Brentford, I would like to congratulate Thomas and Brian on their new contracts,' said director of football Phil Giles's press release. 'First and foremost, they are fantastic people to work with and I'm sure everyone at the club will be pleased that they have committed to stay with us until 2025. They have been integral to the success that we've shared over recent seasons, culminating in achieving our shared target of playing in the Premier League. We want to continue to take Brentford forward, to compete with clubs far bigger than us and to see how far we can progress. I am sure that we can build on the success that Thomas and Brian have helped deliver, along with all the other staff and players, and look forward to what I hope will be a successful conclusion to the season and beyond.'

While Thomas and Brian sign on for another three years, another Premier League manager has today lost his job. Claudio Ranieri, who was only appointed in October and has overseen a mere 14 games, has been fired by Watford. The club statement read, in part, 'The Hornets' board recognises Claudio as a man of great integrity and honour, who will always be respected here at Vicarage Road for his efforts in leading the team with dignity.' It seems they have that much respect for him they can afford him less than four months in the job.

Tuesday, 25 January 2022

Thomas Frank has been charged by the FA with improper conduct following the red card he received after the defeat by Wolves. He has until Thursday to contest the charge but, given his comments after the match about controlling his emotions, it seems that is probably going to be unlikely.

Brentford have accepted an invitation to take part in the Atlantic Cup in Portugal in February. The competition, founded in 2011 by former Arsenal and Sweden player Stefan Schwarz, is normally played between teams from Scandinavia and northern and central Europe, whose leagues have a winter break. The Bees will be sending a second-string squad over to the Algarve for the tournament as the Premier League will be in operation at the same time. It is the first time an English side will have been represented in the competition. The other teams taking part are FC Copenhagen, Midtjylland and Brøndby from Denmark, Halmstads BK from Sweden, Breiðablik UBK of Iceland, Vålerenga of Norway and Russia's FC Zenit Saint Petersburg.

In a somewhat surprising move, Watford have appointed Roy Hodgson as Claudio Ranieri's replacement. There is no doubt that Hodgson knows what he is doing as he has been in charge of some big clubs in his time, such as Liverpool and Inter Milan, and he led Fulham to the 2010 Europa League Final, where they were beaten by Atlético Madrid. Plus, of course, he was in charge of England for a while as well as having managed Switzerland and Finland. He had previously worked with the Pozzo family, who currently own Watford, during a spell at Udinese in Italy. It is the 15th managerial change the Pozzos have made since they took over in 2012. One wonders how a team is going to progress with such constant change. Each new manager will have his own ideas, coaching staff he wants to come with him and thoughts of potential signings, and the players have to get used to the new regime's ideas. Very rarely does success happen overnight. Time, it seems, is something that doesn't exist in Watford.

Wednesday, 26 January 2022

Following on from Pontus Jansson, Thomas Frank and Brian Riemer, now Bryan Mbeumo has put pen to paper on a contract extension, expiring after the 2025/26 season. He originally joined Brentford in 2019 from the French club Troyes and immediately made himself a first team regular, initially playing up front with Ollie Watkins and Saïd Benrahma, and then beginning the following season as a partnership with Ivan Toney after the departures of Watkins and Benrahma.

'I am very pleased that Bryan has decided to extend his contract with us,' commented Frank. 'He has been an important player for us since he arrived in 2019. He had a fantastic first season in the Championship and just as good a follow-up year last season as he developed other parts of his game. His Premier League performances have been even more impressive. As everyone knows, Bryan has hit the woodwork seven times this season. Margins have gone against him, but he has given us a lot. He has been a constant threat to our opponents. I am also very pleased that we have a chance to maximise Bryan's potential. We are only seeing the start of what he will be able to produce. He has a brilliant future ahead of him.'

Another player who is thought to have a brilliant future ahead of him is Brennan Johnson, the Nottingham Forest player heavily linked with a move away from the City Ground, with Brentford, Leeds and Newcastle reportedly interested.

Forest manager Steve Cooper, though, is desperately trying to hold on to his young talent. Speaking after yesterday's 3-0 win over Barnsley, Cooper said of Johnson, 'I am more than hopeful that he will still be here [after the transfer window closes], I am sure of it. That is more than good, it is very good. We do not want to be taking his performances for granted, he did look a threat, didn't he? Even just getting the two left-sided defenders booked in the first 12 minutes, I was thinking, "Keep getting at them, Brennan." His assist was brilliant for Yates's goal and his finish for his own goal was brilliant. He is a talented boy. We love him.'

Thursday, 27 January 2022

With the transfer window closing on Monday evening, the media are ramping up the transfer rumours as, indeed, most of the clubs are probably ramping up their efforts to get new players in. Brentford are featuring quite heavily in the headlines today.

Firstly, a few sources are reporting that Christian Eriksen's proposed deal to join the Bees could be concluded this weekend. Any potential agreement, though, does not have to be done and dusted by Monday's deadline as Eriksen is a free agent and therefore he isn't bound by the usual rules and regulations placed on selling clubs. He has apparently been training in Amsterdam with Jong Ajax, the club's reserve team who are currently being managed by the former Dutch international defender John Heitinga. It was with Ajax that Eriksen began his senior career, playing there between 2010 and 2013. The Eriksen to Brentford talk isn't going away, so could it actually happen?

Secondly, the German newspaper *Bild* is reporting that the Bees are looking to strike a deal for Werder Bremen forward Eren Dinkçi. It also claims that Bremen have blocked Brentford's approach but Thomas Frank 'won't give up' in the chase for his signature.

The third piece of transfer news involves an outgoing. Dominic Thompson has joined Ipswich Town on loan for the rest of the season. Thompson has made five appearances for Brentford so far in 2021/22 – two in the Premier League, two in the League Cup and one in the FA Cup – and is looking forward to joining up with the League One side.

'The club can give me a platform to grow,' says Thompson on iFollow Ipswich, the club's official streaming service. 'Ipswich came on to my radar two or three weeks ago and I am really happy to have the move done. I spoke to the manager and the first chat I had with him really inspired me. I'm really looking forward to working with him and the group here and hopefully developing my game.'

There will be more Brentford representation at the World Cup as Iran, complete with Saman Ghoddos in their squad, beat neighbours Iraq 1-0 to book their place at the finals. With six wins and a draw from their seven qualifying matches, Iran are ten points clear of third-placed United Arab Emirates with three games to play.

Friday, 28 January 2022

After his sending off against Wolves and subsequent FA charge, Thomas Frank will not be appealing the imposed fine. A club statement reads:

'Brentford FC head coach Thomas Frank has accepted a Football Association fine. Thomas was charged with a breach of FA rule E3.1 following Brentford's Premier League match against Wolverhampton Wanderers last Saturday, 22 January. Thomas admitted the charge and accepted the standard penalty. He was given an £8,000 fine. The FA charge was that Thomas's language and/ or behaviour towards referee Peter Bankes after the final whistle was improper. Thomas accepted this charge and the financial penalty. Brentford FC has no further comment to make on this matter.'

Saturday, 29 January 2022

There are no fixtures this weekend as the Premier League have scheduled a mini break. This one weekend off does nothing to appease the calls from certain managers to have a proper break at this time of year. As for some of the other European competitions, the German clubs have a month off, with the leagues in France, Italy and Spain generally closing for about three weeks. This time, of course, certain quarters are questioning why the free weekend is not being used to catch up on some of the games that have been postponed so far this season due to COVID. The Premier League, though, are insisting that the free weekend remains.

Mads Bistrup has joined Nordsjælland on loan for the rest of the season. Brentford's press release reads: "There were a few clubs who were interested in loaning Mads during this transfer window, but Nordsjælland seemed like an obvious choice. Their manager is Flemming Pedersen who used to work here at Brentford, so we know he will be in good hands. They also have a very good reputation for playing and developing young players. Mads now needs to play in a run of consecutive matches in order to progress to the next level. We wish Mads well and look forward to welcoming him back in the summer."

Sunday, 30 January 2022

There are reports today that Brentford, along with Watford, West Ham and Fulham, are interested in recruiting Kai Wagner from Philadelphia Union in the US's Major League

Soccer. Wagner is a German full-back who made the journey to Philadelphia from Würzburger Kickers in 2019. The transfer window closes tomorrow so any immediate deal will have to be done quickly.

Monday, 31 January 2022

Ladies and gentlemen, it has happened. Read the following sentence slowly and just think about the words: Christian Eriksen has signed for Brentford. The deal is, as expected, a short-term one until the end of the season. He has completed a medical assessment and will join the club subject to international clearance.

'I am looking forward to working with Christian again,' said Thomas Frank on Brentford's website, brentfordfc.com. 'It has been a while since I last coached him, and a lot has happened since then. Christian was 16 at the time and has become one of the best midfield players to appear in the Premier League. He has won trophies all over Europe and become the star of the Danish national team.

'We have taken an unbelievable opportunity to bring a world-class player to Brentford. He hasn't trained with a team for seven months but has done a lot of work on his own. He is fit but we will need to get him match fit and I am looking forward to seeing him work with the players and staff to get back to the highest level. At best, Christian has the ability to dictate games of football. He can find the right passes and is a goal threat. He also has very, very good set piece delivery, both from corners and direct free kicks. He is a player you can find with the ball, and he will come up with a solution to the problem in front of him. Christian will also bring experience of top-level football to the club.'

Eriksen himself recorded a message for the Brentford supporters on social media:

'Hi everyone, this is Christian Eriksen. I'm happy to announce that I have signed for Brentford Football Club. I can't wait to get started and hopefully I'll see you all very soon.'

Inter Milan also posted a message wishing Christian well. 'Good luck for your new adventure,' it read. 'We are happy to see you back out on the pitch.'

Eriksen began his career in the Dutch Eredivisie at Ajax, with whom he won three championships. He signed for Tottenham in 2013, quickly becoming one of the most effective midfield players in the Premier League. In 2020 he signed for Inter Milan, winning Serie A in the 2020/21 season. Eriksen made his international debut for Denmark in 2010 against Austria and was the youngest player to play at the World Cup in South Africa that summer. Denmark failed to qualify for the 2014 tournament but were present in 2018 in Russia where Eriksen helped them through the first group stage only to be beaten on penalties by Croatia in round two. Of course, we all know what happened at the European Championships last summer during the Denmark v Finland match. He currently has earned 109 international caps, scoring 36 goals for his country.

What will he be able to manage at Brentford during the last part of the season? That will be seen between now and May. One thing is for sure, though – he wouldn't have been signed just for the sake of a few headlines.

One of the other players who has been heavily linked with a move to the Bees is Keane Lewis-Potter of Hull City, but it seems that is a transfer that will not be happening. The Tigers' new owner, Acun Ilıcalı, speaking to Hull Live, said of the potential move, 'We are very proud to have a player in our club that has seen an offer as big as that come in. I think they will pay more. At this moment, even if they offer £20m, I will not sell him. I want him to continue showing his talents with us. In life, everything has a time and timing is very important and I don't think it is the right move now. We just bought the club and we want to move it forward together.'

Even though Lewis-Potter stayed put, there was some movement between west London and Hull today, as Marcus Forss joined the Tigers on loan until the end of the season.

'Marcus is a striker we have a lot of belief in,' Thomas Frank told brentfordfc.com. 'For the future benefit of Marcus and Brentford, it is important that he gets more consistent game time. He needs to start a lot of games and show week in week out that he is a striker that can score goals. Marcus did that very well when he was on loan at Wimbledon and we believe he can help Hull for the rest of the season. This loan move will also help Marcus and Brentford. It will make him a better player than he is already.'

There is also another outgoing move today with Charlie Goode travelling north to Sheffield United on loan for the rest of the season. Goode has featured eight times for the Bees this season but has missed the last six weeks after suffering an injury in December.

Tuesday, 1 February 2022

After a frantic last day of activity, the transfer window last night slammed shut.

As expected, given their new-found wealth and precarious situation at the wrong end of the Premier League table, Newcastle United were very busy, strengthening throughout the team. Their first signing was the England international defender Kieran Trippier, who joined from Atlético Madrid, having spent the last three years in Spain following his move from Tottenham in 2019. Burnley centre-forward Chris Wood soon followed Trippier to St James' Park in a move that not only strengthens them but weakens one of their relegation rivals. Bruno Guimarães was next through the door, arriving in the north-east from French club Lyon. Guimarães is a defensive midfielder with three international caps for Brazil to his name. They also brought in Aston Villa defender Matt Targett on loan.

Having found themselves without their first choice centre-forward, Burnley moved to replace Wood with Wout Weghorst, who joined from German side Wolfsburg.

Aston Villa also had a good window. They brought in full-back Lucas Digne from Everton, apparently beating competition from Newcastle, Chelsea and West Ham for his signature. They also captured midfielder Philippe Coutinho from Barcelona. Coutinho's move is a loan deal until the end of the season, but it was a smart one from Villa. He hasn't been a regular for the Catalans and he already knew manager Steven Gerrard from their time together at Liverpool. Another arrival was central defender Callum Chambers from Arsenal.

Everton had a busy time, not only bringing in new players, but also a new manager. They recruited Vitaliy Mykolenko from Dynamo Kiev as a direct replacement for Digne at left-back as well as Nathan Patterson from Rangers. Strangely, both deals were sanctioned for Rafael Benítez just days before he was sacked. Frank Lampard then arrived to replace Benítez in the hotseat and immediately set to work. His first day as Everton manager was transfer deadline day and he brought in Dele Alli from Tottenham on a permanent deal and Donny van de Beek from Manchester United on loan. Both players had been short of game time at their previous clubs and will no doubt have plenty to prove.

At the top of the table, Manchester City received the biggest transfer fee of the window when they were paid £50m by Barcelona for their forward player Ferran Torres. They invested £17m of that money in a replacement for Torres in Argentinian striker Julián Álvarez from River Plate. Liverpool also purchased a new forward, Colombian wideman Luis Díaz, who joined from Porto.

In the World Cup qualifying matches that are played tonight, Saman Ghoddos once again represented Iran as they beat the United Arab Emirates 1-0 in Tehran.

Wednesday, 2 February 2022

A really interesting interview with Thomas Frank has been posted on website coachesvoice.com, in which he talks about the tactics he employed against Arsenal in the opening game of the season.

'The reason why we set the team out like this [3-5-2],' he says, 'was that we wanted to carry on from the season before with the back three because we think that is a big help for us in terms of defending well, and we think the team is better with a back three or back five when we need that sometimes. Going into a league that we know is maybe the toughest league in the world, you need to be able to defend well. So that's why we kept that. We had the three midfielders we also had from last season, in terms of we think that gave us stability and we also had two willing runners that can run around the two strikers. And then two strikers that look very, very strong together.'

Over in Kingston, Jamaica, Ethan Pinnock's hopes of playing at the World Cup have been ended as Costa Rica beat their hosts 1-0 in the latest qualifying match. Jamaica needed to win all of their remaining three qualifiers and also rely on other results going their way. Former Arsenal forward Joel Campbell, now affiliated to Club León of Mexico, scored the only goal of the game.

Roy Hodgson gave his first press conference as Watford manager today and explained how he got the job at Vicarage Road:

'The thought of working with players every day has always been something that I knew I would find hard to resist. I thought I would find it a bit easier to resist than I have actually found it, so that's why this job, when it came up, really was one that I was never going to turn down because it was, quite literally, the siren call from a mermaid as the sailor passes by on his ship. They got the right mermaid going past the right ship, if you like.'

I don't know about anyone else, but it was his use of the phrase 'quite literally' that sparked my interest, here. The dictionary defines 'literally' as 'being used to emphasise the truth and accuracy of a particular statement'. That being the case, let's just go through the recruitment process of Watford Football Club, as revealed by Roy Hodgson ...

'The thought of working with players every day has always been something that I knew I would find hard to resist. I thought I would find it a bit easier to resist than I have actually found it, so that's why this job, when it came up, really was one that I was never going to turn down.'

OK, no problem so far. I can understand how an experienced coach, who has held positions all over the world, is missing the interaction with a group of players. Plus, of course, he wants the chance to see if he can still cut it. Completely understand. However …

'It was, quite literally, the siren call from a mermaid as the sailor passes by on his ship. They got the right mermaid going past the right ship, if you like.'

Don't forget, according to Mr Hodgson, this statement was 'quite literally'. So, it seems, when Watford want to hire somebody, they don't go through the normal process of coming up with a list of candidates, inviting them for an interview and then choosing their preferred option, maybe even after inviting one or two back for a second interview. Rather, the board of directors leave sunny Hertfordshire and head for the even sunnier Greek coast. Once there, instead of relaxing on the beach in Kefalonia or Corfu or one of the other islands in the Ionian Sea, they journey on to the island of Aeaea which, according to the Greek poet Homer, is where the sirens dwell. When they reach their destination, instead of looking for the nearest taverna to sample the finest moussaka or souvlaki, depending on personal taste, washed down with a shot or two of the local ouzo, they head to the rocky shores and disguise themselves as mermaids.

While they were hatching their plan, Hodgson just so happened to also be in the same part of the world (or did the Watford directors have this foreknowledge and actually go out to snare Mr Hodgson himself?). He has either hired a sailing vessel of some sort or is enjoying a nice cruise round the Greek islands. Which of these, we cannot be certain, as his statement to the press did not specify. Whichever way it was, he sailed past and found himself captivated by the enchanting melody he could hear emanating from the rocky shores of Aeaea. It is at this point that he either steers his boat towards the beautiful choral refrain that is tickling his ears or jumps overboard from his cruise liner and swims towards the hypnotic chanteuse. Unfortunately, it turns out that he, like many other mariners of tales of old, has been deceived. A siren, though taking the same form as a mermaid, isn't as helpful and good natured as her half-woman-half-fish cousin. A siren is an evil version whose combination of haunting song and stunning good looks puts sailors into a trance so they can lure them to their watery deaths or, in Mr Hodgson's case, Vicarage Road.

So, going by Hodgson's statement to the press, the Watford board of directors are actually sirens masquerading as mermaids who, presumably at some given point in the future, are planning on showing their true selves as not a group of men trying to keep their football team in the Premier League, but a group of mermaids. Even more than that, not just mermaids, but sirens about to cause havoc having lured another poor unsuspecting internationally renowned football manager into their trap. Perhaps they will do it in the team bath or showers at some point after a training session as, as we all know, mermaids reveal their true selves when in water. If he hasn't done so already, let's hope it isn't raining when Brentford visit Watford on 16 April!

An interesting recruitment process.

Thursday, 3 February 2022

The Times today runs a piece on Brentford's signing of Christian Eriksen and how Thomas Frank's relationship with him helped the transfer to go ahead. Of course, the story begins on that fateful evening during the European Championships last summer.

'We had a nice dinner and prepared everything for this big Denmark game,' says Frank. 'I clearly remember when I saw the situation that something was wrong. I could see from the way he fell over. I get goosebumps now speaking about it. It was very dramatic and sitting there with two children means you know how it must feel to see your son [collapse]. Half of the Denmark team I have coached myself. I know all the Danish players one way or another; the head coach, Kasper Hjulmand, is a personal friend, I have friends among the staff, so it was very emotional. I was shocked.'

Fortunately, thanks to the brilliance of the medical staff, Eriksen recovered and was fitted with an internal mini defibrillator. This meant, though, that his contract with Inter Milan had to be terminated due to the Italian rules forbidding players having heart monitoring devices.

'In the middle of December, I gave him a call,' says Frank. 'Just as at Wolves, where there is a Portuguese connection, here we have a Danish connection, which always helps. So, in the middle of December I gave him a call. We had a good chat about things, he sounded interested, he could see the project and a way to come back and play football at a good club in a good environment, with a coach he knows, and hopefully we can help him to come back to his highest level.'

In his pre-weekend press conference today, Frank outlined the plan for Eriksen's integration into the Brentford match day squad:

'My first feeling is excitement. He is a top player with lots of experience. The players are delighted, happy and pleased we managed to get a top player to the club. I am glad he decided to come to us. Besides being a top player and superstar, he is very humble and down to earth. That is a big quality. Because of what happened, some of the bigger clubs weren't interested to take the chance. He will arrive on Sunday and will train with the team on Monday. That will be his first training session.

'Of course, I have been speaking to him a lot the last few weeks, more since December, but he has a physical coach and they had a Zoom meeting with our head of performance this week to make sure we hand over everything in the best way. He has been running a lot and training a lot. His foundation is fine. Another is to get him up to match fitness. It is hard to say when he will be available, I will know a lot more after Monday.'

As for where Eriksen could potentially be in the pantheon of Brentford players, Frank is not playing it down:

'With this crazy experience he chose to do something he knows – the Premier League, London, a club where he knows some of his team-mates and he has a connection to me. Imagine speaking to our fans when we were in League One and saying we would be in the Premier League in six or seven years' time and he would be playing for Brentford. It is a little miracle. It is potentially the greatest signing ever for the club. I spoke to a fan last night and he mentioned a guy about 70 years ago who was at potentially the same level. I think it will be an unbelievable day the day Christian steps on to the pitch. You guys have seen him performing as one of the best in the Premier League and what happened to him in June was crazy and a shock for us. The day he returns, it will be emotional.'

There is further good news with regard to players who are currently out injured. Goalkeeper David Raya and midfielder Josh Dasilva are both well on the road to recovery.

Frank said, 'Both of them played in a friendly against Aston Villa on Tuesday and both of them played around 65 minutes, so that was very positive. David looked his normal self so now I just need to speak to my staff and our goalkeeping coach about potentially starting him on Saturday. For Josh Dasilva, that was his third game. He played 45 and 45 for the B team in similar friendlies like this one. Now he's played 65 and scored a goal. I watched the game back. There's a bit of intensity and the pressing game before he's up to his normal level but that was very positive and I would say we've managed to "sign" three players this January window – Raya, Dasilva and Eriksen.'

One man who may be missing from the match on Saturday is Frank himself. He has returned a positive COVID test and has therefore been unable to take any of the week's training sessions. If he returns two negative tests in line with the government's regulations he can join up with the team at Everton. If not, Brian Riemer will be in charge.

Brentford B's first game in the Atlantic Cup in Portugal ended in a 2-1 defeat at the hands of Icelandic side Breiðablik UBK. Tristan Crama scored Brentford's goal after Breiðablik had taken a two-goal lead through Damir Muminovic and Kristinn Steindórsson. The Bees' next match is against the Danish team Brøndby on Tuesday.

Saturday, 5 February 2022

As it turns out, Thomas Frank does return the required COVID test results and is able to take his place in the dugout today. There is further good news in that David Raya is back between the sticks after his injury lay-off and Josh Dasilva is back as one of the substitutes. The FA Cup fourth round tie away at Everton was always going to be a tough one but, with the added spectacle of Frank Lampard taking his place in the home dugout for the first time, the crowd are going to be up for it and the players are going to want to impress their newly installed boss.

After a fairly quiet start to the game, the sides not being helped by a swirling, blustery wind, the contest burst into life after half an hour. André Gomes stung Raya's hands with long-range effort, forcing the Brentford keeper to push his strike over the bar. From the resulting corner, swung in by Demarai Gray, Everton's Colombian defender Yerry Mina, on as a replacement for the injured Ben Godfrey, muscled his way through a crowd of bodies to get to the ball first and head into the net at the back post past a helpless Raya to notch the first goal of the new Lampard era.

After taking the lead, Everton stepped up the tempo. A long ball from Gray presented Richarlison with a half chance but the ball just wouldn't sit down and he hooked it over, the presence of Pontus Jansson making him rush the shot. Jansson was on hand to stop the same player again shortly afterwards, an important interception on the stretch halting Richarlison's run on goal.

It wasn't all Everton, though, as Brentford had a decent chance of their own. Following some good work down the right, Kristoffer Ajer worked the ball to Sergi Canós who turned inside and let fly from the edge of the box. The ball was heading for the top corner before a flying save from Jordan Pickford kept the hosts in front.

The second half had only just started when Allan's through ball found Richarlison in a dangerous position on the edge of the Brentford penalty area between two defenders. As Raya came out to meet him, Richarlison knocked the ball past him and into the net to double the lead and give Everton a stranglehold on the game.

Brentford needed a quick reply and they almost pulled one back immediately as Ivan Toney was released down the right behind the Everton defence. He pulled the ball back across the six-yard box but it just eluded Mads Roerslev as he came sliding in, and it was cleared to safety. The relief only last for a moment though, as Brentford continued to exert the pressure and a slide-rule Christian Nørgaard pass found Toney free in the penalty area. He took a touch and went round Pickford but was caught by his flailing arm and Brentford had a penalty and a way back into the tie. For the second time this season, Toney faced Pickford from 12 yards and, for the second time this season, he calmly knocked the ball past the England keeper.

A couple of minutes later it very nearly got even better for the visitors as Raya's long throw launched a quick break down the right. The ball was cleared but only as far as Canós who knocked it back into the danger area. Toney knocked it past Pickford as it bounced up between them, but the ball, possibly held up slightly in the wind, didn't quite have enough on it to reach the net and it was cleared away before crossing the line.

Having survived the scare, Everton pushed forward to consolidate their advantage and, as with the first goal, it was a corner that proved to be Brentford's ultimate undoing and firmly turn the match the way of the home team. Gray's out-swinging delivery was inadvertently headed by Roerslev back towards his own goal and straight to Mason Holgate who touched it in to restore the Toffees' two-goal lead.

Brentford sent on Dasilva to replace Roerslev for his first appearance in almost a year but, as the clocked ticked down, Everton took the sting out of the game by knocking the passes around and making the Brentford players chase the game. Following one such pattern of play, just as time was running out, Alex Iwobi played in Andros Townsend who turned inside before placing the ball beyond Raya's reach.

So, Lampard's reign at Goodison Park begins with a victory by four goals to one and Brentford exit this season's FA Cup. One good thing to come out of the game was a return to first-team action of both Raya and Dasilva. They are going to be very welcome additions back into the squad as the season enters what you feel will be a crucial stage. After facing Manchester City on Wednesday, Brentford play Crystal Palace and Arsenal before coming up against Newcastle, Norwich and Burnley in successive matches, teams who currently occupy three of the bottom four league places.

'I do think it wasn't a 4-1 defeat,' said Frank afterwards. 'They had four chances and scored four goals. Very efficient by Everton so fair play to them. I do think that we played a good first half, very aggressive, very intense, front-footed. It was a very, very even game then – they created nothing, we created nothing. Then they scored a goal on a set piece that was very avoidable. Second half we adjusted things but then we concede after three minutes. Fair bit of play by Everton for that goal, but there were a few things we could have done better. Then we had a good spell, got the 2-1 goal, we get another chance but then concede on another set piece. The big disappointing thing today was conceding two set-piece goals.'

Looking at the returning players, he was a lot more positive, telling the media, 'It was so good to see David

Raya out there again today and he played a good game, and we know he will raise his standards over the coming weeks. Josh Dasilva's return made me smile. We've lacked the quality on the ball he can bring, but he has quite a few more steps to take before he is at the top level.'

Everton: Pickford; Holgate, Keane, Godfrey (Mina 14) Coleman, Allan, Gomes, Mykolenko (Kenny 73); Gray (Iwobi 88), Richarlison (Tosun 88), Gordon (Townsend 73)

Brentford: Raya; Ajer, Jansson, Bech Sørensen; Roerslev (Dasilva 72), Jensen, Nørgaard, Janelt (Baptiste 63), Henry (Stevens 83); Canós (Ghoddos 72), Toney

Sunday, 6 February 2022

The FA Cup threw up more surprise results this weekend. On Friday evening, Middlesbrough, who currently sit just outside the play-off places in the Championship, travelled to Old Trafford to face Manchester United and came away with a victory on penalties after a 1-1 draw. United went ahead, Cristiano Ronaldo also missed a penalty, but Middlesbrough came back to force extra time and take the game to spot-kicks, where they triumphed 8-7, the 16th penalty being the only one that was missed.

Bournemouth, currently third in the Championship, were beaten 1-0 at home by National League Boreham Wood. The only goal of the game came from their veteran captain Mark Ricketts. The draw for the fifth round gave Boreham Wood the reward of a trip to Goodison Park to play Brentford's conquerors, Everton. Not only are Boreham Wood the last non-league team left in the last 16 of the competition, but they are also the only team left who are not from either the Premier League or the Championship.

Nottingham Forest, who beat Arsenal in the previous round, continued in their exploits by thrashing their east Midlands rivals and FA Cup holders Leicester City 4-1.

There were so very nearly two more massive shocks. Plymouth Argyle of League One visited Chelsea and were only beaten 2-1 in extra time after they had taken the lead. Not only that, but Kidderminster Harriers, who play in the National League North, were a whisker away from producing the greatest FA Cup shock of all time. They hosted West Ham and took the lead after 19 minutes. It wasn't until added time at the end of the 90 minutes that the Hammers got their equaliser, and it wasn't until added time at the end of extra time that they got their winner. Had Kidderminster managed to hold on for that extra couple of minutes at the end of normal time, they would have become the first team from below the fifth tier of English football (the four divisions and the National League) to beat one from the top level of the footballing pyramid.

Over at the Africa Cup of Nations, the trophy has been won by Senegal. The final against Egypt, with the spectacle of Liverpool's front two Sadio Mané and Mo Salah up against each other, finished 0-0 and went into a penalty shoot-out. It was Mané who came out on top as he converted the winning spot-kick. Ironically, he also missed one during the match, but stepped up to take Senegal's fifth in the shoot-out and this time he made no mistake. It was Senegal's first victory in the tournament, having twice been runners-up, in 2002 and 2019.

Tuesday, 8 February 2022

During Thomas Frank's press conference today, he confirmed that Christian Eriksen won't be playing a part in tomorrow's game at Manchester City, but that he is fitting in well:

'It is very good to see him out there. I spoke to Christian after training and he's just very pleased and happy to be part of a team and a club again. Because of the way he is, he is blending in fantastically with the culture we have here. One thing is for sure, he will not play against Manchester City. We'll take it day by day. He is looking good, but we need to get some match minutes into him in a friendly before we get him out there.'

On tomorrow's opponents, Frank is remaining realistic, 'If we go and get something out of the match it will be one of the biggest surprises in this year's Premier League. Manchester City are the clear number one in the league, playing some brilliant football and having a fantastic season. Taking that aside, it is still 11 versus 11 tomorrow night. We are looking forward to a massive challenge, maybe our biggest of the season, but it is about believing that you can get something out of it and giving it a massive go.'

City manager Pep Guardiola took some time during his meeting with the media today to also talk about Eriksen:

'It is great news that he came back to play the game that he loves and the game he does exceptionally well. I am pretty sure they took all the right measures so that he will not suffer this scare again. Fortunately, he can come back, and it will be nice to see him tomorrow.'

Yet another manager talking about you-know-who is the Tottenham boss Antonio Conte. When asked about whether he had thought about their teaming up again – he was Eriksen's manager at Inter Milan – Conte said that he thought more time would be needed:

'Honestly, I was surprised about the situation because in my mind, honestly, I thought Christian needed more time before coming back to play in England. For sure, Eriksen is part of Tottenham's story. To come back here would be a good opportunity for him, for me, for the club. Now he's signed for Brentford, but only six months, and we'll see what happens.'

It seems that Conte and Eriksen are, at least for the moment, sharing digs. Conte is currently living in a suite in a hotel, as his wife and daughter are still back in Italy.

The Italian said, 'It happened that I met him in the same hotel that we were both staying in. We were lucky to meet each other, we didn't prepare the meeting. It was only a coincidence to see him with his family but, I repeat, it was great for me to see him with his family. I'm the first person to be happy to see him again on the pitch because we spent a really good time at Inter Milan together. We won the league, we spent two important seasons together. I wish him all the best for the future, and you don't know what will happen. It would be good for me to have him again, to work together.'

Sounds to me like he's opening the door for Eriksen to return to Tottenham.

Brentford B's second game in the Atlantic Cup saw them register a 1-0 victory over Brøndby, a particularly good result as Brøndby are the current reigning Danish league champions. Nathan Young-Coombes scored the only goal of the game after just seven minutes. Jaakko Oksanan won possession in the midfield area and slid a through ball forward to Young-Coombes, who finished with a well-taken chip from an acute angle. The next game is scheduled for Friday against Halmstads of Sweden.

Wednesday, 9 February 2022

Before the game against Manchester City at the Etihad even started, Brentford were dealt a blow when Ivan Toney was ruled out due to a calf injury, and both Bryan Mbeumo and Yoane Wissa were deemed not fit enough to start. With the three missing, they went into the match with a strike partnership of Saman Ghoddos and Sergi Canós.

The game itself bore an uncanny resemblance to the first encounter at the Community Stadium in December. City, as expected, had the majority of the ball, as they tend to do in every match they play. Brentford, though, were resilient and David Raya was rarely troubled.

The Bees limited their hosts to speculative chances, both João Cancelo and Aymeric Laporte having efforts that flew wide of the target. They did threaten when Riyad Mahrez swung in a low cross aiming for Raheem Sterling who was arriving at the far post, but Raya got down to push it away from danger.

For their part, Brentford were not completely on the back foot and Frank Onyeka saw his header saved by Ederson after Mathias Jensen's shot had been blocked and scrambled away for a corner.

Five minutes before the half-time interval, Sterling danced his way into the left side of the penalty area and, as he approached the touchline, Mads Roerslev slid into the challenge. Unfortunately he was nowhere near the ball, took out Sterling, and a penalty was awarded. Mahrez stepped up to take the spot-kick and expertly dispatched it into the top corner.

The final moments of the half saw City almost double their lead when Sterling's cross fizzed across the box with nobody able to apply the finishing touch. At the other end,

Rico Henry played a one-two with Ghoddos and found himself one on one with Ederson. His effort beat the keeper but was heading wide. As Canós tried to get to the loose ball, Ederson recovered to touch it clear.

The early stages of the second half saw City try to kill the game off. Cancelo weaved his way into the area before testing Raya down to his left, and the same player blasted wide from distance. Bernardo Silva also saw his effort unable to beat Raya. Brentford sent on Mbeumo and Josh Dasilva in an attempt to stem the tide, and Mbeumo soon found himself with a half chance from Christian Nørgaard's pass but he was crowded out just as he was about to pull the trigger.

The game was put to bed with 20 minutes to go, City's second coming from a defensive error. Raya had the ball at his feet but dissected his own defenders and played it out straight to Sterling. As the England forward tried to fire it back past him, Raya recovered to make a brilliant flying save but the rebound went straight to Kevin De Bruyne who steered his shot into the net. Brentford did have one more decent chance after that, but Wissa saw his shot blocked and steered to safety.

Speaking after the match, it was put it to Thomas Frank that he would be disappointed with both goals that Brentford conceded.

'Looking from a defensive performance perspective,' he said, 'I think it was almost perfect. If you look at the two goals we gave away – a penalty that we should never have given, we should not slide down inside the penalty area, and the second one obviously a big mistake from David – so that is the disappointing thing because, if you look at the first half, yes, City is dominating like they do against almost every team here, but we made it so difficult for them. We had a strong structure, discipline, mentality, effort, but at the decisive moments we don't take it. Rico Henry had a good chance, a good opportunity, and then we get punished in the other end. So, yeah, it's just that spell where we make these mistakes we shouldn't make, but the overall performance, we are pleased with that, and that is the bit that needs to give us confidence.'

The league table now reads, bottom upwards: Burnley 14 points, Watford 15, Norwich 17, Newcastle 18, Everton 19, Leeds and Brentford both 23. Burnley still have games in hand.

That is now five straight league defeats, and the critics will no doubt start to make a bit of a thing of that. Yes, it is a bad run, but let's not forget those five matches were all against sides who occupy top-ten places in the Premier League table – Southampton, Liverpool, Manchester United, Wolves and Manchester City. There are games coming up on the horizon that are far more likely to shape Brentford's destiny than these. After playing Crystal Palace and Arsenal, the next three opponents are Newcastle, Norwich and Burnley. Decent results there will do a lot of good when it comes to the end of season reckoning. In fact, Brentford still have to play every other team currently below them in the table, with the last two games of the season being against Everton and Leeds. It's not panic stations yet, but any points picked up now are going to be good ones.

Manchester City: Ederson; Stones, Dias, Laporte, Cancelo; De Bruyne, Rodrigo, Silva; Mahrez (Grealish 67), Foden (Gündoğan 71), Sterling

Brentford: Raya; Ajer, Jansson, Pinnock; Roerslev, Onyeka (Wissa 70), Nørgaard, Jensen, Henry; Ghoddos (Mbeumo 62), Canós (Dasilva 62)

Thursday, 10 February 2022

BBC Sounds have today released an interview with Christian Eriksen as part of their series *The Sports Desk*.

'I'm very happy to be able to do it again, to be able to play football,' he began by saying, 'to be involved and to be the professional footballer that I was before. I'm very happy, very pleased that it is possible now. It's been some tough months but I'm happy where I am now.'

He was asked how grateful he is to Brentford for giving him this chance. 'A lot,' was the instant response. 'For me and for my family, the next six months was the perfect situation. We pretty much know the area, it's close to where we were for many years in north London so yeah, first for my family and then also to get the chance to stay in the Premier League and to get to know the people here. Of course, I knew the coach before and a lot of my team-mates are from Denmark, so it's an easy group to fall in to.'

The interview finishes with Eriksen being asked whether he believes he can get back to the level he was previously at and whether he will have to change his style of play at all, and he was adamant he would continue where he left off:

'I feel like me like before, so I don't see any reason why I couldn't get back to the same level.'

Whenever Eriksen does make his Brentford bow, it's going to be a big and emotional occasion. Crystal Palace on Saturday is probably pushing it a bit, but then the games to come are against opponents where the stakes and emotion may be even higher. Arsenal were his deadly rivals when he was a Tottenham player, then Newcastle, Norwich and Burnley are going to be big games in the course of the season. After that are Leicester who are no strangers to footballing tragedy themselves after their owner Vichai Srivaddhanaprabha was killed in a helicopter crash shortly after leaving their ground in 2018. Plus, of course, Leicester's goalkeeper is Kasper Schmeichel, Eriksen's Danish international team-mate who was on the pitch when he collapsed. The only thing we do know for sure is that when Eriksen does pull on the Brentford shirt for the first time, the entire footballing world will be watching, holding its breath.

Friday, 11 February 2022

Thomas Frank today confirmed that Christian Eriksen is raring to go but won't be involved against Crystal Palace.

'I think he's fine, he's training well, and he looks the quality player we know he is,' is the manager's assessment. 'It's a joy watching him play football, it is so natural for him, so that's fantastic to see but he will not be available for the team tomorrow. That would be too early after just one week. We will have a friendly game on Monday where he will play minutes and that's the right way to do it.'

Frank's opposite number tomorrow, Crystal Palace manager Patrick Vieira, also made mention of Eriksen. 'This is a happy story,' he told the press. 'To see him back on the training field and playing games I think is something we can enjoy. He loves the game and for him to be back on the field and to do what he loves is something we can all be happy about.'

Brentford B's final game in the Atlantic Cup today ended with a 2-1 defeat at the hands of Swedish team Halmstads BK, with all the goals coming in the first 15 minutes. Nathan Young-Coombes gave Brentford the lead with his second goal of the tournament, converting a low cross from Myles Peart-Harris. The Swedes, though, were level only a couple of minutes later, Marcus Olsson heading home from a corner. The winner came in strange circumstances. An attempted clearance by Daniel Oyegoke smashed against Tristian Crama and the ball rebounded back past his own goalkeeper. The result meant that Brentford finished their games with three points courtesy of their victory over Brøndby.

The tournament winners were Russian team Zenit Saint Petersburg who won all three of their matches. They were 1-0 victors over Midtjylland, they beat Brøndby 2-1 and overcame FC Copenhagen 5-4 on penalties after a 1-1 draw.

Saturday, 12 February 2022

David Raya is featured in an interview on the Sky Sports website in which he talks about getting back into the team after his long injury lay-off.

'It's amazing to be back after such a long time of injury,' he says. 'You don't know what you have until you miss it, so it was a bit of a shock. I've never been injured, it was my first long-term injury and when the news was that I was going to be out for four or five months I had to accept it as soon as possible to work hard on my rehab and be back as soon as possible.'

The question then came up of Raya wearing a dinosaur costume on his first day back at training (see: 10 January). His response leaves more questions than answers, I fear:

'I had that costume in the back of my car for two months, so I just wore it.'

Sorry, hang on, it was just in the back of the car? Even more bizarrely, the interview then just moves on. No, wait, don't stop there – I now have a thousand more questions that need answering. Or maybe it's just me. Maybe I just don't drive the right sort of car. Mine came with air conditioning and CD radio as standard, not giant dinosaur costume. Am I missing out on something here?

Before Brentford v Crystal Palace kicks off, Christian Eriksen takes to the pitch to be presented to the home supporters. There is rapturous applause from all corners of the ground, including from the Crystal Palace end. He waves to all the fans before taking his seat in the stand.

The match itself took a little while to get going. When it did, most of the action was played out in the midfield with Brentford having slightly the better of the possession. What chances were carved out were, for the most part, half chances, with neither goalkeeper being overly extended. Rico Henry had a shot that seemed to be heading for the bottom corner of the net deflected just wide of the post and Christian Nørgaard saw an effort fly wide.

There was a shout for a penalty when Ethan Pinnock's long throw into the area was knocked clear by Palace defender Marc Guéhi's arm. Instead of awarding a penalty, the referee gave a free kick to Crystal Palace as he adjudged that Guéhi had been pushed by Nørgaard. The Brentford players appealed and the Video Assistant Referee was consulted. When the decision came back it confirmed the referee was right to have awarded the free kick, minimal thought the contact was.

The Bees' best efforts as the half drew to a close came from the wide positions. Firstly, Sergi Canós tricked his way along the right flank and played in Bryan Mbeumo but Palace goalkeeper Vicente Guaita was quick to come to meet him and Mbeumo was unable to steer his effort past him and into the net. Shortly afterwards, on the opposite touchline, Mathias Jensen got in behind the full-back and he played in a dangerous low cross towards Yoane Wissa. Just as he was stretching to convert, Joel Ward got back to intercept the cross and snuff out the danger.

The visitors' best chance of the half came when Brentford sloppily conceded possession in the middle of the park. Odsonne Édouard took advantage, advanced into space and played the ball through to Jordan Ayew. Fortunately for the Bees, Ayew waited too long before unleashing his shot and he lashed it harmlessly wide of the post. The let-off gave Brentford one last chance to go in ahead but, after some good interplay between Henry and Nørgaard, from Mbeumo's cross, Canós headed wide.

The second half was more stop-start than the first, but the introduction of Josh Dasilva gave Brentford another attacking option and he was in the middle of many of the better moments. A good run took him to the touchline but his cross just evaded Wissa.

As Brentford pressed for the opening goal, Guaita made a flying save from a Pontus Jansson header and Mbeumo's shot was blocked before testing the Palace keeper.

In the final moments, Wilfried Zaha went down under Henry's challenge and it was the visitors' turn to ask for a penalty. Again the decision went to VAR and, although there was contact, it was deemed not enough to warrant Zaha's fall to the floor and play continued. The very last action of the match saw Joachim Andersen let fly at the Brentford goal, but David Raya kept it out and, with Andersen charging in for the rebound, gathered the ball in to safety at the second attempt. The referee called a halt to the proceedings and, for the second time this season, the teams reached a 0-0 stalemate.

'The big positive is we got the clean sheet,' said Thomas Frank afterwards. 'I think we have performed to get other clean sheets where we didn't get them, but today we gave one big chance away on our own mistake to Ayew and that's it. I'm very pleased that we are so solid and difficult to play against, I think that's a big thing. I think we need to have more quality in the final third.'

When talking about whether Brentford should have had a penalty, Frank was magnanimous, unusually so for a manager who had seen his team denied a spot-kick.

'The penalty incident, when you watch it back, I don't think it was penalty,' he conceded. 'I hate that rule with the handball. I agree he put his hand out and blocked the shot or the cross or something, 100 per cent. But no, he got a push, he was out of balance when it was touching the hand. I would have hated that given.'

With Ivan Toney being missing again, will he be OK to take his place in the line-up to face Arsenal next time out? 'He will be assessed during the week and we will do everything we can to get him available. It's not like we can say he 100 per cent will be, but that is something we are hoping for and could be realistic. Of course, we would love to have our top scorer out there on the pitch, but Wissa is a good striker who can play and can score goals, but of course I would love to have Ivan on the pitch.'

Brentford: Raya; Ajer, Jansson, Pinnock; Canós (Baptiste 86), Jensen, Nørgaard, Janelt (Dasilva 61), Henry; Wissa (Ghoddos 82), Mbeumo

Crystal Palace: Guaita; Ward, Andersen, Guéhi, Mitchell; Gallagher, Hughes (McArthur 66), Schlupp; Ayew (Olise 77), Édouard (Mateta 72), Zaha

Monday, 14 February 2022

Southend United were the visitors for a friendly today that must have put a smile on Thomas Frank's face for a few different reasons.

Reason 1: A 3-2 win.

Reason 2: More to the point, Christian Eriksen played 60 minutes without, seemingly, suffering any ill effects. He was busy throughout his time on the pitch and even set up one of the goals.

Reason 3: A hat-trick from Josh Dasilva. His first came when Eriksen won possession just inside the Southend half and played it forward for Dasilva to touch it past the advancing goalkeeper; for the second he found a bit of space in the penalty area to give him time to steer a through ball past the keeper; and the third was a curling effort from the edge of the box into the corner of the net.

Reason 4: Could we have witnessed a promising Eriksen-Dasilva understanding and partnership blossoming? Now that really *would* be a boost for the last three months of the season.

Thursday, 17 February 2022

The results of the Premier League Fan Engagement Survey have been released and Brentford have come out top of the tree. The survey took place between November and January and was carried out on behalf of the Premier League by a research and strategy consultancy company called Yonder.

Supporters from all the Premier League clubs were invited to take part in the survey, answering questions and giving opinions on subjects like how their favourite club is run, the customer service communication with supporters, stadium facilities, and even the atmosphere within the stadium during matchday. The results are collected and, to make the rankings fair, they are determined on average responses. Brentford topped the league in such categories as family friendly environment, toilet facilities, attitude and performance of club staff as well as overall matchday experience.

'We are really pleased and proud of these results,' said chief executive Jon Varney. 'It has been a monumental effort for us to adjust to life in the Premier League and to fully open our new stadium to our fans. Our staff have worked so hard, so I want to thank them for contributing to this. It has been a real team effort across every department. I would also like to thank our fans for their patience and understanding whilst we made the transition from Griffin Park to our new home. Despite the inevitable teething problems we encountered, the togetherness shown throughout the club is something the fans and staff should be very proud of.'

It's nice to know that in these days of big finance, mega marketing and money, money, money – it's no coincidence that the richest clubs are the most successful clubs, and the most successful clubs and the ones that wield the power – that Brentford do seem to genuinely think about making the supporters' visit to the Community Stadium as enjoyable and comfortable and problem-free as possible.

Friday, 18 February 2022

Brentford take on Arsenal tomorrow – assuming Storm Eunice which has been battering the UK today doesn't have a resurgence and force postponements – in the return fixture of Brentford's first Premier League match. One man who won't be playing a part in the game is Christian

Eriksen. Thomas Frank confirmed in his press conference today that Eriksen needs a little more time:

'Christian looked good in the 60 minutes he played, he is looking good in training, he feels well and he is in a good place. But he's been out for seven months. Normally you need a proper pre-season, but he came into us with a good foundation, so he doesn't need six weeks, but this Arsenal game is just one step too early. We have another good opponent in a friendly game on Monday behind closed doors that will really be beneficial for him, so we are aiming for the Newcastle game.'

One man who may or may not be playing a part in the game is Ivan Toney. He has missed the last couple of matches against Manchester City and Crystal Palace with a calf injury.

'Ivan has done some light sessions so we will assess him in the morning and see how close he is,' said Frank. 'Of course, he is a player that we would really like in our team, or at least in the squad. We'll see tomorrow and I'll take the final decision then.'

One man who will more than likely be playing a part in the game, even if it is as a substitute, is Josh Dasilva. He has been on the bench for the last three games as he returns from his long-term hip injury. Dasilva was a product of the Arsenal academy and it was when he was coming through the ranks that he was converted from a winger to playing in a more central position. He made three appearances for the Gunners, all in the League Cup, and is sure to want to get some action against his former club. Dasilva has previously spoken to *The Independent* about his time at Arsenal, his change of position and being coached by Thierry Henry.

'At first I was reluctant to change position,' he admitted. 'I just wanted to get on the ball and enjoy myself. But he [Thierry Henry] and Kwame Ampadu [another Arsenal coach] sat me down and went through all the basics with me. You have to get the credentials to be a midfielder. Tactically he [Henry] improved my game a lot. Every time you were with him, you learned something different. For the first week, you're just starstruck. He's won everything, but once you got to know him, he became one of us. You could chat to him about anything and he would always tell you exactly how it is, never beat around the bush. He helped me a lot to make that transition.'

Saturday, 19 February 2022

There were some kind words for Christian Eriksen from Tim Sherwood on talkSPORT today. Sherwood had been Eriksen's manager at Tottenham for a time between the reigns of André Villas-Boas and Mauricio Pochettino.

'He really could make the difference,' said Sherwood of how Eriksen could influence the rest of Brentford's season. 'It's not only what he delivers on the pitch, but also what he delivers in the dressing room. The attitude and conduct is magnificent, the best I have ever seen from any professional. Amazing. Amazing trainer. His influence on Harry Kane was unbelievable. He was out there practising his craft all the time. You might say, "Surely you are a footballer, you always need to do that," but they don't. They waste training days. This boy didn't waste a training day.'

Today's match at the Emirates Stadium began with both teams looking to put an early stamp on things. Sergi Canós had to block Ben White's header from a corner and David

Raya was called into action to stop Alexandre Lacazette shortly afterwards.

There was also one crazy bit of action that began in the Brentford penalty. Bukayo Saka was tackled by Josh Dasilva, got back on the loose ball, had his shot deflected again by Dasilva and the deflection ricocheted the ball into Raya's face. When it dropped, Dasilva once more was first on it and this time he released Bryan Mbeumo for a counter attack. He raced away but saw his shot blocked to again send Arsenal straight back up the other end. Kieran Tierney crossed for Lacazette to touch the ball in, only for VAR to rule that he had been in an offside position.

From then on, the home side gained control of the possession and probed for the breakthrough. Thomas Partey shot wide and both Lacazette and Martin Ødegaard had efforts blocked before they had a chance to trouble Raya. Cedric Soares saw his goalbound effort stopped by a flying block from Yoane Wissa. Arsenal appealed for a penalty, claiming that Wissa had actually blocked the ball with his hand, but once again the Video Assistant Referee ruled against the Gunners and the half ended scoreless.

The second period began as the first ended, with Arsenal exerting the pressure, and the opening goal came after just three minutes. Lacazette found a bit of space in the midfield area and moved it to Emile Smith Rowe. He advanced into the Brentford penalty area and placed his shot across Raya into the far corner of the net.

The goal jolted Brentford into action and they came close when Vitaly Janelt released Mbeumo behind the defence. The ball, though, had just too much on it, and Mbeumo was just unable to bring it under control enough to worry Aaron Ramsdale in the Arsenal goal.

The hosts got a firm grip on proceedings when Partey made strides into the Bees' danger zone before finding Saka in space just outside the area. Saka brought the ball under control before firing past Raya to make it 2-0.

Brentford did pull one back right at the end of the match. A free kick was swung in by Saman Ghoddos and headed clear by Soares. The loose ball fell to Janelt who fired it towards goal. His effort was blocked but fell to Christian Nørgaard who fired it home. One quick VAR check later confirmed the goal was a good one but there was no time for Brentford to push for the equaliser, the strike coming after 93 minutes. It was Nørgaard's second goal of the season following his effort in the opening game against the same opponents.

'It was a fair and square win for Arsenal, no complaints there,' admitted Thomas Frank after the match to the gathered press. 'First half Arsenal had a lot of the ball, but you expect that when they're playing at home. They are competing for the top four, they had a point to prove, but I'm very pleased with the way we defended. We had a good structure. Yes, they had some shots and lots of corners, but they didn't have many big chances. We were not good enough on the ball, we didn't take care of it and threw it away too quick to be a threat in the other end. In the second half that was a better part, we progressed more up and the pitch and created a few dangerous situations, but not enough.'

Frank was well aware that the teams below Brentford picked up points today, but he wasn't giving much away about the pressure that is coming from the lower positions.

'It's just one game at a time, we need to focus on ourselves, that's the only thing we can do anything about.

It's what we've done in the last three years. In the next session we'll evaluate the game and make sure we do things better going into the next game and do everything we can to get the three points. We're very aware, of course, that we haven't got that many points lately. I think there are reasons for that, but the positive is we have a fully fit squad available and that will help us.'

Arsenal: Ramsdale; Cedric, White, Gabriel, Tierney; Xhaka, Partey; Saka, Ødegaard, Smith Rowe (Pépé 75); Lacazette (Nketiah 83)

Brentford: Raya; Ajer, Jansson, Pinnock; Canós (Ghoddos 84), Dasilva (Baptiste 68), Nørgaard, Jensen (Janelt 44), Henry; Mbeumo, Wissa

Sunday, 20 February 2022

Thomas Frank was asked about it yesterday and, quite rightly, said that Brentford can only concentrate on their own performance, but at least half an eye needs to be kept on the teams below them in the league.

The table is so close, and this weekend's results have not been good ones. While Brentford were being beaten by Arsenal, many of their direct competitors picked up points. Of the teams below them in the table, Burnley beat Brighton, Watford scored their first victory under Roy Hodgson against Aston Villa and Newcastle gained a draw at West Ham.

It leaves the table looking this way, from 11th position down:

Leicester 27 points, Aston Villa 27, Crystal Palace 26, Brentford 24, Leeds 23, Everton 22, Newcastle 22, Watford 18, Burnley 17, Norwich 17. Out of those teams, Brentford have played more games than anyone and Burnley have played fewest. If any of those teams go on a decent run they could quite easily climb out of trouble but, on the other hand, a losing streak could well mean curtains.

From Brentford's perspective, you get the feeling that the next little cluster of matches are going to be vital. Their run of games from now until the end of March are against Newcastle, Norwich, Burnley and Leicester. Good results from these and we should (*should*) be able to breath a bit more easily in the last part of the season.

What, then, do Brentford need to do? Thomas Frank often says in his post-match interviews that he is pleased with the overall way the team performs and chances are being made, but the ball just needs to hit the back of the net a bit more often. Sounds obvious, but reading down the results thus far, Brentford have lost by just a single goal on seven different occasions and drawn five. That is easy to say, of course, but the Premier League is the best, certainly the most competitive, top-level league in the world. Getting Ivan Toney back in the team after his injury could be crucial and Christian Eriksen's inclusion may be a game-changer. It is certainly going to be an exciting and, probably, scary end to the season. But that's why we all love the game of football, right?

Monday, 21 February 2022

As advertised by Thomas Frank last Friday, Brentford played another behind-closed-doors friendly today, travelling to Glasgow to take on Rangers. As was the case in the last friendly last Monday, all went well for Brentford, mission accomplished. Christian Eriksen came through unscathed having played 80 minutes and once more had an influence on the proceedings.

After 15 minutes, Eriksen swung in a corner from the left that was met by the head of Mathias Jørgensen who nodded home. Rangers equalised halfway through the first period thanks to Amad Diallo and then took the lead after Brentford keeper Álvaro Fernández saved a penalty and Diallo was fastest to react and knock in the rebound. The Bees made it 2-2 not long into the second half, again from an Eriksen assist. This time he played in a free kick, Tristan Crama got there before his marker and the ball was flicked into the Rangers net. Eriksen was replaced by Ryan Trevitt for the last ten minutes of the match, the next stage of his reintroduction complete.

All looks to be going well in the plan for Eriksen to be back involved in first team action for the match against Newcastle on Saturday. It certainly would be a big lift in Brentford's fight to stay in the Premier League.

Tuesday, 22 February 2022

Following yesterday's friendly match against Rangers, there is an interview with Christian Eriksen on Brentford's Twitter profile.

'The minutes are getting more and more, and I feel good,' says Eriksen. 'It was a tough test in the last week or so. The game against Southend was tough but I'm happy to be out there. I feel like I'm in a good place, mentally going into the games and body-wise, which is the most important at the moment, and I'm actually a bit surprised that my body is acting as it is. Of course, I've been training hard, but I didn't expect it to feel as good as it is now, it's definitely something very positive.'

Sounds like good news. Eriksen seems happy, Thomas Frank says that he is also happy with the progress, so could we see him make his Brentford debut for the match on Saturday?

Wednesday, 23 February 2022

Fresh from their Atlantic Cup exploits, Brentford's B team today had a friendly against Monaco in France. Monaco are currently sixth in Ligue 1 behind runaway leaders Paris Saint-Germain, Marseille, Nice, Strasbourg and Rennes. It was a good test for the Bees, as Monaco fielded a strong side including the likes of current internationals Aleksandr Golovin of Russia and Germany's Kevin Volland, along with Cesc Fàbregas who has won over 100 caps for Spain.

The hosts went ahead just after the half hour when Maghnes Akliouche hit a long-range shot that deflected past Brentford keeper Roco Rees and might have had a second when Golovin's effort hit the post.

Five minutes before half-time, Brentford were level when Daniel Oyegoke played in Nathan Young-Coombes to strike low past Monaco goalkeeper Radosław Majecki. He also almost gave Brentford the lead after the break when he chipped Majecki only to see the back-pedalling defenders bundle the ball clear.

With ten minutes to go, Monaco scored the winner thanks to Eric Ayiah. He jinked his way into the box and finished past substitute keeper Ben Winterbottom to seal the victory.

Even though it was a defeat, the young Bees team need not be too downhearted as they pushed a top team from an elite league all the way. It is said that you learn more form defeats than victories, and the experience will certainly do them good.

Thursday, 24 February 2022

Brentford have today announced that they plan to install barrier seats at the Community Stadium for next season. The plan is for the whole of the West Stand and part of the away end to be licensed safe standing areas. Last year, the government announced that they would allow safe standing areas at Premier League and Championship grounds, with trials having taken place since January. Manchester United, Manchester City, Tottenham, Chelsea and Cardiff City were chosen to trial the scheme. The first fixture in the trial was Chelsea v Liverpool on Sunday, 2 January.

'It has always been our preferred option since the move to the new stadium,' said Brentford's operations director, Alan Walsh, 'to convert the West Stand to safe standing if the legislation changed. The feedback we received from our fans in our recent survey endorsed that position, so we are pleased to confirm that we have made the decision to proceed. We thank everyone who contributed to that consultation process.'

The sports website TEAMtalk today claims that Brentford are one of the teams who are showing an interest in Blackpool winger Josh Bowler. The Bees are apparently in competition with Leicester City, Nottingham Forest, Norwich and Wolves for Bowler's signature in the summer.

Friday, 25 February 2022

There is only one story that the sports media is interested in today.

'He will be in the squad, and he will get on the pitch tomorrow.' Guess who Thomas Frank was talking about.

'It will be amazing,' said the boss in his press conference prior to the game against Newcastle. 'It is a big day, definitely for all of us, but especially for Christian and his family when he will walk on to that pitch. For me personally, of course, and for everyone involved in football who saw what happened, it's another of those reminders that we need to remind ourselves that we are privileged to do what we do and be alive and we need to appreciate every day, every moment, which is very difficult in life, but a good reminder for us all.'

Eriksen's upcoming Brentford debut isn't the only piece of good news. 'For maybe the first time this season we have all players available, which is positive,' says Frank. 'This also means Ivan Toney will be involved in the squad tomorrow. That's a huge positive going into the final part of the season.'

Another positive from Brentford's point of view is that Watford, Leeds and Norwich were all beaten in midweek games, the only winner from the bottom part of the table being Burnley who beat Tottenham. This leaves the bottom three as Norwich at the foot of the table with 17 points, Watford in 19th with 18 and Burnley 18th with 20. Norwich have now played the same number of games as Brentford although that will change tomorrow, of course, and Watford have one game in hand on the Bees but are six points behind. Burnley are now only four points behind but have played three games fewer. Newcastle are next on 22 points, just two behind Brentford, which makes tomorrow's match a big one.

Saturday, 26 February 2022

It's a big day. You have a home match against one of your rivals in the relegation dogfight, the squad is pretty much back to full fitness in time for the last big effort going into the final third of the season, the player who is potentially the biggest and most important signing in your club's history is going to make his debut and the crowd are buzzing with expectation. What's the last thing you want to happen? How about your midfield playmaker getting sent off after only ten minutes?

A Newcastle corner was swung in and knocked clear to the edge of the area. Matt Targett ran in but Josh Dasilva was there fractionally before him. Dasilva tried to put his body in between Targett and the ball in order to pirouette past the Newcastle man and bring it away. Unfortunately, Dasilva went over the ball into Targett's ankle and they were both left on the ground. The referee initially gave a free kick to Brentford but, on advice from VAR, revisited the incident on the pitchside monitor. In slow motion the incident looked an awful lot worse than what Dasilva intended (we must assume) and the official reversed his decision and brandished the red card. Jonjo Shelvey took the free kick but it went harmlessly straight at David Raya.

From then on it was always going to be an uphill struggle. Brentford had Raya to thank for keeping them in it as he produced fine saves from a Chris Wood header and was then down quickly to stop a low cross from Joe Willock reaching Targett. Raya couldn't keep the visitors out indefinitely, though, and was unable to stop Joelinton opening the scoring. Ryan Fraser jinked his way down the left flank and his cross was met firmly by the Brazilian whose header arrowed into the corner.

Just before the half-time break, things got even worse when the second goal came on the breakaway after a Brentford corner. A long clearance reached Fabian Schär on the halfway line. Schär got the better of Rico Henry and played the ball across to Willock who galloped up in support. Raya was helpless as Willock curved his shot round him into the net.

Two goals and a man down at half-time, it was going to need something special to turn things around. Time to turn to Christian Eriksen. Six minutes into the second period, Eriksen came on for Matthias Jensen to a rapturous reception, even from the Newcastle fans. Just 259 days since he collapsed in that Denmark v Finland match, here he was back on a football pitch again. Ironically and perhaps a little poetically, it was Jensen who replaced Eriksen that day.

Eriksen's arrival gave Brentford that little boost. He immediately started to spray the ball around in the manner to which we were accustomed to seeing during his time at Tottenham and, for a while, the Bees looked dangerous. Christian Nørgaard sent a curling effort just too high, and Bryan Mbeumo had a dangerous-looking shot blocked. Ivan Toney also came off the bench after missing the last three games to add to the threat but, with a player short, it was just too much of an ask for Brentford and the points headed north.

Naturally, the game's two major incidents dominated Thomas Frank's post-match press conference.

'I think it was a completely random situation,' he said of Dasilva's sending off, 'and unfortunately he's given Josh a red card. I understand with VAR and the perception of it why it was given, but everybody who knows and understands football sees he's tried to step in front of the ball, tried to put his foot on it but unfortunately he hits his leg, and apparently that's a red card.'

Frank was, of course, more upbeat on Eriksen's return to action, 'I think for everyone involved in football it was a big moment. It was fantastic to see he got a big reception stepping on to the pitch. Newcastle fans, fantastic. All our fans, of course, fantastic, and everyone else involved. Big moment for Christian and his family. It was nice to see and hopefully now he can only talk with his feet and speak about football instead of everything else.'

Brentford: Raya; Ajer (Canós 72), Jansson, Pinnock, Henry; Jensen (Eriksen 52), Nørgaard, Janelt; Dasilva, Mbeumo, Wissa (Toney 62)

Newcastle United: Dúbravka; Krafth, Schär, Burn, Targett; Joelinton, Shelvey, Willock (Lascelles 83); Murphy (Guimarães 64), Wood, Fraser (Almirón 90)

Sunday, 27 February 2022
Leeds have today parted company with manager Marcelo Bielsa. Their recent form has been somewhat alarming, having picked up just a single point in the last six games, losing the last four with a goal aggregate of 17-2. They are currently a point behind Brentford, two above the relegation zone.

Bielsa led Leeds to promotion two seasons ago, after a 16-year absence from the top flight, and finished ninth in the Premier League last year. There has been no immediate replacement installed. He is the ninth Premier League manager to have lost his job this season.

It is reported today in *The Sun* that Brentford are looking to sign Millwall winger Tyler Burey in the summer. Burey has been out on loan at Hartlepool but has returned to Millwall, scoring two goals in seven appearances.

The first major silverware of the season was won by Liverpool today as they beat Chelsea in the League Cup Final at Wembley. In a dramatic game, Chelsea had three goals and Liverpool one disallowed for offside as the match finished 0-0 and went to penalties. Nobody was missing from the spot and every player who finished the game took their turn. Only the 22nd penalty failed to hit the net as Chelsea goalkeeper Kepa Arrizabalaga, who was brought on by manager Thomas Tuchel in place of Édouard Mendy especially for the shoot-out, ballooned his shot over the crossbar.

Tuesday, 1 March 2022

After the dismissal of Marcelo Bielsa, Leeds have appointed the American Jesse Marsch as their next head coach. Marsch had previously been with Montreal Impact and New York Red Bulls before moving to Germany where he had stints with Red Bull Salzburg and RB Leipzig.

Thursday, 3 March 2022

There has been a lot of talk from Brentford's supposed transfer targets today. Hull City's Keane Lewis-Potter, Millwall's Tyler Burey and Brennan Johnson's manager at Nottingham Forest, Steve Cooper, have all spoken out.

'I don't worry too much about Brennan because he is a very calm guy,' Cooper is quoted as saying in the *Daily Mirror*. 'He is quite interested in his football, really, and training well and getting ready for the next game. He will be looking at stuff from the last game he has done and aspects to improve on. I don't worry one bit about any side-shows going on around him. As for contract talks, I am sure there is stuff going on in the background, but my job and Brennan's job is just to work as hard as we can and win as many games as we can. We'll leave the other stuff to other people.'

In an interview with the website News at Den, Burey acknowledged there had been reports of other clubs being interested in him.

'I don't focus on that,' he said. 'My focus is on Millwall, on me working hard, enjoying my time here and loving football. I want to keep learning new things, so all the other stuff on the outside I just clear out of my head. I know what I need to focus on which is trying to start every week, playing well and doing my job on the pitch. The other stuff is not my focus.'

Finally, speaking to Hull Live, Lewis-Potter also refused to be drawn into any speculation:

'I play for Hull City and that's all I'm going to concentrate on. It's about helping the team and we need to push higher up the table, and I think we've got the players to do that, so we need to start putting the performances together.'

Interestingly, none of the three dismissed the speculation, so maybe that's something to keep an eye out for during the summer.

Friday, 4 March 2022

There is a really good exclusive interview in the *Daily Mail* with Thomas Frank. He talks about life as a coach and how it is addictive but also draining. His background in the game also makes him appreciate what he has got right now.

'I said to myself when I started here that I would be a head coach for ten years and I have seven years left of that,' he says. 'I still mean it but also it could be that in ten years you meet me and I'm still doing it. Maybe even here at Brentford. For someone like me who was never a player it's pretty cool to be here right now. I look and there is Ronaldo on the field, Salah. It's normal to me now but

I know there are bigger things out there. It's not the only thing I can do.'

Frank is asked about his plans for the rest of the season. What will he be saying to his players? 'I try to speak about being brave, cool, aggressive and that's a big thing. Play forward. Turn up. Press high. We win or we learn. I try to be direct with any criticism without killing people as who does that help? But of course, they need to know if they can do something better. I try to show lots of positive situations. So we want to press high? Here are three situations where it was perfect and we created chances. I try to reinforce the positive messages.'

Another Brentford player in print today is Bryan Mbeumo who is featured in the *Metro* newspaper. He has been interviewed ahead of tomorrow's crunch game against Norwich City.

'Every game is important but of course the next two are big ones and we will do everything we can to try to win as always,' he says, also keeping in mind the meeting with Burnley the following weekend. 'We will stick together and try to get that winning feeling back. We will do everything to get out of this. We have to stick with the plan, to talk with each other and be together, like we are always.'

Mbeumo joined Brentford from French team Troyes, and he says that moving to London was like another world:

'Troyes is not so big! There is so much to do in London and I like to have a walk. I've had the chance to go and discover new places. I also play a lot of video games and watch football on TV – other Premier League matches, the Championship, Ligue 1, and also basketball, tennis and Formula One. I always wanted to play in the best leagues in the world. I enjoy it here and have had some great experiences, like promotion from the Championship, which made me very happy. The Premier League is, of course, much harder than the Championship, and quicker, but I am very happy to be playing here.'

Looking forward to tomorrow, Norwich manager Dean Smith hinted at his press conference that his players really do need to be looking to take something from the match:

'A loss against them means that they're ten points ahead of us as well, so it's a big game for us. We know they're one of the clubs that came up with us last season, we know how hard it is to stay in the league in the first season, so it's a big game for both clubs and we're looking forward to it. I don't think any game is a must-win at the moment, but it's certainly a must-not-lose. We're going into each game knowing that we have to try to win now. We're running out of games, we know, there's a dozen left, and it's a big game for both teams.'

Saturday, 5 March 2022

The Bees arrived at Carrow Road knowing that they really could not afford to be beaten today. Christian Eriksen is in the starting line-up as is Ivan Toney. Three points today would do Brentford the world of good and put Norwich in trouble.

The match started with both teams looking like they knew they needed something, as an open, flowing game produced chances at either end. Norwich had the first opportunity as Billy Gilmour played a one-two with Teemu Pukki before playing in Milot Rashica, but David Raya got down well to stop his shot. Raya also blocked an effort from Pukki to keep the game scoreless. Brentford, for their part, also had chances at the other end. Eriksen crossed for

Bryan Mbeumo to volley wide and Sergi Canós was denied by Norwich keeper Tim Krul.

The all important opening goal came just after the half hour mark. Ethan Pinnock launched a long throw into the Norwich penalty box that fell to Canós, and his shot was turned aside by Krul. Eriksen swung the corner into the near post, Kristoffer Ajer got a flick on and Toney, lurking at the back post, lost his marker to knock the ball in.

Having taken the lead, Brentford began to look a lot more comfortable, with Eriksen bringing a calmness to the play. He was getting the ball and finding little pockets of space to operate in, his obvious class showing. He almost played in Canós for a second, but the Spaniard was crowded out before he could get his shot off.

The second half began in the same vein, with Brentford looking the most likely to score again. Another Eriksen corner landed in the danger zone, Pontus Jansson got in front of his marker but received a boot in the face. The Video Assistant Referee was consulted and returned a verdict of dangerous play and a penalty was awarded. Krul tried to play the mind games with Toney as the striker put the ball on the spot, advancing back and forth from his goal line, but the Brentford man was having none of it and just kept turning away. When the kick was finally taken, he coolly dispatched it into the bottom-left corner to double the lead.

The two-goal cushion soon became three. Christian Nørgaard played a through ball to Toney who was taken out by a challenge by Ben Gibson and, again after a VAR consultation, a penalty was awarded and Toney had a chance to claim the Bees' very first Premier League hat-trick. He put his spot-kick in the same place as the previous one, safely out of reach of Krul's dive and, barring a catastrophe, the points were Brentford's.

VAR continued its busy afternoon as Norwich thought they had pulled one back when Rashica shot low past Raya. Replays showed, though, that Pukki was offside in the lead-up. Still not content with merely awarding two penalties and ruling a goal out, the Video Assistant Referee stepped in again when Mbeumo thought he had made it four. Pinnock took a throw-in to Toney who played it back to him and, from Pinnock's cross, Mbeumo's header was saved but he put the rebound past Krul. This time it was ruled that Pinnock was slightly offside when he received the ball back from Toney before putting his cross in.

There was just enough time for Pukki to grab a consolation in injury time, but it was too little too late for the home side and an important match ended with Brentford's first three-point haul since the win against Aston Villa at the start of January.

Norwich City: Krul; Byram, Hanley, Gibson, Williams (Aarons 81); Gilmour (Rowe 74), Normann (Lees-Melou 81), McLean; Sargent, Pukki, Rashica

Brentford: Raya; Ajer (Roerslev 75), Jansson, Pinnock, Henry; Janelt, Nørgaard (Onyeka 59), Eriksen; Mbeumo, Toney, Canós (Wissa 82)

Monday, 7 March 2022

On Sky Sports's *Monday Night Football* show tonight, former Liverpool defender Jamie Carragher analysed the Christian Eriksen effect on Brentford's performance against Norwich.

'What I thought was really interesting,' said Carragher, 'was his role within the team. He played deeper than where we would normally associate him when he played for Tottenham, where he would be more between the lines, trying to find the final pass. He was more of a playmaker. He played part of a midfield three, just to the left, but slightly deep.'

Carragher highlighted a few passes Eriksen played in order to set attacks going, comparing him to the former Italian international Andrea Pirlo who, towards the end of his career at Juventus, moved back from an attacking role to playing in front of the defence in order to get things going for his team.

It was a good weekend for Brentford. Not only did Eriksen play 90 minutes and look good, and not only did Toney get back to scoring ways by taking the match ball home with him, but most of the other teams at the bottom end of the Premier League table were beaten. Out of the bottom seven, only Brentford and Newcastle picked up any points. Reading from the bottom up, Norwich and are now ten points behind the Bees on 17 points after 27 games, Watford lost to Arsenal and are on 19 points having also played 27 and Burnley are third bottom on 21 after 26 games due to their loss to Chelsea. Then come Everton who lost at Tottenham on 22 points although they have only played 25, Leeds on 23 after 27 as they were beaten by Leicester in Jesse Marsch's first game in charge and then Brentford who have 27 points.

Even though they have played 28 matches, more than anyone else, it is still handy to have a four-point gap, meaning that even if the team below won their game in hand they would still be a point behind. One place and one point above Brentford are Newcastle who beat Brighton. They are unbeaten in eight league games and look to be pulling themselves out of trouble. With many of the aforementioned teams yet to play each other, there are no doubt more twists and turns to come and, interestingly, Brentford's last two games of the season are away at Everton and at home to Leeds.

At the top, it is a two-horse race. Manchester City are six points ahead of Liverpool but have played a game more, with Chelsea in third a further ten points behind. Arsenal are in fourth spot and look to be in a race for the final Champions League place with Manchester United, West Ham, Tottenham and Wolves.

Tuesday, 8 March 2022

The EFL have been running a competition to find the best goal of this season's League Cup, and the votes are in. The winner is – drum roll, please – Yoane Wissa. His overhead kick against Oldham Athletic in the third round topped the poll. After each round, the EFL ran an online vote for the best goal of that particular stage of the competition, and the winners were pitted against each other for the overall prize.

Wednesday, 9 March 2022

The Liverpool v Chelsea penalty shoot-out in the League Cup at Wembley at the end of February was, by all accounts, a bit of a marathon, with Liverpool coming out 11-10 winners. That, however, is nothing compared to what happened tonight in the Ernest Armstrong Memorial Cup match between Washington and Bedlington at the Ford Quarry Football Hub in Sunderland. The match finished in a 3-3 draw and went to penalties. As in Liverpool v Chelsea, the spot-kicks kept hitting the back of the net but, unlike the Wembley final, when the first one was missed, what would have been the winning penalty was also missed. And so it went on until, after 54 kicks, Washington were the eventual winners by a score of 25-24. Unsurprisingly, the marathon shoot-out has gone down as a world record. The *Guinness Book of World Records* lists the previous longest as 48 kicks in the match between KK Palace and Civics in the Namibian Cup in 2005. Wouldn't you have hated being the player who missed the final one?

Thursday, 10 March 2022

Tonight was a good night for Brentford. They didn't play, but Norwich, Watford and Leeds all did and they were all beaten. It seems very uncharitable to want other teams to lose, but they are direct rivals in the table. All three have now played the same number of games as Brentford and are four points behind (Leeds), eight points behind (Watford) and ten points behind (Norwich). The Bees' next game is against another relegation rival on Saturday as Burnley visit the Community Stadium. Three points from that one would be very handy indeed. The other team to make up the bottom six, Everton, are five points behind Brentford but have three games in hand. They do, though, have to get points from those games otherwise they are going to be in trouble.

Saturday, 12 March 2022

This afternoon's big match against Burnley was one of not many chances with the defences being on top. The nearest either team came to opening the scoring was when Christian Eriksen's shot from the edge of the box was pushed wide by Burnley keeper Nick Pope. Soon afterwards, the visitors also had an opportunity, but Dwight McNeil headed a cross wide of the goal from eight yards out. Just as half-time was approaching, Sergi Canós crossed for Bryan Mbeumo whose effort may have found the far corner of the net but for the intervention of Burnley defender James Tarkowski who slid in to clear in the nick of time. The loose ball found its way to Vitaly Janelt but Nathan Collins's intervention meant he couldn't get his shot off.

The second period opened up a little more and Janelt had another opportunity but saw his header land on the roof of the net. At the other end, Maxwell Cornet chased down a Rico Henry back-pass but David Raya got down well to block his effort when it looked easier for Cornet to score. Jay Rodriguez came closest to breaking the deadlock with a long-range effort that had Raya beaten, only for the ball to come back off the crossbar.

With time running out, Eriksen gained possession to the left of the Burnley penalty area and made some space before crossing for Ivan Toney at the back post. The cross was pinpoint accurate and Toney's downward header beat Pope and Brentford had a vital lead. That's two starts and two assists from Eriksen.

The two combined again in time added on for injuries when Eriksen played in Toney behind the visitors' defence and, just as in last week's game against Norwich, he was taken down and a penalty was awarded. VAR was consulted to decide the severity of the punishment and, in addition to the spot-kick, Collins was shown a red card. Again, just like last week's game against Norwich, Toney picked himself up and converted the spot-kick. That's five goals in two games for Toney, and it seems he is finding his top form just at the right time.

A huge cheer greeted the final whistle, with everyone well aware that Brentford's 2-0 victory had secured a vital three points in the fight for survival.

At the press conference after the match, a lot of the focus was on the impact that Eriksen has made, and the chance that Thomas Frank took in bringing him to London.

'For me it was not a gamble,' said Frank, 'I was pretty convinced he would help us. If we could do that, it would be a fantastic signing. Maybe the best signing ever for Brentford, or maybe the most important, depending how you measure it. For me it was not an injury, it was a heart condition, so he wouldn't have lost any speed or anything. Of course, there is a mental issue that we had a lot of talks about, but when he is quite decisive in taking a decision, "I want to play, I want to play in the World Cup," then you know that he is pretty calm and clear about what he wants. I think he is top quality. We have seen a few times this season against us, Man City here, 1-0 win, De Bruyne with an unbelievable cross. Today we had that quality from Eriksen.'

Brentford: Raya; Ajer, Jansson, Pinnock, Henry; Janelt, Nørgaard (Jensen 81), Eriksen; Mbeumo (Onyeka 90), Toney, Canós (Wissa 75)

Burnley: Pope; Roberts, Collins, Tarkowski, Taylor; Lennon, Westwood, Brownhill, McNeil; Weghorst (Rodriguez 67), Cornet

Elsewhere today, Manchester United beat Tottenham 3-2 with Cristiano Ronaldo bagging a hat-trick. His career goals tally is now an astounding 807, a number that may well have made him FIFA's all time record scorer. There is some confusion as Josef Bican, who played in Austria and Czechoslovakia in the 1930s, '40s and '50s, as well as international football for both countries having changed citizenship, is registered with FIFA as having scored 805, but they do say it is an estimated total. The Czech FA has him registered with 821 while other sources say he actually managed a whopping 950 goals. This total, though, includes games for amateur, reserve and regional teams. Whatever the true amount of Bican's goals is we will probably never know with absolute certainty. This being the case, FIFA are now recognising Ronaldo as football's greatest ever goalscorer. Their top five reads: Ronaldo 807, Bican 805, Romário 772, Lionel Messi 759 and Pelé 757.

Monday, 14 March 2022

The weekend's results have made things even more interesting at Brentford's end of the table. The Bees' victory over Burnley did them the world of good, and they are now eight points above the drop zone on 30 points. Leeds are four points behind on 26 after they beat Norwich 2-1 with the winner coming on 95 minutes. The Canaries thought they had salvaged a point after themselves equalising in injury time but lost to pretty much the last kick of the game. Everton and Watford are both on 22 points, Burnley have 21 and Norwich are beginning to be left adrift on 17. The number of matches played is a bit more even now, too. Brentford, Leeds, Watford and Norwich have all played 29, Burnley have played 27 and Everton 26. Newcastle look to have pulled themselves out of trouble. Before yesterday's defeat at Chelsea they had been unbeaten in nine.

The top of the table is also becoming very interesting. Liverpool are on a run of eight straight wins and have clawed back Manchester City's lead to just four points. The Reds also have a game in hand and a better goal difference.

The race for the top four, and therefore the Champions League spots, is also hotting up. Chelsea are third, seven points behind Liverpool on 59, then come Arsenal on 51,

Manchester United on 50, West Ham with 48, Wolves have 46 and Tottenham 45. It is looking like Manchester City, Liverpool and Chelsea will finish as the top three, and of those in the race for fourth, both north London teams look to be decently placed as they are the ones with the games in hand. But, of course, you never know.

Tuesday, 15 March 2022

Christian Eriksen has been called up to the Denmark squad for their friendly matches against the Netherlands and Serbia at the end of the month.

'Christian is in pretty good physical shape,' said Denmark coach Kasper Hjulmand. 'I saw him against Burnley last Saturday where he was the best player on the pitch. He is a player who thinks faster than most people do.'

After recovering from his cardiac arrest, Eriksen has always stated that his goal was to play at the World Cup. It seems that now he may well have the chance.

Friday, 18 March 2022

David Raya has been called up to the Spain squad for the first time as they look forward to friendlies against Albania and Iceland next week. He replaces Manchester United goalkeeper David De Gea.

'It is part of the tracing we do with the goalkeepers,' said Spanish team manager Luis Enrique, of his choosing Raya. 'He is a player who is doing very well. I really want to see him in the context of the selection. He has the necessary profile to play for us.'

It is certainly an achievement for Raya to be called up to the international scene as Spain have traditionally had some of the world's best goalkeepers, and they also tend to display longevity. Their current number one is Unai Simón who currently has 20 caps to his name, and De Gea has 45. Before their era, however, Iker Casillas was the custodian, and he won an astounding 167 caps. Prior that, Andoni Zubizarreta had the gloves for 126 appearances. Before him, Luis Arconada played 68 times. The three of them were mainstays of the team since 1977. There were one or two others who made a handful of appearances, but that was it – just a handful. So, for Raya to gain inclusion, he certainly must be doing something right.

Looking forward to this weekend's match away at Leicester, Thomas Frank says that he has impressed to his players how important it is to continue playing like they believe they belong in the Premier League.

'We know results are nice, but they need to be backed up by the performances, so our consistency in producing good performances gives us something to believe in,' he told his press conference. 'The more free-flowing you can play, without thinking about the consequences, the better you will play. The last two games were close games, which is natural because the wins mean a lot. In general, we have been reinforcing that we need to be brave, be cool and be aggressive. The more we can enforce that on the training pitch the better.'

As for Sunday's fixture, Frank says of Brentford's opponents, 'We know it is going to be difficult. They have maybe not hit the highest level this season compared to the last two seasons where they were fighting for Champions League football and playing unbelievable football, but they are still a top team who, on their day, can beat all the top six teams. I am aware that Leicester have conceded some goals, but I am also certain that Brendan Rodgers, his staff and players, will do everything they can to avoid conceding, so that can be a battle in this game.'

He was also asked about Christian Eriksen's future. Could he stay at Brentford? 'I think that's a discussion between Christian and the club. If you ask me, of course I hope that he will stay for a longer time. I am convinced and sure that he is happy with life right now. He has come to a club where we have a very good environment and a good atmosphere and I'm pretty sure that he likes that a lot, and he knows a lot of people here. He is here to the end of the season and there are some options afterwards. I think it is realistic to keep him, 100 per cent, but I am also aware that there are bigger clubs out there who could be potentially interested. I think there's a lot of things that need to be drawn into perspective in football and in life for Christian, so let's see. I'm just enjoying having him here. I don't think it is time to focus too much on what will happen at the end of the season.'

Sunday, 20 March 2022

The Bees travel to Leicester without Christian Eriksen who is out with COVID. It is a blow as he has brought that extra bit of quality to the Brentford midfield and, of course, his through balls and set-piece deliveries have been instrumental in creating goal scoring opportunities in the last couple of games.

The match started with both teams playing some nice stuff, but there was a lack of penetration at either end. The ball was being played around nicely in the middle section, but attacks tended to fizzle out 25 yards from goal. In fact, when the opening goal was scored after 20 minutes, it was from the first effort on target.

Leicester frontman Harvey Barnes moved inside from the left flank and played the ball back to full-back Timothy Castagne. The Belgian took one touch to cue himself up and fired an unstoppable shot that arrowed into the top corner of the net with David Raya beaten all ends up. Absolutely no fault can be attached to Raya, and it seemed that even Castagne himself couldn't believe it by his running off with his hands on his head.

After the goal, the game began to open up a little more and the opportunities began to come for both teams. Almost immediately, Yoane Wissa made strides down the left wing and knocked the ball inside for the arriving Mathias Jensen who hit it first time. Unfortunately for him, the shot flew straight at Kasper Schmeichel, whereas a yard or so either side would have made it very difficult for the keeper indeed.

It wasn't too long before the second goal arrived and, unfortunately, it was a second for Leicester. James Maddison won a free kick 25 yards from goal and picked himself up to strike a beauty into the net. He lifted the ball over the defensive wall and into the near corner, once again leaving Raya grasping at thin air. Two goals down and there was absolutely nothing Brentford's keeper could have done about either of them.

The second half began with Leicester looking to put the game to bed. Raya was called into action to stop both Kelechi Iheanacho and Maddison again to keep Brentford in the game. As the half wore on, though, the Bees began to get the upper hand and looked the most likely to score the next goal. Pontus Jansson had a couple of opportunities, firstly heading over from a corner and then seeing his shot deflected wide after a loose ball was won by Vitaly Janelt.

From the resulting corner it was Jansson once more who was on the end of it, but Schmeichel acrobatically tipped it over the bar.

Still Brentford pressed and the Foxes once again had Schmeichel to thank as he stopped Bryan Mbeumo's close range header from hitting the target. He was helpless, though, to prevent Wissa reducing the arrears with five minutes to go. Shandon Baptiste, on as substitute for Janelt, strode forward and, when he was challenged, the loose ball fell to Mbeumo. He played it in to Wissa who struck it into the corner from 22 yards, a goal that was reminiscent of his effort against Aston Villa in January.

The last few minutes saw Brentford press for the equaliser but it just would not come. Ivan Toney had an attempt blocked and Mbeumo was again denied by Schmeichel. The final whistle called a halt to an entertaining encounter, but one from which Brentford head back to London with nothing to show for their endeavours.

'I think fair play to Leicester, in the first half they were the better side,' conceded Thomas Frank afterwards. 'That said, we didn't give a chance away in the first half, they decided to put two in the top corner. The free kick, well done to Maddison, and a worldy by Castagne where he hits that one out of 100, with all due respect to him. If you want to win in the Premier League you want a team not to score two worldies.'

Leicester City: Schmeichel; Justin, Söyüncü, Amartey, Castagne (Evans 64); Tielemans, Mendy, Dewsbury-Hall (Soumaré 79); Maddison, Iheanacho (Daka 86), Barnes

Brentford: Raya; Ajer (Roerslev 66), Jansson, Pinnock, Henry (Fosu 74); Jensen, Nørgaard, Janelt (Baptiste 56); Mbeumo, Toney, Wissa

Monday, 21 March 2022

It's funny how just one round of matches changes things, isn't it? A week ago Brentford were looking to be in a strong position in comparison to their relegation rivals, but this weekend's fixtures have thrown it all up in the air again. There were only a few games due to the FA Cup quarter-finals, but those that were played saw Brentford beaten and both Leeds and Everton win. And what's more, Leeds got their winner in a 3-2 victory over Wolves in the 91st minute and, worse than that, the only goal in the Everton v Newcastle game came after 99 minutes. Those results mean that Leeds are now just a single point behind Brentford having played the same amount of games and Everton are five points behind but have three games in hand. Burnley, Watford and Norwich are currently occupying the three relegation places. This is how the table currently looks:

14 – Newcastle, 31 points, played 29
15 – Brentford, 30 points, played 30
16 – Leeds, 29 points, played 30
17 – Everton, 25 points, played 27
18 – Watford, 22 points, played 29
19 – Burnley, 21 points, played 27
20 – Norwich, 17 points, played 29

It looks like Norwich are going to struggle to stay up and Watford are going to have to produce a Herculean effort to retain their Premier League status when you look at their points tally and games played compared with the others. It becomes even more interesting when you see who the other teams have left to play, before we even get to the final day (deep breath):

Newcastle: Tottenham, Wolves, Leicester, Crystal Palace, Norwich, Liverpool, Manchester City and Arsenal

Brentford: Chelsea, West Ham, Watford, Tottenham, Manchester United, Southampton and Everton

Leeds: Southampton, Watford, Crystal Palace, Manchester City, Chelsea, Arsenal and Brighton

Everton: West Ham, Burnley, Manchester United, Leicester twice, Liverpool, Chelsea and Brentford;

Burnley: Manchester City, Everton, Norwich, West Ham, Southampton, Wolves, Watford, Aston Villa and Tottenham.

And just look at what the fixture computer has thrown up for the last day of the season: Arsenal v Everton, Brentford v Leeds, Burnley v Newcastle.

Just try to work out who is staying and who is going down from that little lot! No wonder managers always say they are just concentrating on one game at a time. Really, you could make a case for any of those clubs to stay up or go down, couldn't you?

Looking at that fixture list, and I know it doesn't always work out like you would think it should, Everton have the toughest run-in. The funny thing about football, though, is that you just never know for certain what will happen. Your favourite team can look like world-beaters in one game and then be totally useless in the next. That is why we love it. Or should that be, 'That is why we are driven completely mad by it and for some reason let it completely spoil our mood even though, in reality, it does not actually matter one jot to our lives whether our team are playing in the Champions League or fighting relegation into non-league, although of course it does, it's vitally important to our very existence and, try as we might, we just cannot bring ourselves to admit that it is only a game'?

So, who is your money on? It's going down to the wire, isn't it?

Tuesday, 22 March 2022

It is reported today in *The Sun* that, thanks to his scoring exploits for Brentford's B team this season, Nathan Young-Coombes is appearing on a few clubs' radar. It is claimed that Southampton, Crystal Palace, Bournemouth and Queens Park Rangers are all interested, with the Bees open to a loan move so he can gain some experience, but they do not want him to leave permanently.

There is more good news regarding players extending their contracts. Earlier in the year, Pontus Jansson and Bryan Mbeumo, as well as Thomas Frank and Brian Riemer, re-signed, and the latest to add his name to the list is Rico Henry who has signed on until 2026.

'I am very pleased that Rico has signed another contract with us,' said Frank. 'He has had a top time here. He has been here a long time and we are pleased that he wants to continue to grow with us. Rico has seamlessly made the step up to the Premier League. Defensively, he is fantastic, and you can see the way he defends one on one against some great attackers. He is also contributing up the field with the way he can arrive in the penalty area, as we have seen this season. There are bits to work on, but it is great that he will continue his development with us.'

Henry came through the ranks at Walsall before making the move to the Bees in 2016, where he was reunited with his former boss at the Bescot Stadium, Dean Smith, who was then manager at Brentford. He has now played over 150 games for the Bees in all competitions.

Friday, 25 March 2002

Some very important matches are being played in the latest international break, with World Cup play-offs happening throughout Europe. The ten qualifying group winners are automatically through to the finals, with the three remaining European spots being decided via play-offs involving the 12 non-winners with the best records in their respective qualifying groups. There are six semi-finals, with three finals deciding who will play at the World Cup in Qatar next winter.

There is one big shock as North Macedonia win 1-0 in Italy to go through to their final where they will play Portugal. How big a shock? European champions Italy are ranked six in the world and North Macedonia are 67th. In the Portugal v Turkey semi-final, with the score at 2-1, Turkey were awarded a penalty in the 85th minute, which was taken by their captain Burak Yılmaz. Unfortunately for him, he put his kick over the bar, Portugal scored again, the match ended 3-1 and the Portuguese will play North Macedonia for a World Cup place.

That was yesterday, and today Yılmaz has announced his retirement from international football. He told the Turkish media that he was 'in shock' and added, 'The match was my last with the national team, there needs to be a change. It is a final decision stripped of emotions, one that is taken rationally. The change needs to happen.'

It is a sad ending for a player who has won 77 international caps, scoring 31 goals for his country. He represented Turkey at two European Championships, in 2016 and 2020, and has won league titles and cups competitions in both Turkey and France, but is he going to be remembered for one shot that didn't hit the target?

OK, let's play a game. What is the first thing that comes to mind when you think of the playing career of Gareth Southgate? Anyone vote for England's Euro '96 semi-final shoot-out with Germany? What about Stuart Pearce? The Italia '90 World Cup semi-final, perhaps? But just how fair is this? Southgate won 57 England caps as well as two League Cups with Aston Villa and Middlesbrough, always held himself with dignity. Pearce played for England 78 times, was his country's captain, a legend at Nottingham Forest and one of the most feared opponents for many a right-winger.

What, then, does one think when the names Lionel Messi and Cristiano Ronaldo are mentioned? Two of the greatest players of all time? Goal after goal after goal? What about such descriptions as 'genius' or 'magic' or 'phenomenal'? To be fair, all apt descriptions. That being the case, guess which two players have missed more penalties than any others?

Messi 30, Ronaldo 29.

Saturday, 26 March 2022

England's international friendly game against Switzerland at Wembley provided another landmark for Harry Kane. His 49th goal for his country put him level with Bobby Charlton in the scoring charts, with only Wayne Rooney ahead of him on 53.

The Swiss took the lead in the game thanks to a well-placed header from Breel Embolo, with Luke Shaw hammering home the equaliser just before half-time. Kane's winner came from the penalty spot after VAR adjudged that Steven Zuber had handled from a corner.

Over in Spain, David Raya made his full international debut to become the first Brentford goalkeeper to represent his country. Ferran Torres opened the scoring for Spain before Albania equalised with five minutes to go. It was a strange one for Raya to concede his first international goal, as a long ball forward – more of an interception than a pass – was headed against Albanian forward Myrto Uzuni by Spanish defender Pau Torres, with the rebound pinging past Raya. Spain's winner came in the last minute from Dani Olmo.

Yoane Wissa scored for the Democratic Republic of Congo in their 1-1 draw with Morocco in the first leg of their World Cup play-off. The second leg is on Tuesday.

Finally, he wasn't going to be outdone by any of his team-mates, was he? Who? Oh, come on, as if you don't know who I'm talking about! Denmark's friendly with the Netherlands in Amsterdam saw Christian Eriksen's return to international football. He came on as a second-half substitute and, with his first touch of the ball – his *first touch* – he steered it into the top corner of the net. Denmark were beaten 4-2 but the main thing was Eriksen being introduced back into the international fold. Just where will the Christian Eriksen story end? Is he going to lead the Danes to World Cup glory? Let's just settle for his leading the Bees to Premier League safety, shall we?

Tuesday, 29 March 2022

It is reported in the *Daily Record* that Bayern Munich youngster Christopher Scott is the subject of a transfer tug of war between Brentford and Celtic. Scott is an attacking midfielder of Ghanian descent who had represented Germany at youth level but has seen his first-team chances limited. It's another one of those let's wait and sees.

England's second friendly of the international break ended in a 3-0 victory over the Ivory Coast, with former Brentford striker Ollie Watkins, now at Aston Villa, opening the scoring. Further goals from Raheem Sterling and Tyrone Mings sealed the win, in what is now the national team's record run without defeat. The last time England lost (not included are penalty shoot-outs – anyone remember last summer's European Championship Final against Italy?) was a 2-0 defeat to Belgium in 2020, 22 games ago.

Unfortunately there was World Cup heartbreak for both Yoane Wissa and Frank Onyeka as the Democratic Republic of Congo and Nigeria were beaten in their respective play-off matches. Wissa's Congolese team lost 4-1 to Morocco in Casablanca, with Nigeria bowing out on the away goals rule after a 1-1 draw with Ghana after the first leg had ended scoreless.

In happier news, Christian Eriksen was back at the Parken Stadium in Copenhagen, the scene of you know what. He was given the captain's armband for the friendly with Serbia and led by example as he steered in a cracking goal from the edge of the box, the third in a 3-0 win. He departed the action after 80 minutes to a standing ovation, handing the captain's armband to Kasper Schmeichel.

Friday, 1 April 2022

A few media outlets are reporting that Brentford are among the frontrunners to sign Scotland international Aaron Hickey. The young defender, who earned his first two Scotland caps this past week, is currently playing with Bologna. He was first mentioned in transfer news in January, and the talk is refusing to go away. Reports say that Newcastle are also in the running for his signature, as are AC Milan if he chooses to stay in Italy. The suggestion is, however, that he may favour a move to London to secure more playing time than he may be guaranteed elsewhere.

One player who has put pen to paper on a Brentford contract is Vitaly Janelt. He has become the latest Bee to re-sign with the club, his new contract taking him to 2026.

'I think Vitaly is a prime example of when we succeed with our recruitment and development of a player,' was Thomas Frank's assessment. 'We are good at finding young talented players and maximising their potential. Vitaly came to us from the German second division, and we saw a lot of good things in him. He was able to come in and be part of the team right from the off.'

With Janelt signed up and speculation about Hickey, what about the player who Frank described earlier this season as 'potentially the greatest signing ever for the club'?

'I don't think it is any secret that we would like it to continue,' Frank told reporters when asked in his press conference about the possibility of keeping Christian Eriksen on. 'I'm pretty convinced that Christian is enjoying it here, but I am also convinced that nothing will be decided until the end of the season from either side. I guess I will get a lot of these questions every Friday and I will try to answer them in the best possible way, but I think it is clear that we would like to continue with Christian.'

Over in Qatar, the draw for next winter's World Cup (it still doesn't sound quite right, does it?) takes place. England are the seeds in Group B and are drawn to play against Iran, the USA and the winners of the play-offs involving Scotland, Wales and Ukraine, which are yet to take place.

Brentford players (hopefully) representing the Bees in the finals could be David Raya in the Spanish squad, Saman Ghoddos of Iran, and Denmark could be featuring three Bees in Christian Eriksen, Mathias Jensen and Christian Nørgaard.

The opening game of the finals will be the hosts, Qatar, against Ecuador.

What are the chances, then, of England meeting Denmark in the final? If both teams win their group and continue to progress, they will meet in the quarter-finals; if one of them wins their group and the other qualifies as runners-up, a final meeting is possible.

Saturday, 2 April 2022

Brentford travelled the short distance to Chelsea knowing that only Manchester City have come away from Stamford Bridge with three points this season. The Bees were not overawed, though, and started the game well. Ivan Toney had a couple of efforts, one a header from a cross from Bryan Mbeumo but he was stretching a bit too much to direct his header on target, and one where his low shot was saved by Édouard Mendy low at the near post. For Chelsea, Mason Mount fired wide and Hakim Ziyech brought the best out of David Raya. Mount found Ziyech in a bit of space on the right, he cut inside and his effort was heading into the top corner but for a flying Raya who tipped it over the crossbar.

It was still scoreless at the break, but it didn't take the home team long to break the duck in the second half. Antonio Rüdiger picked up the ball 30 yards from the

Brentford goal and let fly. The ball rocketed past Raya and in off the post.

Brentford, though, didn't give their hosts time to settle and build on their lead. Almost immediately they were level. Christian Nørgaard found Mbeumo on the edge of the penalty area and Mbeumo knocked the ball to the in-rushing Vitaly Janelt who drilled his shot past Mendy.

Four minutes later, Timo Werner found himself in on goal but Kristoffer Ajer made a last-ditch block and the ball went out for a corner. The kick was cleared away and Mbeumo turned past Ziyech and his pace took him clear. As the Chelsea defenders came to close him down, he slipped the ball inside to Christian Eriksen who had galloped up in support. As Mendy came out to him, Eriksen touched his shot over him to net his first Brentford goal and put the Bees 2-1 up.

Shortly afterwards, a long clearance from Raya found Toney who knocked it on to Mbeumo who gave it straight back to his strike partner. Toney's first-time pass pierced the Chelsea defence and Janelt found himself one on one with Mendy. The angle was tight but he lofted the ball over the keeper and Brentford had a two-goal lead. It was a lovely team goal and, from being one down, 12 minutes later they were 3-1 ahead. Janelt has only just signed a new contract and, if this is the upshot, then get him to sign weekly deals!

Chelsea, as you would expect, piled on the pressure to get back into the game and Raya was called into action to stop N'Golo Kanté, then Havertz thought he had reduced the arrears when he converted from a cross but VAR showed that he had used his hand to control the ball and the goal was chalked off. The same player also headed wide, but when the next goal arrived it was another for Brentford.

Yoane Wissa had only been on the pitch for two minutes after replacing Mbeumo and, with his first touch of the ball, he knocked it in after Eriksen had played a short free kick to Nørgaard who crossed high into the box. Toney got a touch on it, the Chelsea defence failed to clear properly and Wissa ran on to the loose ball to hit it home past Mendy. Chelsea 1 Brentford 4.

Yes, I know – rub your eyes and read that again. Chelsea 1 Brentford 4. Chelsea are the reigning European champions and Brentford are a bus stop in Hounslow. It was the first time the Bees had won at Stamford Bridge since 1939. And there is no way that anyone can say the victory, and the margin of victory, was undeserved.

After the game, Thomas Frank was, as you can imagine, delighted, 'In football you work so hard, so many hours, every day, every week, every month, every year, and a lot of times you don't think you get what you deserve for all the hard work you put in, you can't control all the randomness in football. Today everything clicked and winning here at Stamford Bridge against the European champions with a well deserved almost complete performance, that's a little bit unreal.'

He was, of course, asked about Eriksen scoring his first goal for the club, '"Please save some goals for Brentford after scoring two for Denmark," I said to him. Christian is a top player, it's an ongoing fairytale and I'm very pleased, of course. What he brings to the team in terms of ability on the ball, calmness, you can always give it to Christian and he will find a solution, plus he will always provide goals or assists. He gives to the team with his personality – he's not a big presence like Ivan – but he's a big presence on the ball and the way he presents himself.'

Regarding the Toney-Mbeumo partnership, Frank commented, 'I think both of them are very dynamic and have done unbelievably well for us. Ivan could have scored some goals, but I think sometimes people forget how good a link-up player and a good passer he is. That pass for Vitaly was perfectly weighted.

'But Bryan Mbeumo I think actually deserves more praise today. Why I always play him is I trust him because he presses high, he works defensively hard, he runs in behind and he is also a goal threat. Today I'm just very, very proud of being part of Brentford with these players and staff, and I could enjoy the moment with the fans. Coming here to Stamford Bridge and winning 4-1, and deserving to win with an almost complete performance, it's a big moment for me personally.'

Chelsea: Mendy; Azpilicueta, Silva, Rüdiger, Alonso (James 55); Mount, Loftus-Cheek, Kanté (Lukaku 64); Ziyech, Havertz, Werner (Kovačić 64)

Brentford: Raya; Ajer, Jansson, Pinnock; Roerslev, Eriksen, Nørgaard, Janelt (Jensen 81), Henry (Canós 88); Toney, Mbeumo (Wissa 85)

On *Match of the Day*, the three studio pundits quite rightly purr over Brentford's performance. Gary Lineker calls the win 'an absolutely truly stunning victory, probably one of the best in their history'. Alan Shearer agrees with Thomas Frank about the front two, saying, 'It's not very often you see two top class centre-halves like Rudiger and Silva given the runaround like they were today from Mbeumo and Toney. They didn't score but they didn't half play their part in the game, and they made it very, very difficult for that Chelsea defence.' Micah Richards, though, focuses on Eriksen, 'He's totally transformed the way they play. He was all over the pitch. Brentford only had 30 per cent possession today but it's what they did with it, and I just though he was excellent. He's always looking forward and it's just effortless and this is what Brentford have been missing.'

Sunday, 3 April 2022

In a piece by Jamie Redknapp for the *Mail on Sunday* today, the former Liverpool midfielder says that he hopes Christian Eriksen stays at Brentford.

'He's writing a new chapter with a lovely club, and it would be nice to see him continue his footballing fairytale,' says Redknapp. 'Eriksen may have his pick of clubs when he's a free agent in the summer, but he seems happy at Brentford and I'd like to see him thrive there.'

Monday, 4 April 2002

Christian Nørgaard is interviewed on talkSPORT following the sensational win at Chelsea. Not only was it a great day for the club, it was also a milestone for him as he made his 100th appearance in Brentford colours.

'It's hard to describe,' he said. 'Coming to Chelsea as a Brentford fan for the first time in the Premier League and winning 4-1 must feel unbelievable. I'm sure our fans had a good night out and celebrated with lots of beers. It's a massive win. I'm not going to say we have survived in the Premier League already, but this was certainly a big, big step towards that.

'We are all still aware we have a job to finish, but the belief in the squad is that we should aim as high as possible and that means more than just avoiding relegation. We are all very happy with the win but also the performance. To go to Stamford Bridge and win 4-1, it's a feeling that is quite hard to describe.'

Friday, 8 April 2022

Yoane Wissa and Frank Onyeka have spoken to BBC Sport Africa about how they have settled into life at Brentford. Both players were signed in the pre-season, Wissa from Lorient in France and Onyeka from Danish club Midtjylland.

'I'm still dreaming,' said Wissa. 'I'm dreaming with my eyes, you know? It was hard at the beginning because I came from another country, playing with new players, a new language. I think it's the intensity, to be honest, because when you're watching TV you don't feel the intensity. But when you go out on to the pitch you feel the intensity, the hardness, the work, because the people work hard to be here.'

Wissa began his career with Châtearoux before moving to Angers. A couple of loan spells followed, one at Stade Laval and another with Ajaccio, and he made a permanent switch to Lorient. Wissa established himself in the Lorient side, helping the team to the Ligue 2 championship in 2020. At the end of the following season he crossed the Channel to newly promoted Brentford.

'For me,' confirmed Onyeka, 'playing in the Premier League at this time is a dream come true. I came from Denmark straight into the Premier League. It's not been easy. I'll say it is really a massive step. When I first came, I played a lot of games, went to the AFCON [Africa Cup of Nations] and I've not been in the team that much. Normally they say they don't give the players a song, but my first game I got a song from the fans, which is really nice because I feel like "oh, the fans are close to the players, they love the players". I think it goes "Super, super Frank, super, super Frank, super, super Frank", and then they say something in between that I don't really know!'

Onyeka moved to Midtjylland from Ebedei in Nigeria and quickly established himself in the Danes' midfield. He played over 100 games from Midtjylland and earned his transfer to Brentford on the back of his performances in the 2020/21 season, including ten in European competition.

Sunday, 10 April 2022

West Ham arrive at the Community Stadium looking for a win to help them in their quest for a European place next season. They are currently in sixth position and look to be in a fight with Arsenal, Tottenham and Manchester United for fourth, which will secure qualification for next season's Champions League. Liverpool and Manchester City are battling it out for the title and Chelsea look to be fairly safe in third.

Ivan Toney and Bryan Mbeumo's partnership caused problems for the Hammers right from the off. Mbeumo had a decent chance from a Rico Henry cross, but his header didn't really test Łukasz Fabiański. He did test the keeper shortly afterwards, though. David Raya's kick was flicked on by Yoane Wissa and Toney's first-time through ball found Mbeumo on the corner of the penalty area. His snap shot forced Fabiański into a flying save at his near post. Not long before half-time, the Toney-Mbeumo link ended with Mbeumo's attempted curling effort flying past the far post.

Just before the break, a dangerous free kick from Christian Eriksen flicked off the head of West Ham's Czech defender Vladimír Coufal and landed on the roof of his own net with Fabiański beaten. From the resultant corner, the ball pinged around dangerously in the area and ended up with Eriksen on the edge. He took aim but didn't hit it as he would probably have liked and was denied by Fabiański's diving save.

A couple of minutes after the resumption, Kristoffer Ajer found Toney in a bit of space. He steered the ball first time into the path of the on-rushing Mbeumo who sped past his marker and clinically knocked the ball beyond Fabiański and in at the near post.

Brentford continued to press, and it wasn't long before they had a second. Christian Nørgaard found Henry in a bit of space on the left wing and, after a one-two with Wissa, made his way to the byline and crossed to Mbeumo who was waiting at the far post. Mbeumo knocked it back across goal for Toney to nod past a helpless Fabiański.

It could have got even better for the Bees, but Mbeumo volleyed over after Vitaly Janelt had crossed following a bit of a scramble in the West Ham goalmouth.

As for the visitors, the closest they came was in the closing stages when former Brentford man Saïd Benrahma had a long-range effort deflected on to the roof of the net.

That's four wins out of five in the league, following the victories over Chelsea, Burnley and Norwich, a run spoilt only by the loss at Leicester. It was also Brentford's first double of the season, after having beaten the Hammers 2-1 at the London Stadium in October.

'I think it was close to a complete performance,' said a delighted Thomas Frank afterwards. 'It was the first time all season that we have more or less controlled the game from the minute one to minute 90. Winning 2-0 against a very good side, a side in the quarter-final of the Europa

League and challenging for the top four, and restricting them to just five shots, that's "wow" for me. I'm very proud of the performance, it was possibly even more complete than the Chelsea one. The way we did it shows how far we have come. It is a combination of a top performance and a good win, that's the big thing. Of course I look at the table, but I want to focus on the next game.'

Brentford: Raya; Ajer (Roerslev 82), Zanka, Pinnock, Henry; Janelt (Jensen 69), Nørgaard, Eriksen; Mbeumo (Canós 78), Toney, Wissa

West Ham United: Fabiański; Coufal, Dawson, Zouma (Diop 29), Cresswell; Souček, Rice; Bowen, Lanzini (Benrahma 57), Fornals; Antonio (Vlašić 66)

Monday, 11 April 2022

Ivan Toney is today quoted in the *Evening Standard* that he is sure that Christian Eriksen will extend his stay at Brentford beyond the end of the season:

'He sets a certain standard for himself and the team and we have to come up to that and play above that, so with him coming in its great for all of us. I'm sure he will be here [next season], let's see what happens.'

On the subject of whether he feels that the team are safe from relegation after yesterday's win, Toney's response was, 'Yeah, 100 per cent. I felt like we were safe before, the players we have got in the team. I feel like we've got more than enough to stay in the league. We were feeling closer and closer and better. I think I was more happy for Bryan to score [against West Ham] than myself. That is the partnership we have. We know each other's games, he knows the runs I will make and I do his. He puts it in the danger zone and I'll be there.'

13 August 2021 – Sergi Canós scores Brentford's first ever Premier League goal, against Arsenal at the Community Stadium

Brentford 2 Arsenal 0, Premier League life gets off to a dream start

Ethan Pinnock celebrates after scoring against Liverpool

David Raya thwarts West Ham's Jarrod Bowen during Brentford's 2-1 victory at the City of London Stadium

Rico Henry nets against Newcastle in a 3-3 thriller at St James' Park

Ivan Toney slots home the only goal of the game against Everton from the penalty spot

Thomas Frank after the victory over Everton

Christian Nørgaard gets to grips with Cristiano Ronaldo during Manchester United's visit to the Community Stadium

Yoane Wissa and Mads Roerslev, Brentford's scorers in their 2-1 win over Aston Villa

The greatest signing in Brentford's history? Christian Eriksen resurrects his career in west London …

… makes his Brentford debut against Newcastle at the Community Stadium …

… and scores his first Brentford goal against Chelsea at Stamford Bridge.

The greatest result in the club's history? Pontus Jansson and David Raya after beating Chelsea 4-1

Ivan Toney completes his hat-trick in a vital 3-1 win at Norwich

Kristoffer Ajer slots home against Southampton for his first goal in Brentford colours.

Vitaly Janelt in control against West Ham.

Rico Henry heads Brentford's winner against Everton at Goodison Park.

Brentford's last goal of the 2021/22 season as Sergi Canós' header hits the back of the Leeds net.

Thomas Frank speaks to the supporters after the last game of Brentford's historic first Premier League season.

Thanks, everyone – see you next year!

Tuesday, 12 April 2022

It is widely reported that a whole host of clubs are queueing up to sign Christian Eriksen when he becomes a free agent again in the summer. His old club Tottenham are, naturally, one of those mentioned and have been linked ever since he started playing again at Brentford. For a while now, if you believe what is written, they have been in a race with Manchester United for his signature assuming, of course, he doesn't continue on with the Bees. Now, though, there are other names being talked about as possible destinations. Newcastle, with the money from their new Saudi Arabian owners, have apparently entered the fray, along with Aston Villa, Crystal Palace, West Ham and Everton. The thing is, if it turns out that Eriksen does say that he will be leaving Brentford when the season ends, you'll be hard pushed to find a club who won't be interested in taking him on.

It is also suggested that Shaktar Donetsk winger Mykhaylo Mudryk is back on Brentford's radar. Reports of their potential interest first surfaced in December, and he is once again being linked. Mudryk has played a handful of games for Donetsk and spent some time on loan with both Arsenal Kyiv and Desna Chernihiv. His name keeps coming up in connection with a transfer to London, so maybe that is something to look out for in the summer.

Wednesday, 13 April 2022

So how is the relegation battle going, then? We know that Brentford got another three points to pull further clear at the weekend, but what about elsewhere?

Newcastle arrested a recent slump to get back to winning ways. A 1-0 victory over Wolves turned things around after they had lost their previous three, with Leeds

3-0 winners over Watford and Norwich beating Burnley 2-0. The loss at Carrow Road has plunged the Clarets right back into the mire. They had previously beaten Everton to give themselves a morale-boosting three points, but the defeat puts them right back in trouble again. Everton beat Manchester United by a single goal to give their survival hopes a lift, although they sit just above the relegation zone on 28 points. Below them, Burnley have 24, Watford are on 22 and Norwich occupy the bottom spot with 21. Above Everton in 16th are Leeds with 33 points, then come Newcastle on 34 and then Southampton (where did they suddenly come from!?) who have 36, the same as Brentford.

I can't really believe that I am writing that Everton are in the mix to go down. I mean, they're Everton, one of the biggest and most successful teams in English football. Aside from Arsenal, who have been in the top flight since the 1919/20 season, Everton have been in the top division longer than anyone else, since 1954/55. Surely they are too good to go down, aren't they? The thing is though, the table never lies. If you are relegated it shows that, after a 38-game season, you were one of the worst three sides. It is the same at the top. Nobody has ever won the league championship by fluke and not deserved to do so. You can win the FA Cup if things are going for you a bit, but that is only six games (or eight if you are outside the top two divisions and don't enter the competition in the third round). The league, though, is different. Where you finish at the end of the season is where you deserve to finish. Which other teams have been 'too good to go down'?

In the 1992/93 season, the dreaded phrase kept being repeated about Nottingham Forest. Under Brian

Clough they had been league champions and won the European Cup twice in successive years, but in his final season, despite having players such as Stuart Pearce, Roy Keane and Clough's son Nigel in their ranks, Forest went down.

Ten years later, in 2002/03, it was West Ham's turn. Four years previously they had finished fifth, the second-highest league position in their history, but here they slipped through the relegation trapdoor even though their squad included David James, Glen Johnson, Nigel Winterburn, Rio Ferdinand, Joe Cole, Michael Carrick, Freddie Kanouté, Les Ferdinand and Paolo Di Canio. Too good to go down? On paper, absolutely. As we all know, though, football is played on grass, not on paper.

The biggest event of all, perhaps, happened at the end of the 1973/74 season. Norwich and Southampton were relegated, but who went down with them? Manchester United. Six years before, in 1968, they had won the European Cup with a squad that included Alex Stepney, Paddy Crerand, Nobby Stiles, Bobby Charlton, Denis Law (although he missed the final due to injury) and George Best. Now, though, they were a shadow of their former selves and learned the hard way that name and reputation mean nothing.

Are we adding the Everton team of 2021/22 to that list? They have some tough fixtures left, including matches against Liverpool, Leicester twice, Chelsea and Arsenal. Then again, their win against United might just have given them the kick they needed.

It's even closer at the top, although only two teams are in it for the championship. Manchester City and Liverpool fought out a 2-2 draw on Sunday to leave City top with 74 points and Liverpool second, just a single point behind. Both teams have seven games remaining. Any slip-ups now could prove costly. The two play each other next weekend as well, this time in the FA Cup semi-final, and they are both still in the Champions League, with their quarter-final second legs being played tonight, City against Atlético Madrid and Liverpool v Benfica. The best two teams in the land at the moment? Without a doubt.

Thursday, 14 April 2022

The *Northern Echo* is reporting that Newcastle are confident of sealing a deal for Christian Eriksen in the summer, ahead of the other clubs who are reportedly interested in him. The newspaper says that Newcastle are looking for a flagship signing and Eriksen is the man who fits the bill. Newcastle's Saudi-based backers showed in the January transfer window that they are willing to provide the finance that manager Eddie Howe needs and, with Eriksen available on a free transfer the thought is even more appealing.

German sports magazine *Kicker* has published an interview with Vitaly Janelt. In it, Janelt says that the German national team manager, Hansi Flick, has spoken with him about a call-up. Janelt is quoted as saying, 'I met him by chance when we played Arsenal in February. That's when he ran into me in the tunnel and we had a quick chat. Because Bernd Leno was sitting on the bench at Arsenal, he actually had to be there because of me. He also confirmed that to me. I think that he has me on his radar.'

Janelt has so far represented Germany at Under-15, 17, 19, 20 and 21 level. He began his career at RB Leipzig before moving to VfL Bochum. He joined Brentford in 2020 and has been a fixture in the midfield ever since.

He was also asked if he would return to Germany if a Bundesliga club registered interest in signing him:

'I'm very relaxed here. Whatever comes comes, but I'm not waiting for an offer. Before the extension [the contract extension signed a couple of weeks ago] there were enquiries from the Bundesliga and other major leagues. At the moment I am happy at Brentford.'

Friday, 15 April 2002

Shock news comes out of Burnley today as they announce that manager Sean Dyche has been relieved of his duties after ten years at the club. Dyche joined the Clarets in 2012 when he succeeded Eddie Howe, who had left for Bournemouth. He led Burnley to promotion into the Premier League in the 2013/14 season, but they returned to the Championship the following year. In 2015/16 they were again promoted and each season since it has been generally regarded that Dyche had been doing a terrific job in keeping them up. He even guided them into the Europa League for the 2018/19 season, the first time Burnley had qualified for European competition for 51 years.

Burnley chairman Alan Pace released a press statement reading, 'Firstly, we would like to place on record our sincere thanks to Sean and his staff for their achievements at the club over the last decade. During his time at Turf Moor, Sean has been a credit both on and off the pitch, respected by players, staff, supporters and the wider football community. However, results this season have been disappointing and, while this was an incredibly difficult decision with eight crucial games of the campaign remaining, we feel a change is needed to give the squad the best possible chance of retaining its Premier League status.'

Dyche's sacking means that he is the tenth Premier League manager to lose his job this season behind Xisco Muñoz, Steve Bruce, Nuno Espírito Santo, Daniel Farke, Dean Smith, Ole Gunnar Solskjær, Rafa Benítez, Claudio Ranieri and Marcelo Bielsa. Burnley's Under-23 coach Mike Jackson takes temporary charge.

Thomas Frank was asked for his reaction during his press conference today. 'I am massively surprised,' he said. 'I do not know what happened behind the scenes, but looking from the outside, and as Brentford head coach, there are a lot of things we can learn from a club like Burnley. They were promoted, relegated and then promoted again and they have been here six or seven years in the Premier League. It is remarkable what they have done. Sean Dyche and his coaching staff and everyone at the club have done an unbelievable top job.

'I think Sean Dyche deserves a lot of credit and they should build a statue of him outside Turf Moor because what he has done is incredible, every season going into the Premier League with probably bottom three or four budget and then still being able to compete. And not just survive, but to get at least a couple of top-ten places, is a fantastic, remarkable job. Looking from the outside, I think they would have had a better chance keeping him to survive because he knows everything. But, of course, I don't know everything.'

As one club says goodbye to its manager, it appears that another is close to appointing their next one. Manchester United are seemingly reaching an agreement with Ajax boss Erik ten Hag to take over at Old Trafford. Interim boss Ralf Rangnick has been in charge of team affairs since the dismissal of Solskjær in November.

Saturday, 16 April 2022

Brentford make the trip to Hertfordshire today knowing that victory at Watford will have a big impact on the rest of the season. The bottom five – Norwich, Watford, Burnley, Everton and Leeds – are beginning to look like they are coming slightly adrift and need to start picking up some points. They can't really afford to let the teams higher up the table get too far ahead with games beginning to run out. It's going to be a tough afternoon for Brentford.

The opening period saw the teams trying to suss each other out, with most of the action happening in the midfield. On the 15-minute mark, however, Brentford got their noses in front. Ethan Pinnock launched a long throw into the Watford danger area which was flicked on at the near post by Kristoffer Ajer. As the ball fell, Christian Nørgaard arrived unmarked to sweep the ball past Watford keeper Ben Foster.

After conceding, the home side began to get more of a hold of the game and the efforts on goal began to come without really testing David Raya too much. João Pedro fired wide from long range and Ismaïla Sarr was thwarted by an important Rico Henry block. In fact, the closest Watford came to equalising was when Ajer's miskick flew past Raya but, fortunately for him, also went past the post.

Early in the second half, Ivan Toney had a chance to make it 2-0. He escaped the Watford defence to get on to the end of a Christian Eriksen free kick but he only half-hit his shot and it bounced wide of the goal. Almost immediately, Brentford were made to pay. A cross from Kiko Femenía just evaded Sarr but the loose ball came to Emmanuel Dennis who had time to set himself before firing it into the roof of the net. The assistant referee's flag was raised for offside against Sarr, but the VAR check overruled the call and the match was level.

Watford pressed for the winner, hemming Brentford in. Samir dragged an effort just wide and Dennis had a free kick touched on to the bar by Raya. As for Brentford, the closest they came was from a speculative effort from Toney from fully 35 yards that caught Foster unawares but bounced just wide.

As the 90 minutes passed and the game entered time added on, Watford broke forward once more. Joshua King found a bit of space on the left and teed up Dennis. His effort was blocked but the loose ball fell to Moussa Sissoko six yards out. A last-gasp challenge from Pontus Jansson hooked the ball away from Sissoko but, at the same time, also took it away from Raya who had come out to meet it. King pounced but could only hit the post. The ball bounced out straight to Imran Louza who had the simplest of tasks to tap in and win the game for Watford. Inexplicably, though, he somehow managed to knock his effort wide from the edge of the six-yard box, right in the middle of the goal. Nobody in the ground could believe he had missed and, to compound his misery, Brentford went straight up the other end and claimed the points themselves. Bryan Mbeumo was impeded and from the resulting free kick, Eriksen found Jansson powering through the defence to nod in the winner. It was an amazing finish to the match, a match that was ultimately won in Scandinavia. A goal each from Denmark and Sweden with assists from Denmark and Norway.

'It's been in many ways a crazy season for us, a remarkable season,' said Thomas Frank afterwards. 'We are now on 39 points and we will try to keep focused on winning the next game and finishing as high as possible. We always wanted to be an asset to the Premier League, we always wanted to finish as high as possible, or aim as high as possible, always wanted to focus on the next game, always have that laser focus. I think that's why we are on 39 points. That's why we did well in the beginning, that's why we came through the wobble, that's why we are doing very well now. I'm just happy that we are on a decent amount of points, but I want more.'

Watford manager Roy Hodgson was asked what he made of Brentford's season. 'They are organised, and they are strong,' he responded. 'They know the type of football that they want to play, and all the players have bought into that. They have some very good individuals. They had that even before Christian arrived and now they've added that side of their game.

'They are always going to be a very, very difficult team to beat because there are no obvious failings in their team, there's no obvious weakness, and they do have some very, very good strengths. Not least of all their long throw and their corners and wide free kicks to all the big players they have. They are where they are because that is where they deserve to be. I wouldn't go as far as to say that they really deserve to be going back to Brentford with three points today, I don't know their performance really merited that. But I mean, I would say that their position in the league, and what they've done in the league, is a credit to the club and in particular to Thomas Frank and his staff and all the players he's worked with. They are where they are because that's where they deserve to be.'

Watford: Foster; Femenía (Cathcart 87), Kabasele, Samir, Kamara; Sissoko, Louza, Kucka (Cleverley 84); Sarr, João Pedro (King 84), Dennis

Brentford: Raya; Ajer, Jansson, Pinnock (Bech Sørensen 21), Henry; Janelt (Jensen 74), Nørgaard, Eriksen; Mbeumo, Toney, Wissa (Ghoddos 66)

Sunday, 17 April 2022

This year's FA Cup Final will be between Liverpool and Chelsea. The semi-finals were played at Wembley this weekend, with Liverpool defeating Manchester City 3-2 and Chelsea beating Crystal Palace 2-0.

The first semi-final to be played at Wembley was in 1991 when Tottenham and Arsenal were drawn against each other. The traditional venues for semi-finals were Villa Park, Hillsborough (we don't need to go into what happened there two years previous), Old Trafford and stadiums of that ilk, but in 1991 the FA decided that the only sensible option was to stage this particular occasion at Wembley. This would stop 50,000 people travelling from north London up to Birmingham, or Manchester, or wherever, causing chaos on the roads and reducing any potentially volatile situations. The rivalry was, and still is, a deadly one. The Wembley option here – Stamford Bridge was the other potential venue considered – was a reasonable one.

Two years later, in 1993, the two sides were drawn to play each other again, with the other semi-final being a Sheffield derby, Wednesday against United. The FA again decided to use Wembley and this time both matches were played there, one on the Saturday and one on the Sunday. For no apparently obvious reason the 1994 semis were also played at Wembley, but a return to other neutral grounds was made in 1995. In 2003, the FA announced that from 2008 all semi-finals would be played at the new Wembley Stadium once it had been built.

Every year at semi-final time, there are football supporters of a certain age (I hold my hands up, here) asking why the matches are being played at Wembley. For the first ten years of the competition, from 1872 to 1881, the semi-finals and finals were both played at the Kennington Oval, but from 1882 onwards, various neutral grounds up and down the country were used, as would be the case for 110 years until that Tottenham v Arsenal match of 1991.

There are generally two schools of thought about this. One says that it is nice to have the games at Wembley as it gives the supporters a good day out and more players the chance to sample the Wembley atmosphere and to say that they had played there. The other says that Wembley should be reserved for the finals and England internationals and that playing there should be the pinnacle of a player's career and should be something special. To play semi-finals there as well takes a little bit of the sparkle off the final and makes it slightly less hallowed ground. I guess it's just another one of those pointless debates as the FA will do exactly what they want anyway.

Tuesday, 19 April 2022

The results from the weekend mean that even if Brentford do not get any more points this season, they cannot be caught by Norwich and just two more points will put them out of the reach of Watford, the two teams who occupy the bottom two places in the league table. After his team were beaten by the Bees, Watford manager Roy Hodgson was asked whether his players were capable of keeping the club in the Premier League. Of course, he wasn't going to say no but, at the same time, he did acknowledge that it would be an extremely difficult task.

'One has to believe, one has to keep faith, one has to take some sort of heart from their desire and commitment and effort during the second half,' Hodgson told reporters. 'You just have to hope that in six times 95 minutes more, they will be able to do that. And maybe, who knows, we will pick up points where no one expects, and we will get ourselves back into the race. But it's not the right moment in time to start predicting that from the next game onwards we are now going to sweep the board and kill all opposition that we find in front of us. Because, if I say that, people will laugh at me.'

If Watford do win the rest of their matches they will amass 40 points, the amount that always seems to be the target. Time and time again we hear managers talking about the magic 40-point mark, but is it really the case?

If you look at the final tables from all the Premier League years since its inception in 1992 (or, more accurately, from the 1995/96 season due to the first three years having a Premier League of 22 teams), 40 points does seem to be fairly safe, but it is not a complete certainty. Both Sunderland and Bolton have been relegated with 40 points and in the 2002/03 season West Ham went down with 42. The average amount of points scored by teams who have finished in 18th position, the third relegation spot, is 35. The lowest points a 17th-placed team has scored is 28, by Fulham last season.

Will 40 points be enough this time? Burnley are currently 17th on 25 with seven games to go so, if they win all seven, they will end on 46. Considering they have won only four matches all season, you would say that they are up against it to avoid the drop. It is still fairly difficult to predict, though, as Burnley's remaining fixtures include games against Watford and Newcastle and they still have both matches to play against Aston Villa, who have slid down the league to suddenly be sixth from bottom. As games run out, though, it is looking more and more like three from Norwich, Watford, Burnley, Everton and Leeds.

Thursday, 21 April 2022

There is a lot of talk in the media surrounding the future of Ivan Toney. Clubs who are supposedly interested in taking him from Brentford include London rivals Arsenal and West Ham. The Gunners are short of strike power due to their sale of Pierre-Emerick Aubameyang to Barcelona in January and it is widely believed that Alexandre Lacazette will also be leaving north London in the summer. As for the Hammers, they are looking to build on their good showing this season. They are currently into the semi-finals of the Europa League and also challenging for fourth spot in the Premier League. The other club said to be interested in Toney is Newcastle United, where he had his first taste of the big time after his transfer from Northampton. Toney only made two appearances for Newcastle before being loaned out and eventually sold. Would he return there? Would he prefer to stay in London? Will he stay with the Bees? It will be interesting to see how many Brentford players are going to be linked with moves away as the season draws to a close, now that they have shown what they can do in the spotlight of the Premier League. It's going to be an interesting summer at the Community Stadium.

News comes out of Old Trafford this afternoon that Manchester United have appointed Erik ten Hag as their new team manager. He will make the move from Ajax at the end of the season, taking over as permanent boss from interim coach Ralf Rangnick. He will have a big job to do as, for a couple of years now, there has been scathing criticism of the team from the media, fans and former players alike.

Saturday, 23 April 2022

Another big day for Brentford, and also for Christian Eriksen, as Tottenham visit the Community Stadium. Eriksen, of course, played over 200 games for Tottenham before his move to Italy with Inter Milan. It is bound to be an emotional day for him.

Brentford started the match showing the confidence that comes with five wins out of the last six. The first sighter came when Bryan Mbeumo was fed by Mathias Jensen 20 yards out. Mbeumo took a touch but pulled his shot wide of Hugo Lloris's left-hand post. Mbeumo's strike partner Ivan Toney was a constant thorn in Tottenham's side, and it was his aerial strength that almost contributed the opening goal. Eriksen's corner was met powerfully by Toney from eight yards out but his header cannoned on to the crossbar and was scrambled clear by a relieved Tottenham defence. Not long beforehand, the same two players had combined but this time Toney's effort was blocked and cleared before he could get to the rebound.

In the second period, Brentford carried on where they left off and continued to take the game to their opponents. A mistake in the visitors' defence led to a chance for Eriksen but his long-range effort was deflected wide. The corner that followed was only half cleared by Lloris, Mads Roerslev played it back into the danger zone and Pontus Jansson's header had Lloris beaten but was headed off the line by

Harry Kane. The ball only dropped as far as Eriksen and this time Lloris got down well to keep out his low shot.

Still the home team pressed, and in the closing stages Eriksen floated in a free kick into the packed penalty area. Again it was Toney who won the ball and his header once more beat Lloris but this time he saw the ball bounce back off the far post. The ball came quickly back to Mbeumo whose snap shot hit the side netting.

Tottenham's closest attempt at breaking the deadlock was right at the end of the match when Dejan Kulusevski's cross was met acrobatically on the volley by Kane. His scissor kick beat the outstretched hands of David Raya but also beat the far post and went out to safety. It was pretty much the last piece of action as the final whistle blew to end an entertaining game with the Bees earning another good point, although they will be disappointed not to have won all three.

Had either of Toney's headers that came back off the woodwork gone in, it may well have been all three as their opponents didn't manage a single shot on target in the whole game. Another bonus was the reintroduction of Josh Dasilva to first-team action as he came on as a late substitute in place of Jensen.

After the match, Thomas Frank was delighted with his teams effort, especially considering the tinkering to the line-up that had to be made.

'Normally when we go to a back three we have Ethan Pinnock and Kristoffer Ajer and the next one in line is probably Zanka, so we decided to put Mads Roerslev in as an outside centre-back and then we normally would have played Sergi Canós, but he was also out, so we decided to play Saman Ghoddos,' he explained to reporters. 'We also had maybe our best performing player this season,

Christian Nørgaard, also out in the number six position. So, we have the second-best player in four positions up against a Tottenham side that are fighting for Champions League. That's a massive credit to the players, first and foremost, to the staff who have done everything to prepare them and to the structure we have in the team. And then, on top of that, we deserved to win. It's great.'

Brentford: Raya; Roerslev, Jansson, Bech Sørensen; Ghoddos (Wissa 78), Jensen (Dasilva 78), Janelt, Eriksen, Henry; Mbeumo, Toney

Tottenham Hotspur: Lloris; Romero, Dier, Davies; Royal (Moura 86), Bentancur, Højbjerg, Sessegnon (Sánchez 74); Kulusevski, Kane, Son

Tuesday, 26 April 2022

A glorious night for the Brentford B team as they won the London Senior Cup, beating Hendon on penalties. Managed by Neil MacFarlane, the Bees were 3-0 winners in the shoot-out after a 1-1 draw.

After 65 minutes it was Hendon who took the lead when Jayden Clarke shot past Brentford goalkeeper Ben Winterbottom, his effort going in off a post. With time beginning to run out, Brentford equalised when Nico Jones flicked an Alex Gilbert free kick past Hendon keeper Ethan Wady to take the match into extra time. No further goals were forthcoming, so the cup had to be decided on spot-kicks.

Samuel Corcoran stepped up to take Hendon's first kick but saw his shot fly over the crossbar. Ryan Trevitt made no such mistake with the next penalty and Brentford took the advantage. Taking Hendon's second kick, Christian Smith produced a carbon copy of Corcoran's effort to make it two misses out of two. Gilbert then fired home for the Bees to pile the pressure on Hendon's next penalty taker, Joe White. This time it was Winterbottom who denied Hendon a goal as he saved the kick leaving Myles Peart-Harris the chance to claim victory. He duly converted and the Bees claimed the trophy for the first time since 1898.

The match was played at Champion Hill, the home of Dulwich Hamlet. The stadium, incidentally, holds the record for the largest attendance for a league game outside of the English Football League when 16,254 attended Dulwich v Nunhead in 1931. It was also used in the 1948 Olympics, staging South Korea v Mexico.

Thursday, 28 April 2022

Ahead of Brentford's forthcoming match against Manchester United at Old Trafford on Monday evening, Thomas Frank tells his press conference that both Christian Nørgaard and Kristoffer Ajer are in the running to return to the team after injury.

Monday, 2 May 2022

'How do Manchester United overcome Brentford?' That was the question that Sky Sports studio guest Roy Keane was asked before kick-off at Old Trafford tonight. Just think about that for a moment. 'How do Manchester United overcome Brentford?'

No, they haven't exactly had the best season in their history and no, they're not going to finish in the top four, but just to have that question asked says an awful lot about how the Bees have been equipping themselves lately, doesn't it? It says an awful lot about how the players have adapted to life in the Premier League this past season and it says an awful lot about Thomas Frank and his coaching staff. How much does it say about them? Let's have a look at the cold hard facts and figures.

Manchester United have won 20 league championships, 12 FA Cups, 5 League Cups, 21 Charity/Community Shields and six European trophies. Brentford's best performance in the league was finishing fifth in the 1935/36 season, they have appeared in four FA Cup quarter-finals and one League Cup semi-final. United's squad currently have 1,019 international appearances between them, including three World Cup winners, two European Championship winners and a Copa América winner, while Brentford's has 274 caps, with 111 of them belonging to Christian Eriksen alone.

As it turns out, the answer to the question 'how do Manchester United overcome Brentford?' is 'give the ball to Cristiano Ronaldo'. It was one of those nights where Ronaldo decided he was going to turn it on. It was he who was the difference between the two sides. Right from the off he was full of flicks and tricks, a wide range of passing and was a constant threat. It was he who drove United on and it was he who provided the cutting edge, in doing so also making space for others.

The mood of the game could, however, have changed dramatically in the very first minute. Right from the kick-off, Christian Eriksen's long pass released Bryan Mbeumo in behind United's defence but Alex Telles recovered to get a challenge in just as Mbeumo was about to pull the trigger. Not long after, Kristoffer Ajer's cross was tipped over by a back-pedalling David De Gea as the Bees penned their hosts in.

The opening goal, scored after nine minutes, settled the home side. United's young forward Anthony Elanga chased down a long ball on the right flank and hooked the ball into the middle. Bruno Fernandes arrived first to knock the ball in past a helpless David Raya.

Having taken the lead, United suddenly looked a lot more assured and Ronaldo started to perform. Just before the interval, Juan Mata broke forward and played a ball into the middle for Ronaldo to fire it home first time. His joy was short-lived, however, as VAR showed that he was marginally offside and the goal was chalked off.

When the second goal did come, it was from the penalty spot. Ronaldo beat Rico Henry to the ball and, as he entered the penalty area, Henry's challenge knocked him from his feet and a spot-kick was awarded. Ronaldo picked himself up and made no mistake. Even though Raya guessed where Ronaldo would put his shot, it arrowed into the corner to give him no chance.

A third came when Ronaldo's cross hit Pontus Jansson but the ball diverted just wide of the post by a flying Raya. The corner was swung in and Raphaël Varane met it on the volley to convert.

As the game closed out, Brentford had a couple of chances to get on the scoresheet. Substitute Josh Dasilva's foray into the United box caused a bit of panic and the loose ball found its way back to him but Varane was there with a desperate challenge to block out the danger. Ivan Toney also had an opportunity but slipped at the vital moment when he found himself in a bit of space with only De Gea blocking his route to goal.

'I'm a bit disappointed,' said Thomas Frank afterwards. 'I think we could have performed better, especially in the first half. We started fantastic, the first five minutes, and then I felt that United were more on top of the game without creating chance after chance. They had one top moment for their 1-0 goal, so credit to them for that situation, but we had three against one in the box so it should be possible to avoid that.'

Manchester United: De Gea; Dalot, Lindelöf, Varane, Telles; Matić (Fred 71), McTominay; Elanga (Cavani 75), Mata (Jones 75), Fernandes; Ronaldo

Brentford: Raya; Ajer, Jansson, Bech Sørensen; Roerslev, Janelt (Dasilva 71), Nørgaard (Jensen 71), Eriksen, Henry; Toney, Mbeumo (Wissa 76)

Wednesday, 4 May 2022

The second legs of the Champions League semi-finals are played this midweek. Yesterday Liverpool overcame Spanish side Villarreal 3-2 after a 2-0 victory in the first leg. Today it was Manchester City's turn to see if they could make it an all-English final. Their first leg match with Real Madrid last week produced a 4-3 win and, as much as that was thrilling, the second leg tonight matched it for drama. City took the lead in the Santiago Bernabéu Stadium after 73 minutes to take firm control of the tie, but Madrid grabbed a late lifeline when Brazilian forward Rodrygo scored right on the 90. City were still heading through but a minute later, the same player scored again to take the game into extra time. Five minutes in Karim Benzema converted a penalty to complete a stunning comeback, Madrid held on and it is they who play Liverpool in Paris on 28 May. Tomorrow it is the turn of West Ham and Rangers to see if they can manage an all-British Europa League final. Both teams lost their first leg matches by a single goal,

West Ham 2-1 to Eintracht Frankfurt and Rangers 1-0 to RB Leipzig.

Thursday, 5 May 2022

West Ham were beaten 1-0 tonight to bow out of the Europa League 3-1 on aggregate to Frankfurt, but Rangers were 3-1 winners over Leipzig to secure an overall 3-2 victory, so the two play each other in the final in Seville on 18 May.

Saturday, 7 May 2022

This is potentially a big weekend. Let's look at the possible connotations.

If Brentford win their match with Southampton today and Leeds are beaten at Arsenal tomorrow, then Brentford are almost certainly safe from relegation. If results do work out this way, even if Brentford lost both of their remaining matches and Leeds won all of their remaining three, both teams would finish on 43 points. Brentford, however, are currently 23 goals better off on goal difference, and there is no way that would turn round in three games.

What about Burnley? Again, assuming Brentford get all three points today and Burnley are beaten by Aston Villa, the best the Clarets can achieve is also 43 points. Goal difference between the clubs is only four in favour of the Bees, so there is still a possibility that the Lancashire club can catch up and overtake. However, their remaining matches after today are against Tottenham, Villa again and Newcastle so, if they were to get 12 points out of their four games, that would be a monumental effort on their behalf.

Which brings us to Everton. They have had a bit of an upturn in the last few matches, having won two and drawn one of their last four. The most they can finish on is now

47. They play Leicester tomorrow and then face Watford, Brentford, Crystal Palace and Arsenal. They may have the upper hand in games left to play but, of course, they have to win them.

And what's this with Southampton all of a sudden? Almost out of nowhere they are now in the bottom six and, if Brentford do beat them today, the most points they can tally when the season ends will be 46. Their last two games are against Liverpool and Leicester, so they could be in for a nervous finish.

What this all means, then, is that Brentford need four more points to make it absolutely impossible to finish in the bottom three and suffer relegation. Realistically, though, Leeds, Burnley, Everton and Southampton are not going to all win all of their remaining fixtures, are they? Even if it came down to it, Brentford's destiny is still in their own hands as their last three games are all against teams below them – Southampton today, Everton next week and Leeds on the last day.

So, what am I actually saying, here? What I'm saying is that there are two ways to look at it, and these two ways are through the eyes of the two types of football fan that there are.

Firstly, the pessimist. Brentford are not safe yet and could still go down, so it is going to be a tense and nervous end to the season and all the good work that has been done since the season kicked off could be thrown away. Those brilliant victories against the likes of Arsenal and Chelsea will mean nothing.

Secondly, the optimist. Job done. There is no way that all teams below them will win all their remaining games. Thomas Frank and the boys have done a fantastic job and can look forward to more Premier League football next season.

As soon as the match started, Brentford took the game to their opponents. In the very first minute a chance almost fell to Christian Nørgaard from a long Mads Bech Sørensen throw but it just evaded Nørgaard's reach. A few minutes later, Rico Henry burst down the wing and fired in a low cross that was scrambled clear with Mathias Jensen lurking.

The early pressure soon told. Bryan Mbeumo broke away and crossed for Yoane Wissa but, just before Wissa was able to pounce, Southampton defender Jan Bednarek knocked it out for a corner. Christian Eriksen's kick reached Ivan Toney at the back post. Toney brought it down and fired it back across into the danger zone for Pontus Jansson to turn it in past Fraser Forster.

Barely a minute later it was two. Bech Sørensen found Wissa on the halfway line, and he touched the ball on to Eriksen as he burst forward. Eriksen's run was halted by a desperate lunge, but Wissa was following up and took the ball forward before calmly curling it into the net from the edge of the box. It was a stunning start to the game from Brentford, and Southampton were visibly rattled.

Not long after, Wissa had the chance to make it three but he somehow managed to put the ball over the crossbar from two yards after Eriksen's free kick had been drilled back across the goalmouth by Toney.

As the half wore on, Southampton began to get more into the game and Armando Broja found himself with a chance to pull one back, but he swung at the ball and completely missed it with only David Raya to beat. The ball was cleared away but only to Adam Armstrong whose long-range effort was acrobatically kept out by Raya. Armstrong did have the ball in the net as the half drew to a close, but the assistant referee's flag was raised and the goal was chalked off.

The second half was a more even affair and attempts on goal became rarer. Raya saved from both Armstrong and Mohamed Elyounoussi and the closest Brentford came to extending their lead was again from a long Bech Sørensen throw, but this time Toney was unable to force the ball home.

As the game was drawing to a close, Mbeumo and Eriksen linked up down the left, with Eriksen's cross causing confusion in the Saints' defence. Josh Dasilva's shot was blocked, with the loose ball falling to Nørgaard who touched it on to Kristoffer Ajer. He swivelled past the attentions of Mohammed Salisu and, as Forster came out to meet him, he slipped the ball through his former Celtic team-mate's legs to wrap up the points. It was Ajer's first goal in Brentford colours.

There was just time for another first as Nathan Young-Coombes came on as a late substitute for Jensen to make his first-team debut.

Brentford: Raya; Ajer, Jansson, Bech Sørensen, Henry; Jensen (Young-Coombes 87), Nørgaard, Eriksen; Mbeumo (Baptiste 81), Toney, Wissa (Dasilva 69)

Southampton: Forster; Walker-Peters, Bednarek, Salisu, Perraud; Ward-Prowse, Diallo (Elyounoussi 64); S. Armstrong (Romeu 83), Redmond; A. Armstrong, Broja

Sunday, 8 May 2022
It's official – Brentford will be a Premier League team again next season! Leeds were beaten 2-1 at Arsenal and are now nine points behind Brentford with three games left. If they

won all three, including against the Bees on the last day of the season, and Brentford lost their last two, they would draw level. There is, however, no way on earth they would overhaul what is now a goal difference imbalance of 27. It's a day to celebrate what a brilliant job has been done at the Community Stadium by all concerned.

Wednesday, 11 May 2022

There are a couple of transfer stories circulating today. The first is concerning the Brazilian defender Marquinhos Cipriano who is currently on loan at Sion in Switzerland from his parent club Shakhtar Donetsk. The online Spanish sports media company AS Sports is reporting that Sion will be looking to buy him permanently but are facing competition from clubs in Germany and England, namely Hertha Berlin, Stuttgart and Brentford.

The second story is surrounding Ivan Toney. The north-east local newspaper the *Evening Chronicle* reports that Callum Wilson believes Toney should ignore all the speculation about his future and that this club and that club will be considering taking him in the summer and stay at Brentford. The reason for this, according to Wilson, is his international ambitions.

'You talk about how he wants to play for England, and he's playing and scoring at Brentford,' Wilson is quoted as saying. 'You go to a bigger team, the competition is bigger, you might not even be playing as much and be on the bench a lot more. Really, then, you're not going to be in Gareth Southgate's mind, so you need to stay relevant and be the main guy. Yeah, he can go to another team, and he might take on that challenge and thrive, but there is always that risk. There are always going to be players, the higher you go, two or three of the same quality players in that position.'

Reading that back, you would think that they are actually quite wise words, especially considering that there has been talk of one or two clubs being interested in Toney, particularly Arsenal and Newcastle. Of those clubs, Arsenal are light on goalscorers at the moment having let Pierre-Emerick Aubameyang go to Barcelona in the January transfer window and with both Alexandre Lacazette and Eddie Nketiah coming to the end of their contracts. Newcastle, on the other hand, do have a few options, with their four main strikers including Allan Saint-Maximin, Joelinton, Chris Wood and, hang on a minute, who's this? It's Callum Wilson! So, the man who is warning Toney off a potential move to Newcastle due to the competition there is one of those providing that competition. Now, I'm not trying to be cynical here, but is he perhaps trying to limit the competition for himself? As he rightly said, 'There are always going to be players, the higher you go, two or three of the same quality players in that position.' And I'm sure that Wilson wants to keep that famous number nine shirt, doesn't he?

Friday, 13 May 2022

The Premier League has announced its nominees for the 2021/22 Manager of the Season award. The first two men on the shortlist are, inevitably, Pep Guardiola and Jürgen Klopp of Manchester City and Liverpool respectively. Guardiola's City are two games away from retaining the title, currently holding a three-point advantage over Liverpool. Klopp's team can still, of course, win the league but they are actually in the hunt for an unprecedented quadruple. Admittedly they need City to slip up, but they could still be champions, they are in this weekend's FA Cup Final against Chelsea, they are playing Real Madrid in the Champions League Final and they have already won the League Cup. It could be an amazing season for them.

Patrick Vieira of Crystal Palace is the third name on the list. He is in his first season as a Premier League manager and has transformed the way Palace are playing. They are an exciting team to watch now with some good flair players and are chasing a top-half finish.

The fourth nominee is Eddie Howe of Newcastle. He arrived at St James' Park with the team in pretty dire straits and staring relegation in the face. Yes, he had the backing of the new owners in the transfer market, but he has done a great job in the second half of the season to lead them not only to safety, but comfortably so.

The fifth and final candidate is Thomas Frank. What a fantastic accolade and, quite rightly, due recognition for what he has achieved with Brentford this season. Again, this is testament to how far the club have come. He is now literally being talked about in the same breath as Klopp and Guardiola.

Saturday, 14 May 2022

It is FA Cup Final day, with Liverpool taking on Chelsea in a repeat of February's League Cup Final. Just like that first encounter the match finished goalless and went to penalties to decide the winner. Unlike that first encounter, the shoot-out ended in a reasonable time but again it was Liverpool who took the trophy. In the regulation five shots, both teams missed once, César Azpilicueta hitting the post for Chelsea with Liverpool's miss coming from Sadio Mané who saw his effort saved by Édouard Mendy. In sudden death, Mason

Mount's shot was saved by Allison leaving Konstantinos Tsimikas to convert Liverpool's winner. Chelsea have now been runners-up in the last three FA Cup finals, in 2020 to Arsenal, 2021 to Leicester City and now 2022 to Liverpool. It is the first time a team has lost three in a row. It also means that Liverpool are still on for an historic quadruple. With the two domestic cup competitions in the bag, they are toe to toe with Manchester City for the league title and also into the Champions League final.

The website footballinsider247.com is claiming that Brentford, along with Southampton and West Ham, are interested in Bright Osayi-Samuel, who is currently playing for Turkish team Fenerbahçe. Osayi-Samuel was born in Nigeria before moving to England when he was a young boy. He made the breakthrough at Blackpool before moving to Queens Park Rangers, where he made over 100 appearances. He transferred to Fenerbahçe in January 2021 and can play either as a winger or full-back.

Sunday, 15 May 2022

Brentford's last two games of the season will have a big impact on who is relegated from the Premier League. Today they visit Goodison Park to take on Everton, with Leeds to come to the Community Stadium next week.

Everton boss Frank Lampard called on his players to start on the front foot and the club's supporters to get right behind the team from the off. And that was certainly what happened. From the moment the referee started the match the noise level inside the ground may well have been heard from west London, and Everton penned Brentford in. Their first decent chance came when Dominic Calvert-Lewin flicked on a long clearance from Jordan Pickford, with the ball landing to Vitaliy Mykolenko. David Raya came out to meet him and got a hand to his attempted lob. The loose ball fell to Richarlison who headed wide under pressure from Rico Henry. A short time later, the same player volleyed an effort wide, but the Toffees' fast start was soon rewarded. Anthony Gordon swung in a free kick, Richarlison hooked it on and the ball was diverted into the net off Calvert-Lewin's chest. It looked like it would be a long afternoon for the Bees, with Everton knowing a victory would keep them safe from relegation to the Championship.

Brentford's first clear-cut opportunity of the game came when Mathias Jensen launched a long clearance towards Ivan Toney as Everton pressed for a second. Toney got himself in front of Jarrad Branthwaite and then was floored as his heels were clipped as he moved clear. The referee not only awarded Brentford a free kick in a dangerous looking situation but, with Branthwaite the last man, a red card was brandished and Everton were down to ten men. Christian Eriksen hit the free kick just wide with Pickford beaten.

From that moment the game changed. Suddenly Brentford had the possession with Everton looking nervous. Jensen had saw chance go begging and Toney was causing all sorts of problems for the Everton back line. The equaliser came from an Eriksen corner. Pontus Jansson made himself a nuisance in the box and the ball fell out to Toney on the right. His low cross made its way to Yoane Wissa who swung it back into the danger zone and a deflection off the chest of Seamus Coleman took it past Pickford.

It was now Brentford who were pressing their opponents back and Toney had an effort which lacked the pace to beat

Pickford, then Bryan Mbeumo saw the keeper push his attempt away. Just on the verge of half-time, Richarlison reached another Calvert-Lewin flick and bisected Jansson and Mads Bech Sørensen, with the latter pulling him down. He picked himself up and stroked the penalty home and Everton were ahead at the break.

The second half continued with Brentford in the ascendancy. After an hour, an Eriksen corner was aimed at the near post where Wissa was waiting. His flicked header looped over Pickford and into the net at the back post to level the scores. As against Southampton last week, Brentford almost immediately scored again. Christian Nørgaard swung in a pinpoint cross from the right on Henry's head and he placed his header into the corner of the net to make it 3-2 to the visitors.

With two minutes remaining, any chance that Everton might have had of getting something out of the game disappeared when they received their second red card of the match. Substitute Salomón Rondón, who had only been on the pitch for four minutes, launched himself into a two-footed tackle on Henry right on the touchline, giving the referee little option but to issue the red. It capped off a miserable day for the Toffees – two players sent off and relegation from the top flight for the first time since the 1950/51 season still a possibility.

Everton: Pickford; Iwobi, Coleman (Rondón 84), Branthwaite, Holgate, Mykolenko; Gomes (Kenny 72), Doucouré; Richarlison, Calvert-Lewin, Gordon (Gray 72)

Brentford: Raya; Ajer (Dasilva 59), Jansson, Bech Sørensen (Janelt 45), Henry; Jensen, Nørgaard, Eriksen; Mbeumo, Toney, Wissa (Roerslev 76)

Tuesday, 17 May 2022

Thomas Frank is making headlines in Leeds today regarding the final match of the season on Sunday. It is a possibility that Brentford could relegate Leeds if they beat them at the Community Stadium and there has been some talk – not by Brentford, incidentally, but up in Yorkshire – that the Bees will be out for revenge. In the last few days, a video has resurfaced of Leeds players Kenny Dallas and Liam Cooper singing a song aimed at Frank after Leeds had won the Championship title at the end of the 2019/20 season. The tension between the sides comes from Frank's comments that Leeds would fear coming to Griffin Park when they were enduring a bad run of results. The game ended in a draw and Leeds went on to promotion while Brentford lost in the play-offs.

'First and foremost, we have to be very professional and win every game for the Brentford fans and also I think it's very important to respect the league and try to do everything we can because, if I was in that situation, I'd expect that from the other teams,' Frank is quoted as saying by Leeds Live. 'Of course, we will put our very best team out there and it's so important to understand we need to do our very best to win. It's nothing about Everton, Burnley or Leeds and I know at my press conference next week I will get a lot of questions about the story and about me and the video, but there is no story there from my perspective.'

Wednesday, 18 May 2022

Christian Nørgaard has been named both the Brentford Players' Player of the year and the Supporters' Player of the Year. It is just reward for Nørgaard who has been outstanding throughout the season, not only adding that extra bit of safety in front of the defence but also in starting and supporting many of Brentford's attacking plays. He wasn't the only winner as Sergi Canós won the Goal of the Season award for his opening-day strike against Arsenal, the Bees' first Premier League goal.

The Europa League Final between Rangers and Eintracht Frankfurt was played this evening, the German team taking the trophy. The game, played in Seville, was another decided by a penalty shoot-out, Frankfurt winning 5-4. The 90 minutes had finished 1-1 with Rangers taking the lead thanks to Joe Aribo and Rafael Borré equalising for Frankfurt. The victory gave Frankfurt their second European trophy, having won the UEFA Cup in 1980.

Sunday, 22 May 2022

The last day of Brentford's first Premier League season. There is an awful lot to play for today although, of course, the Bees themselves are safely in mid-table. Brentford could relegate Leeds as they are level on points with Burnley but have a far inferior goal difference. Burnley play Newcastle and must equal Leeds's result in order to survive.

It promises to be an equally tense afternoon at the top of the table too as either Manchester City or Liverpool can claim the title. City are one point in front and victory over Aston Villa, managed by Liverpool legend Steven Gerrard, will guarantee they retain the championship. Any dropped points, combined with a Liverpool win over Wolves, will mean the trophy goes to Merseyside. First, though, to Brentford v Leeds.

Leeds started the game pushing forward but were unable to carve out many dangerous opportunities. Jack Harrison played an inviting looking low cross into the goalmouth but there was nobody to capitalise, and Sam Greenwood had an effort fly over. Then, on the 20-minute mark, Leeds had the ball in the net. Harrison flicked it into the penalty area where Joe Gelhardt was arriving and he knocked it past David Raya. Leeds were on their way to safety. Hang on a minute, no they weren't. VAR showed that Gelhardt was slightly offside when he received the ball and the goal was cancelled. Hang on a minute, yes they were. Just as Gelhardt wasn't scoring, Newcastle were. Callum Wilson converted a penalty to move Burnley down into the third relegation spot and swap places with Leeds.

Brentford almost got back on level terms when Christian Eriksen's long crossfield pass found Bryan Mbeumo on the right wing. He skilfully played the ball through Junior Firpo's legs before finding Mathias Jensen, in the starting line-up in place of Christian Nørgaard, who had picked up a knock in training. Jensen's delicate chip almost caught Leeds keeper Illan Meslier out but, back-pedalling, he managed to tip the ball over the bar.

In the second half, the deadlock was broken due to an uncharacteristic mistake from Raya. He received a back-pass but played it out only to Leeds dangerman Raphina. He made his way into the box and took the ball round Raya but was taken down by the keeper's flailing leg for a clear-cut penalty. The same player picked himself up and slotted the ball home from the spot. Things got even better for Leeds a few moments later with the news that Burnley had gone two down, Wilson scoring again for Newcastle. Maxwell Cornet soon pulled one back for Burnley but Leeds were still in pole position to avoid the drop.

Brentford made three substitutions, one of which was Sergi Canós who replaced Rico Henry. He made a big impact after climbing off the bench and got the Bees back on level terms. Yoane Wissa teased the Leeds defence and floated a cross in towards Canós who headed the ball back across goal into the far corner of Meslier's net. It was a pinpoint header and it meant that the relegation jitters were back for Leeds. As Canós ran off to celebrate he removed his shirt and threw it up into the air, earning himself a yellow card. Two minutes later, Canós lunged in at Raphina as he made his way along the right wing, was shown a second yellow and therefore a red. He had been on the pitch for 12 minutes, scored and picked up two bookings. This left Brentford down to nine men as, just before Canós scored, Kristoffer Ajer had been forced to leave the pitch due to injury and so, with all three substitutions having already been made, the Bees were already down to ten.

Naturally, playing with two extra men, Leeds regained the impetus for the last ten minutes and pushed forward knowing that a Burnley equaliser against Newcastle could still send them down. With almost the last action of the season, Raphina swung in a corner that was knocked out by Josh Dasilva. The ball fell invitingly for Harrison who drove it back and into Raya's bottom-right corner to make it 2-1.

The result meant that Leeds were safe and Burnley, who were beaten 2-1 by Newcastle, join Norwich and Watford in slipping through the relegation trap door. Brentford finish in 13th position with 46 points, 11 clear of the drop zone and only 12 points off a place in next season's Europa League.

'Today I think it was a bad football game, to be fair. I don't think there was any natural width, Leeds were nervous with everything at stake. If you had seen our dressing room at the end of the game they were very disappointed and very angry which shows how much the game meant to us. We had big mistakes with the first goal and then the red card,' summed up Thomas Frank afterwards.

What about how the campaign has gone as a whole? 'I had massive belief in this team before the start of the season. I think we showed that we could be an asset to the Premier League and that's what I am most proud of. I'm very proud of the overall performance and how we presented ourselves as players and as a team. Of course, if you want standout moments I think I have three. Arsenal, obviously, the 2-0 win; the Stamford Bridge win against Chelsea; and in December when we beat Watford 2-1. We had so many injuries and had to play with players out of position. Going 1-0 down and the way we were fighting our way back into the game and equalising in the 82nd minute, or something like that, and still going for the win in the end for me shows everything about this team.'

Brentford: Raya; Ajer, Jansson, Bech (Baptiste 70), Henry (Canós 62); Jensen (Dasilva 58), Janelt, Eriksen; Mbeumo, Toney, Wissa

Leeds United: Meslier; Koch, Llorente, Cooper, Firpo; Greenwood (Klich 85), Phillips; Raphinha, Rodrigo, Harrison; Gelhardt (Struijk 71)

The fight for the championship produced a strange old set of circumstances. You would have assumed that both Manchester City and Liverpool would record fairly standard victories against teams in mid-table, especially considering what they were playing for. You can, of course, never assume in football. After only three minutes at Anfield, Liverpool were behind against Wolves thanks to Pedro Neto's goal. Cue an afternoon of celebrations in Manchester. Not so. City's response was to also fall behind as Matty Cash put Aston Villa ahead. Liverpool then equalised thanks to

Sadio Mané and City fell further adrift as ex-Liverpool midfielder Philippe Coutinho gave his old chums a boost by scoring Villa's second.

If Liverpool would go on to win, they would be champions. They duly did their part, Mo Salah and Andy Robertson securing a 3-1 victory. Manchester City, though, aren't the team they are for nothing. With only 15 minutes left, three goals in six minutes from İlkay Gündoğan (two) and Rodri saw that the championship trophy stayed in the blue half of Manchester. It is their fourth championship in five years, a brilliant achievement under Pep Guardiola. Yes, he has all the money to spend, but the players still have to make a team and the way they have performed has been nothing less than beautiful at times. As for Liverpool, there is to be no quadruple but the cup treble is still on.

Wednesday, 25 May 2022

Thomas Frank has missed out on the Manager of the Year award as Liverpool's Jürgen Klopp has been announced as the winner. To be fair to Klopp, it is an understandable choice as the Reds were fighting for a domestic treble right up to the last day of the season and still have the Champions League Final to come at the weekend. It is still a wonderful achievement for Frank to be nominated and is testament to the impact that Brentford have made this season. The player awards went to two Manchester City players with Kevin De Bruyne scooping the Player of the Year trophy and Phil Foden named as the Young Player of the Year.

Saturday, 28 May 2022

Liverpool play Real Madrid tonight to see who will become the champions of Europe. It is the third Liverpool v Real

Madrid final and therefore the most common European Cup/Champions League final in the competition's history. The other two clashes were in 1981 when Liverpool won thanks to Alan Kennedy's winner, and 2018 when Madrid triumphed 3-1, with goals from Karim Benzema and two from Gareth Bale, including a spectacular overhead kick. Liverpool's scorer that day was Sadio Mané.

Tonight's match in Paris sees another 1-0 victory but this time it is in favour of the Spaniards. Vinicius Junior got on to the end of a low cross at the far post to convert the only goal and take the trophy back to its favourite destination at the Bernabéu. It is the 14th time Los Blancos have won the tournament, double the victories of their nearest challengers AC Milan who have won seven. Madrid manager Carlo Ancelotti is now the only manager to have won four European Cup/Champions League titles. He has won two with Madrid, in 2014 during his first stint there and now in 2022, and twice with AC Milan in 2003 and 2007.

Sunday, 29 May 2022

The last loose string of the season is tied today as Nottingham Forest won promotion to the Premier League via the play-offs. A 1-0 win over Huddersfield was enough to return them to the top flight for the first time since the 1998/99 season. This means that Norwich, Watford and Burnley will be replaced next season by Forest, Fulham and Bournemouth. Well done to those three teams, see you next year at the Community Stadium.

EPILOGUE

THE STRIDES that Brentford have made in the last few years have been astonishing. Less than ten years ago the club were in League One, and up until three years back they were a mid-table team in the Championship.

The 2018/19 season saw the Bees finish 11th. Manager Dean Smith had left the club to join Aston Villa barely a month after the season had started, with his assistant Thomas Frank taking over the reins. Frank endured a tough start to his tenure, winning only one of his first ten games in charge. The team gradually stabilised as the season progressed and a mid-table finish was a decent turnaround after their early season woes.

Neil Maupay had scored 25 goals in that 2018/19 season, a record that earned him a move to the Premier League with Brighton. His place as main striker for 2019/20 was taken by Ollie Watkins. It wasn't going forward and scoring goals that had been the problem, however. It was the other end, the defensive side of the game, that had sometimes let them down and it was this part of the team that Frank sought to improve.

There was a flurry of activity in the pre-season transfer market as Frank led Brentford through a bit of a transformation. The first to arrive was Christian Nørgaard. He had endured a difficult time the season before, making only six appearances for Fiorentina in Italy since his transfer from Brøndby in his native Denmark. He was a player already known to Frank due to their time together at Brøndby, Nørgaard as a player, Frank as his coach. As a defensive midfielder, Nørgaard was exactly what Frank wanted to give the defence that extra bit of security.

Next through the door was Ethan Pinnock. He had helped Barnsley to promotion to the Championship the previous season, his defensive displays winning him the club's Player of the Year award.

Pinnock's soon-to-be defensive partner Pontus Jansson joined shortly after from Leeds. Having made his name with Malmö in Sweden, a spell in Italy with Torino followed before his move to England. He had been a regular in the Leeds first team but, after their Championship play-off semi-final defeat against Derby County at the end of the 2018/19 season, Jansson was told by manager Marcelo Bielsa that he wasn't in his plans for the following campaign and to find a new club. Brentford swooped and Jansson made the move south. He was soon made club captain after the departure of Romaine Sawyers to West Bromwich Albion.

Goalkeeper David Raya joined from Blackburn in the same week that Pinnock and Jansson both arrived. He replaced Daniel Bentley, who had been custodian for the previous three seasons, as the club's number one. Raya had come over to England to Blackburn on a scholarship in 2012 from Spanish club Unión Esportiva Cornellà. He progressed through the Ewood Park academy and became a first-team regular in 2017/18.

Having reshaped the defence, Frank recruited midfielder Mathias Jensen from Spanish club Celta Vigo. Jensen's time in Spain was affected by injury – he made only six appearances for the club – and Brentford offered him a new start in London. He had previously burst on to the scene at Danish club Nordsjælland where he had been voted the Danish Football Union's Player of the Year, a fact not lost on his new manager and compatriot.

One more recruit followed, this time a forward. Troyes frontman Bryan Mbeumo, scorer of 11 goals in the French league the season before, became the sixth new face through the door. Mbeumo would add power and pace to the attack and provide a partner for Watkins. With the new signings on board, a renewed optimism for the season ahead and a somewhat international feel to the squad, Frank's team was beginning to take shape.

The new recruits had an instant effect. The defence was more solid – they never conceded more than two goals in a game during the whole season, and they only conceded twice on nine occasions in 52 matches – and they won eight of their last ten games to force their way into the play-offs for the Premier League. They overcame Swansea in the two legged semi-final and faced Fulham at Wembley for a place in the big time. In a stadium empty due to the COVID restrictions, it was their west London neighbours who triumphed, a 2-1 victory seeing them promoted.

In preparation for the 2020/21 season, Frank made a few more tweaks to the squad. Watkins left to move up to Aston Villa and be reunited with his former boss Smith, while Saïd Benrahma also transferred up to the Premier League to West Ham. Watkins's replacement up front was Ivan Toney, a big target man from Peterborough. Toney had scored 20 goals in each of his previous two seasons with the Posh.

Frank also brought in other players from European leagues. Another Dane arrived in the shape of Mads Bidstrup from RB Leipzig in Germany, Vitaly Janelt, a former German youth international, came over from VfL Bochum and, during the January transfer window, Iranian international Saman Ghoddos joined from Amiens in France.

Brentford were once again a force to be reckoned with and repeated the previous season's third-placed finish to once again make it to the play-offs. The first leg of the semi-final against Bournemouth ended in a 1-0 defeat, but a 3-1 victory in the second leg sent the Bees to Wembley once more, this time to face Swansea. Toney, with his 33rd goal of the campaign, and Emiliano Marcondes scored the goals to send Brentford into the Premier League, the club's first foray into the top tier of English football since 1947. Premier League, here we come!

We know the story of the 2021/22 season now. Brentford not only came up against the big boys, but they mixed it with them. They took points off Liverpool, Chelsea, Tottenham and Arsenal, four of the top five. The only exceptions were against champions Manchester City, and those games were only lost 1-0 and 2-0. They scored more points than the other two promoted sides, Norwich and Watford, combined. They were involved in some extremely exciting matches – 3-3 draws against both Liverpool and Newcastle spring to mind – and who can forget the 4-1 victory at Chelsea? They have received plaudits from supporters, pundits and press alike and Thomas Frank was a nominee for the Premier League's Manager of the Season award.

Then there is Christian Eriksen. One of the finest players of his generation, one of Denmark's greatest ever players. Would he have signed had he not known Thomas Frank for years? Well, who knows? Frankly, who cares? Because he did. Christian Eriksen signed for Brentford. The Community Stadium could see first hand what they had been watching on their television sets for years. The man is a class apart. Frank has called him possibly the greatest ever signing the club has made.

Will he still be at Brentford next season? Let's hope so. But even if he isn't, let's just applaud what he has done for the club. He not only came in at a difficult period of the season and helped steady the ship with his personality, influence and brilliance on the pitch, but he made Brentford's story known, not just locally, not just in Denmark, but worldwide. Just consider some of the headlines and where they came from:

'Eriksen Signs For Brentford Months After Cardiac Arrest At Euro 2020' – France 24, France

'Eriksen Signs For Brentford On Deal Until End Of Season' – *Marca*, Spain

'Eriksen Signs For Brentford' – Pulse Sports, Nigeria

'Christian Eriksen Confirms Incredible Return, Signs For Brentford' – NBC News, USA

'Eriksen Signs For Brentford Months After Cardiac Arrest' – *Arab News*, Saudi Arabia

'Christian Eriksen Signs For Brentford FC' – *India Today*, India

Not bad for a bus stop in Hounslow.

SEASON 2021/22 STATISTICS

Premier League

13/08/2021	Brentford 2 Arsenal 0
21/08/2021	Crystal Palace 0 Brentford 0
28/08/2021	Aston Villa 1 Brentford 1
11/09/2021	Brentford 0 Brighton 1
18/09/2021	Wolverhampton Wanderers 0 Brentford 2
23/09/2021	Brentford 3 Liverpool 3
03/10/2021	West Ham United 1 Brentford 2
16/10/2021	Brentford 0 Chelsea 1
24/10/2021	Brentford 1 Leicester City 2
30/10/2021	Burnley 3 Brentford 1
06/11/2021	Brentford 1 Norwich City 2
20/11/2021	Newcastle United 3 Brentford 3
28/11/2021	Brentford 1 Everton 0
02/12/2021	Tottenham Hotspur 2 Brentford 0
05/12/2021	Leeds United 2 Brentford 2
10/12/2021	Brentford 2 Watford 1
26/12/2021	Brighton & Hove Albion 2 Brentford 0
29/12/2021	Brentford 0 Manchester City 1
02/01/2022	Brentford 2 Aston Villa 1
11/01/2022	Southampton 4 Brentford 1
16/01/2022	Liverpool 3 Brentford 0

19/01/2022   Brentford 1 Manchester United 3
22/01/2022   Brentford 1 Wolverhampton Wanderers 2
09/02/2022   Manchester City 2 Brentford 0
12/02/2022   Brentford 0 Crystal Palace 0
19/02/2022   Arsenal 2 Brentford 1
26/02/2022   Brentford 0 Newcastle United 2
05/03/2022   Norwich City 1 Brentford 3
12/03/2022   Brentford 2 Burnley 0
20/03/2022   Leicester City 2 Brentford 1
02/04/2022   Chelsea 1 Brentford 4
10/04/2022   Brentford 2 West Ham United 0
16/04/2022   Watford 1 Brentford 2
23/04/2022   Brentford 0 Tottenham Hotspur 0
02/05/2022   Manchester United 3 Brentford 0
07/05/2022   Brentford 3 Southampton 0
15/05/2022   Everton 2 Brentford 3
22/05/2022   Brentford 1 Leeds United 2

FA Cup

08/01/2022   Port Vale 1 Brentford 4
05/02/2022   Everton 4 Brentford 1

League Cup

24/08/2021   Brentford 3 Forest Green Rovers 1
21/09/2021   Brentford 7 Oldham Athletic 0
27/10/2021   Stoke City 1 Brentford 2
22/12/2021   Brentford 0 Chelsea 2

Goalscorers

Ivan Toney	14
Yoane Wissa	10
Bryan Mbeumo	8
Marcus Forss	6
Sergi Canós	4
Vitaly Janelt	4
Rico Henry	3
Pontus Jansson	3
Christian Nørgaard	3
Kristoffer Ajer	1
Shandon Baptiste	1
Christian Eriksen	1
Saman Ghoddos	1
Mathias Jørgensen	1
Ethan Pinnock	1
Mads Roerslev	1
Own Goals	2

Appearances

Álvaro Fernández	16	(PL 12)	(FAC 0)	(FLC 4)
Jonas Lössl	3	(PL 2)	(FAC 1)	(FLC 0)
David Raya	25	(PL 24)	(FAC 1)	(FLC 0)
Kristoffer Ajer	28	(PL 24)	(FAC 2)	(FLC 2)
Charlie Goode	8	(PL 6)	(FAC 0)	(FLC 2)
Rico Henry	37	(PL 34)	(FAC 1)	(FLC 2)
Pontus Jansson	39	(PL 37)	(FAC 1)	(FLC 1)
Mathias Jørgensen	10	(PL 8)	(FAC 0)	(FLC 2)
Ethan Pinnock	35	(PL 32)	(FAC 1)	(FLC 2)
Mads Roerslev	26	(PL 21)	(FAC 2)	(FLC 3)
Mads Bech Sørensen	15	(PL 11)	(FAC 2)	(FLC 2)
Fin Stevens	4	(PL 1)	(FAC 2)	(FLC 1)
Dominic Thompson	5	(PL 2)	(FAC 1)	(FLC 2)
Shandon Baptiste	22	(PL 20)	(FAC 2)	(FLC 0)
Mads Bidstrup	8	(PL 4)	(FAC 1)	(FLC 3)
Sergi Canós	34	(PL 30)	(FAC 1)	(FLC 3)
Josh Dasilva	9	(PL 8)	(FAC 1)	(FLC 0)
Christian Eriksen	11	(PL 11)	(FAC 0)	(FLC 0)
Tarique Fosu	3	(PL 1)	(FAC 0)	(FLC 2)
Saman Ghoddos	23	(PL 17)	(FAC 2)	(FLC 4)
Vitaly Janelt	35	(PL 31)	(FAC 2)	(FLC 2)
Mathias Jensen	34	(PL 30)	(FAC 1)	(FLC 3)
Christian Nørgaard	38	(PL 35)	(FAC 1)	(FLC 2)
Frank Onyeka	24	(PL 20)	(FAC 0)	(FLC 4)
Myles Peart-Harris	2	(PL 0)	(FAC 1)	(FLC 1)
Shandon Baptiste	3	(PL 2)	(FAC 0)	(FLC 1)
Halil Dervişoğlu	1	(PL 0)	(FAC 0)	(FLC 1)
Marcus Forss	12	(PL 7)	(FAC 1)	(FLC 4)
Bryan Mbeumo	38	(PL 35)	(FAC 1)	(FLC 2)
Ivan Toney	37	(PL 33)	(FAC 2)	(FLC 2)
Yoane Wissa	34	(PL 30)	(FAC 1)	(FLC 3)
Nathan Young-Coombes	1	(PL 1)	(FAC 0)	(FLC 0)

Final Table

		P	W	D	L	F	A	GD	Pts
1	Manchester City	38	29	6	3	99	26	73	93
2	Liverpool	38	28	8	2	94	26	68	92
3	Chelsea	38	21	11	6	76	33	43	74
4	Tottenham Hotspur	38	22	5	11	69	40	29	71
5	Arsenal	38	22	3	13	61	48	13	69
6	Manchester United	38	16	10	12	57	57	0	58
7	West Ham United	38	16	8	14	60	51	9	56
8	Leicester City	38	14	10	14	62	59	3	52
9	Brighton and Hove Albion	38	12	15	11	42	44	-2	51
10	Wolverhampton Wanderers	38	15	6	17	38	43	-5	51
11	Newcastle United	38	13	10	15	44	62	-18	49
12	Crystal Palace	38	11	15	12	50	46	4	48
13	Brentford	38	13	7	18	48	56	-8	46
14	Aston Villa	38	13	6	19	52	54	-2	45
15	Southampton	38	9	13	16	43	67	-24	40
16	Everton	38	11	6	21	43	66	-23	39
17	Leeds United	38	9	11	18	42	79	-37	38
18	Burnley	38	7	14	17	34	53	-19	35
19	Watford	38	6	5	27	34	77	-43	23
20	Norwich City	38	5	7	26	23	84	-61	22